SEX
LOVE
AND YOUR
Personality

THE NINE FACES OF INTIMACY

SEX LOVE
AND YOUR
Personality

THE NINE FACES OF INTIMACY

By **MONA COATES**, Ph.D. and **JUDITH SEARLE**

THERAPY OPTIONS PRESS
Santa Monica
California

Sex, Love and Your Personality: The Nine Faces of Intimacy

Cover & Book design by Tania Baban-Natal,
    Conflux Press www.confluxpress.com

Cover photo of Mona Coates by Eddie Jacobs

Cover photo of Judith Searle by Tim Vreeland

ISBN: 978-0-9835562-0-6

First published in 2011

Printed in the United States of America

THERAPY OPTIONS PRESS
855 10th Street #208
Santa Monica, California
310.393.5372

www.judithsearle.com

For Eddie

—M.C.

In memory of Basil

—J.S.

TABLE OF CONTENTS ᵕ୬

Acknowledgements   9

Introduction   11

Part I: What Makes a Healthy Relationship?   17

Part II: The Enneagram Types in Intimate Relationships   41

Type One: The Perfectionist in Love   41

Type Two: The Caretaker in Love   72

Type Three: The Achiever in Love   100

Type Four: The Individualist in Love   130

Type Five: The Investigator in Love   160

Type Six: The Loyalist in Love   190

Type Seven: The Enthusiast in Love   222

Type Eight: The Challenger in Love   253

Type Nine: The Peacekeeper in Love   287

Part III: Love That Lasts   323

Appendices   335

    Appendix A: The C-JES Survey   337

    Appendix B: The C-JES Scoring Sheet and Graph   347

    Appendix C: Bibliography   350

The Authors   353

ACKNOWLEDGEMENTS ᦌ

With unending gratitude I wish to acknowledge Judith Searle, my co-author. Her encouragement, her enthusiasm and her belief in the value of my work have been crucial to the realization of this book. From preliminary concept to final manuscript, she provided creative energy, editorial skills, professional Enneagram analysis, hard work and consistency.

Eddie Jacobs, the love of my life, who became my boyfriend when we were in 4th Grade, has provided infinite love and emotional support from the start. His encouragement and belief in this project have sustained me; he has provided invaluable help with proofreading, computer problems and Enneagram ideas and expertise, always questioning and always concerned with accuracy. Our own relationship journey has been an interesting and exciting one; he is truly the fulfillment of my own lovemap.

I am indebted to the many researchers, clinicians, teachers, scientists, authors, students and clients who have contributed to the body of knowledge that make my life's work possible and specifically to the content of this book. To the authors listed in the Bibliography I offer special gratitude and appreciation.

My professional work and training as a certified Enneagram instructor reflect the contributions of many and various experts in this field. However, the exceptional books and trainings provided by Don Richard Riso and Russ Hudson supplied the backbone of my knowledge; I could not have acquired the Enneagram knowledge I have if I were not standing on their shoulders.

Most important, my deepest gratitude goes to my precious and valued clients over these past three and a half decades. To all who have opened their hearts and minds, been courageous and trusting enough to invite me "in" as their therapist and to have made serious changes in their thinking and in their lives, I am most gratified. I thank each one of you for allowing me to share so deeply in your journey

—*Mona Coates*

Without Mona Coates's vast experience as a therapist and teacher, her special expertise in the fields of human sexuality and psychotherapy and her in-depth understanding of the Enneagram, this book would not exist. I am immensely grateful to her for teaching me so much about the varieties of intimate relationships and showing me how a skillful and compassionate therapist can facilitate deep healing in her clients. Her theory of the Five Factors has contributed greatly to my understanding of relationships.

With special gratitude I honor the memory of Basil Langton, who was my life partner for 36 years. Through his love and generosity of spirit I came to appreciate what a profound blessing an enduring relationship with a soul mate can be.

My debts to various Enneagram teachers and colleagues are many, beginning with Oscar Ichazo, who first delineated the Enneagram of Personality and Claudio Naranjo, whose development of Enneagram theory and practice has enriched the lives of all students of the system. I also owe much to Don Richard Riso and Russ Hudson, Helen Palmer, David Daniels, Tom Condon, Jerry Wagner, Ginger Lapid-Bogda Andrea Isaacs, Peter O'Hanrahan, Jennifer Schneider, David Rapkin, Carol Erickson, Carolyn Bartlett, Richard Rohr, Mary Bast and Clarence Thomson, among many others.

—*Judith Searle*

INTRODUCTION ᥡ

Many years ago, during my first year of marriage, I decided to give my new husband (who had recently moved to Southern California from Philadelphia) a surprise party to celebrate his birthday. I reserved a private room in a fine Italian restaurant and invited seven of my close friends with their spouses or dates. I saw this gathering as a perfect opportunity for my beloved husband and my chums to get to know one other better.

Wrong.

My husband hated the party. Although he tried hard to be gracious at the event, he felt as though he'd been blind-sided. He was angry that I would put him in a situation guaranteed to make him feel overwhelmed and anxious.

Bewildered that my generous, carefully planned surprise was seen as an invasion, I felt unappreciated and discounted.

After a difficult period of adjustment for both of us, the marriage survived this episode, but re-establishing trust in social situations took a long time. If I had known then what I know now about personality types, we could have avoided all that misery and misunderstanding. Although I had been a psychotherapist in private practice for 12 years at that time, I was still bewildered by my husband's reaction.

Two years after the unwelcome surprise party, my husband and I were introduced to the Enneagram, an insightful and respectful system of personality typing that gave us invaluable insights into our own and each other's personalities. Finally I understood his distress over the surprise party. We became so fascinated with the Enneagram that we both became certified teachers and I began using this new tool in my marriage/family counseling and sex therapy practice.

Thus, more than 20 years ago, I started down the long road that would ultimately lead to this book, which describes in detail the sex and love problems commonly encountered by each of the nine basic personality types and offers a case-tested template for predicting whether a particular relationship is likely to endure and/or be satisfying.

Apart from a few dedicated hermits and members of some religious orders, it's difficult to think of many people who are not personally interested in finding, maintaining, healing or escaping from an intimate relationship. The plethora of matchmaking services available on the Internet and elsewhere testifies to the eagerness of individuals to find a mate. Yet one of every two marriages in the United States currently ends in divorce, despite the efforts of more than 48,000 marriage and family therapists and 150,000 psychologists.

In my 35 years of practice as a therapist I have worked with a wide variety of individuals and couples. Through all these experiences, I have become aware of Five Factors that have proved reliable in predicting whether a particular relationship is likely to be satisfying and enduring. Although several of these factors relate to the Enneagram, the two most important ones do not.

Part I of this book discusses these predictive factors, in order of their importance. This section also offers a simplified description of the Enneagram system, which—although it is not the primary focus of this book—offers a useful framework in which to consider the way these Five Factors relate to the 54 cases described here. Part II contains chapters devoted to cases that are typical of each of the nine personality types. Each chapter includes six case histories from my clinical practice—three males and three females—that reflect distinctive variations within each type. I have chosen these particular cases because they illustrate not only the Five Factors' value for predicting the success or failure of actual relationships but also the structural problems and natural neuroses of each personality style. Part III looks back on the Five Factors and explores the benefits and limitations of the therapeutic process for individuals and couples.

It is my hope that the information in this book will provide valuable assistance to people seeking a fulfilling and lasting relationship, couples seeking help or simply enrichment and professionals in the field seeking more effective tools to serve their clients.

—*Mona Coates*
Huntington Beach, California

This book was born out of a 15-year friendship between Mona Coates and me that arose initially from our common interest in the Enneagram and our work together on the Board of the International Enneagram Association's Southern California chapter. Seeing Mona's stimulating presentations at IEA Conferences and Southern California chapter meetings, I had for years been urging her to write a book about the Enneagram and intimate relationships, based on her decades of experience as a therapist and sex educator.

After she retired from college teaching in order to devote the bulk of her time to her private practice, I periodically made this suggestion again.

Finally, she said, "I'll do it if you'll do it with me."

I had no hesitation about joining her in the project. And my rewards have been many: a comprehensive education in the varieties of intimate relationship, an increased awareness of the many ways a skilled therapist can offer significant help to clients and the deepening of a treasured friendship.

Perhaps my most significant qualification for this co-authorship has been my good fortune in having had a long and happy relationship with my late life partner, Basil Langton. Hearing the stories of Mona's troubled clients has made me appreciate in a new way the loving connection he and I shared.

It has been an honor and a privilege for me to work on this groundbreaking book. I hope that you, our reader, will be as fascinated as I was by Mona's 54 case histories and that the ideas and information in these pages will contribute to the quality of your life.

—*Judith Searle*
Santa Monica, California

Part I

What Makes a Healthy Relationship?

*A*s a therapist working with couples and individuals for over thirty-five years, much of my practice has been with people who are ultimately seeking a love relationship that lasts or people who are trying to fix an existing relationship in trouble. The innumerable books, movies, television shows, online dating services and web sites that focus on finding the "right mate" demonstrate what a high priority a good relationship is for almost all of us. Yet our high divorce statistics provide eloquent testimony about the difficulties of sustaining a marriage or love relationship over the long term.

Across all economic, racial, religious, political, age-related and cultural groupings of people, certain common problems appear. Typical issues include: communication breakdowns, working hours, money and/or the allocation of money, mistrust, child discipline and sexual differences (e.g., desire, frequency, dysfunction). How people handle such conflicts varies greatly—from complete avoidance to seeking professional assistance (e.g., therapists, ministers, psychologists, social workers and psychiatrists) or attending retreats and communication seminars.

In spite of all attempts to resolve their differences, many relationships seem to falter, then crumble, under the weight of certain issues. Yet there are also couples whose relationship endures through it all. Despite traumatic crises and turbulent conflicts, they remain steadfast, durable and resilient partners.

What can account for such differences?

I've noticed through years of experience that certain factors are good predictors of whether a particular relationship will survive. Some of these are commonly understood and well known (e.g., good communication, safety, trust, empathy, commitment); others are less familiar to most people and usually buried in the unconscious. I believe a better understanding of these factors can help individuals make wiser choices regarding life partners and attain a deeper understanding of themselves. Contributing to the understanding of these less familiar and unconscious factors has been our strongest motive for writing this book.

So often I have heard comments such as:

> "I flipped out of my mind when I first met this woman—lots of interests in common, so we started living together. Over the following months our 'hot to trot' relationship became a bore and so did she. I'm over it and I don't know why."

> "We have fantastic chemistry, but emotionally we can't sustain a real relationship."

> "This guy really turned me on, I couldn't wait to screw his brains out, then it all suddenly ended."

> "She's my best friend, we love doing everything together, but when it comes to being intimate we just fall flat."

> "Everything was fantastic the first night we met and it was all downhill from there. We have nothing in common in terms of how we want to live."

> "I've been with my wife for 27 years and love her dearly, but for some strange reason I'd rather have sex with an anonymous prostitute or use Internet porn to satisfy myself."

> "I really love this guy, we have super chemistry, but I'm afraid he has no interest in anything outside of the physical."

A longtime friend from my college days once confided in me that he had been very drunk at his 30-year high school reunion and indulged in a one-night stand with a promiscuous woman from his senior class. He described it as "the best sex of my life." He remembers that, even while drunk, he ejaculated five times in the same night. The following morning, realizing what he had done, he felt sick to his stomach; he knew he could never reveal such an indiscretion to his precious, fragile wife of ten years. He somehow knew he would never experience such incredible, uninhibited sex with the wife he truly loved. So it is clear that a person can experience great sex with no love involved. A polar-opposite example is a couple in their mid-thirties who came to me for marriage counseling lamenting that both of them lacked any form of sexual desire. They loved each other dearly and were best friends, but neither felt any sexual desire for their partner. They each masturbated separately and knew their libido or biological sex drive was normal. They simply had no sexual interest in one another. I've observed, through years of doing sex therapy and marriage counseling, numerous clients who deeply love and truly like their partner but who have had no sexual contact for several months or, in some cases, for as long as ten years. So, it is equally clear that some people can have a deep and long-term love relationship without experiencing any sexual chemistry.

The Big Picture

Let's take a look at some of the factors that determine an ideal intimate relationship—when a couple can experience deep love, great sex and intimate friendship all at the same time. Years ago I came up with a conceptual framework to help couples evaluate their own partnership. I entitled it: "Love, Liking and Lust: The Ingredients for Successful Love Relationships."

These three important elements still appear to me useful for a couple seeking to assess their relationship:

> • *Love:* unconditional positive regard and valuing of the other's highest good; willingness to sacrifice for the benefit of the partner.
> • *Liking:* being best friends, pals; doing things together; common interests; enjoying one another's company.

• *Lust:* the primal, animal attraction, the physical urge and biological desire to have sex with the other (i.e., chemistry).

The question then becomes: What factors actually determine when—and if—love, liking and lust can develop? I've attempted to boil down my own clinical experience into *the five most essential and fundamental elements* that go beyond the obvious. It is these less known and unconscious factors that are so important for therapeutic insight and for predicting the long-term outcome of a love relationship. These Five Factors are:

1) Compatible Lovemaps
2) High Levels of Psychological Health
3) Matching Personality Subtypes
4) Harmonic Triad Match
5) Complimentary Connection Line

The first of these elements, lovemaps, a concept originally developed by John Money and used by many, is the best way I know of to explain "sexual chemistry." Three of the remaining four factors can best be discussed through a dynamic system of personality analysis known as the Enneagram, which I'll describe briefly in a moment. But first let's take a look at the most important of the Five Factors: the power of two people having compatible lovemaps.

The Lovemap

Money, a distinguished sex therapist and sex researcher, described the lovemap as a mosaic of traits that make up, partly in our conscious mind but mostly in our unconscious, the picture of our ideal mate or lover and what we would do with them. This conglomerate of traits may include many aspects of the personality, how a person behaves socially, certain critical values, race, religion and political persuasion; it often includes physical characteristics such as hair color, height, weight, body shape or a certain look.

But it is also involved with deeply unconscious assumptions and preferences.

For example, one aspect of my own lovemap (that I was unaware of for many years) is my preference for a man who can fix things around the house, the way my dad did. He built our family's home from the ground up, even installing his own water pipes and electric wiring. So I'm attracted to men who can "fix things," and I have little interest in a guy who has no ability as a handyman. (This is most likely because my own family experience led me to believe this is what a "real man" does.)

Another example from my personal lovemap is my attraction to extremely smart men who are on the quiet side. My dad was a solid, stable, introverted salt-of-the-earth man who focused on his family, doing the work and solving every problem. A "party boy," loud-mouth—or even a man as extroverted as I am—would never be the kind of mate I would choose, because my lovemap requires someone more like my beloved dad in order for me to experience real chemistry.

I've heard many psychologists say that we really cannot explain what chemistry is or why it happens between two people. However, I think the closest we've been able to come is through recognizing that any potential mate we're attracted to (when we feel real chemistry) is someone who meets the important criteria of our lovemap. Some of these criteria—both functional and dysfunctional—are determined through our identification and bonding with the opposite-sex or same-sex parent; others are determined by the rejection of one or both parents. Still other criteria develop from cultural ideals, media images, popular personalities or subtle role models such as teachers, neighbors or historic figures.

If there's a deep compatibility of lovemaps between two psychologically healthy people, it can be a match made in heaven. In reality, acting on the surge of instant, powerful chemistry may lead us only to scratch the surface of our lovemap. We might see only about 5 percent of the important variables: perhaps going no deeper than physical appearance, hobbies, diet and career. This is a major problem for couples who get married quickly or start living together shortly after falling in love. As we get deeper into the layers of our unconscious traits, values and belief systems, the honeymoon is often over. We may abruptly fall "out of love" as we discover that our partner is not meeting some of the major criteria of our lovemap—the other 85 things we were looking for and just assumed would be there. Small wonder that the divorce rate in Southern California, where I live and work, is well over 50 percent.

One of the biggest problems is that many of the components of our lovemap are deeply buried in the unconscious and hidden from our awareness. Most of us couldn't fully describe our internal lovemap if our life depended on it. Typically, we become conscious of these specific traits and expectations only when we're shocked by our partner's behavior, when we feel betrayed or violated. It's likely that we didn't know something was part of our lovemap until we were confronted with a crisis that forced awareness into our conscious mind. Only at this point do we realize that certain things are of great importance—and perhaps *not negotiable*.

Does everyone have a lovemap? Yes, but some of us have lovemaps that are unclear, extremely distorted or "vandalized" by traumatic events such as rape or incest or humiliating early sexual experiences that engrave unhealthy ideas and feelings onto our unconscious template for a desirable mate. Not everyone has the wholesome benefit of identifying in a healthy way with one or both parents (especially the one of the opposite sex). Elements of the lovemap can become confusing, contradictory and bizarre under conditions that set up negativity, abuse, neglect or trauma in the person's unconscious beliefs and expectations for a mate and a love relationship.

For example, a person who believes he or she will be used, verbally abused and disrespected has a highly compatible lovemap with a partner who is hateful, abusive and disrespectful. Negative qualities in the lovemap work just as powerfully for establishing real chemistry as the positive ones. This helps explain why so many people continually attract the same kind of dysfunctional, abusive relationships.

Fortunately, there are many resources for changing and healing our lovemaps. For example, we can consciously *choose* to identify with different or more positive role models such as aunts, uncles, therapists, media idols, historic figures or literary heroes. Another example, in response to more complicated issues, is seeking depth therapy to raise our level of consciousness and psychological health in order to actually correct the self-sabotaging and dysfunctional aspects of our lovemap. There is also a plethora of books, seminars, trainings, video/DVD programs and small group experiences that can assist in this journey. In any case, an in-depth understanding of one's lovemap and that of the partner can be a major asset and vehicle for self-awareness and growth within the relationship.

The Enneagram of Personality

During the course of human history there have been many attempts to classify personality types. Aside from the Myers-Briggs Type Indicator (a testing instrument that examines four continuums related to temperament), I've generally found typologies of little practical use in clinical work—especially in couples counseling. The major exception to this is the Enneagram, which I've found extremely useful not only in helping troubled couples and individuals but with *all kinds* of people.

The Enneagram is an insightful, highly refined and respectful system that describes nine basic personality types, what drives them to perceive the world the way they do and how these contrasting worldviews produce nine distinctive constellations of behaviors. Several specific factors developed through the Enneagram are good predictors of long-term success in intimate relationships.

When I was introduced to the Enneagram, I realized that if I really studied this system I could offer much more insight to my clients. So, over the next five years, my husband and I took Don Richard Riso and Russ Hudson's trainings and became certified as Enneagram teachers through them. We also studied with a variety of other teachers. We developed our own Enneagram typing instrument, the Coates-Jacobs Enneagram Survey (C-JES), which I still use daily with my clients.

Finding Your Own Personality Type

Some readers will already know their Enneagram Type, others

will never have heard of this system. If you have studied your type, you may want to skip this section as well as Appendices A and B. On the other hand, if you don't know what your type is, your understanding and enjoyment of this book will most likely increase if you take the time now to complete the latest version of the Coates-Jacobs Enneagram Survey (C-JES) in Appendix A and determine your scores using Appendix B.

Determining your subtype requires a different approach. If you're unsure whether you are basically a Self-preservation, Sexual or Social subtype, please refer to the definitions provided later in this section under "Personality Subtypes."

Having a firm understanding of your own type and subtype, as well as those of your partner, can offer you greater insight into your relationship, as you will see from the cases presented in this book.

Using the Enneagram in Therapy

My work as a therapist has always been highly eclectic. I use whatever is helpful for my clients: Family Systems, Object Relations, Callahan techniques (Thought Field Therapy), clinical hypnosis, Gestalt methods, Reality Therapy, Bioenergetics—whatever the person needs. However, the Enneagram is the most powerful tool I've ever had to explain who the person is and what motivates them. To me as a therapist, the Enneagram is what a hammer is to a carpenter. It's a basic tool that I use in all kinds of individual therapy, couples therapy and family counseling.

It's especially useful for couples because it allows people to gain a profound understanding and appreciation of themselves as well as one another. Reading about the Enneagram makes their thinking about their own personal problems more objective. It depersonalizes some of the pain and conflict, as they begin to more clearly understand the personality structure of their partner, as well as their own.

This is what it did for me in my own marriage—helped me to understand my husband and also to see my own patterns and blind spots in the relationship. For example, before discovering the Enneagram I was aware of my own personality and knew I was extremely extroverted. However, I never put together all the underlying motives that make up my own type. Of course I don't like pain (which is anathema to Sevens), but I didn't realize that avoiding pain had been a major theme in my life ever since I was a kid. People have asked me: "How could you possibly be a therapist if you're a Seven and you don't like pain?" Well, that's exactly why I *am* a therapist—because I'm so committed to getting people out of their pain. In individual therapy or marriage/family counseling I push to resolve the problems, doing everything I can so that people are no longer suffering.

Let's take a brief look at the Enneagram and how it can become a major tool for understanding yourself as well as your partner—thus eliminating much suffering, conflict, pain and misunderstanding.

1. How the Enneagram Works

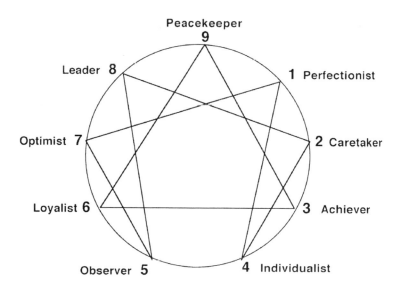

THE ENNEAGRAM

The word Enneagram (pronounced *ANY-a-gram*) in Greek simply means nine-pointed diagram. Though the symbol itself has been known since ancient times, the Enneagram of Personality wasn't developed until the mid-20th century. In the above diagram each of the nine personality types is marked by a point on the circle and each is connected with two other points through interior connecting lines that show the type's affinities.

The Enneagram acknowledges the complexity within every human being, and the system's usefulness to individuals and couples in therapy owes much to its precise mapping of these elements.

Most people who are knowledgeable about the Enneagram refer to the types by their numbers. As I mentioned earlier, I'm a Seven and Judith, my co-author, is a One. In order to make remembering the nine types easier for students, many Enneagram teachers and authors supply names for each type. You can see in the above diagram the names I've found most descriptive. However, it is important to realize that no single label or category can ever fully define the essence of an individual.

The Enneagram is universal, applicable to all cultures and all people throughout time. Using this framework to study personality styles provides an opportunity to learn more about yourself and others. The system is like an x-ray of the human psyche. Just as a skeletal x-ray reveals your bone structure, the Enneagram reveals your personality structure.

Seen through the lens of the Enneagram, differences between people—and human behavior in general—can become quite apparent. Differences in personality type explain why and how you can think, act and feel so unlike your mate. Once you understand these dissimilarities, it's easier to have genuine empathy and compassion for one another.

The insights of the Enneagram offer us tools for understanding, dismantling and healing the sources of our rage, hurt, depression, guilt, shame and despair. The dynamic nature of the Enneagram also gives us "maps" that can guide us toward waking up to our inner self and moving beyond our fears, "hot buttons" and the unconscious limitations of our personality.

The Nine Personality Types

When we look at the nine distinct Enneagram Types, the story of the nine blind people and the elephant comes to mind. In the story each of these individuals describes the animal in relation to the piece he or she has taken hold of—the trunk, the tail, the ears or the massive legs. Since all these people are blind, none of them is able to comprehend the whole elephant. Like these nine blind individuals, each Enneagram style has hold of a genuine piece of the truth. Problems arise when someone assumes that his or her particular portion is the whole truth. Each Enneagram Type represents a habitual way of perceiving the world—one in which our psychological filters allow us to focus on certain aspects of our experience and ignore others.

Let's begin with a thumbnail sketch of the nine personality types and the basic strategies that suggest which piece of the truth each one has hold of:

- **Type One** (The Perfectionist): principled orderly, self-doubting, irritable.
  Strategy: "If I can make myself and everything around me perfect, then I can survive." Fears being wrong, bad or corrupt. Desires to be virtuous, correct and self-controlled.

- **Type Two** (The Caretaker): nurturing, demonstrative, possessive, proud.
  Strategy: "If I can make others love me and depend on me, then I can survive." Fears being unloved, unneeded or unappreciated. Desires to be indispensable, sought after, helpful.

- **Type Three** (The Achiever): goal-directed, competitive, driven, vain.
  Strategy: "If I can establish a public image of myself as a successful person, then I can survive." Fears failure, looking bad or worthless. Desires to be acknowledged as a winner and super achiever.

- **Type Four** (The Individualist): authentic, passionate, depressed, envious.
  Strategy: "If I can make friends with the darkness and become a connoisseur of my own pain, then I can survive." Fears not having a true self, being insignificant or defective. Desires to be unique, self-expressive and noticed for individuality.

- **Type Five** (The Investigator): cerebral, independent, withdrawn, stingy.
  Strategy: "If I can keep my mind focused on gaining enough information, then I can survive." Fears being incompetent, dependent on others or overwhelmed Desires to be knowledgeable, capable and private.

- **Type Six** (The Loyalist): cooperative, authority conscious, suspicious, fearful. Strategy: "If I can stay alert to all possible dangers and find trustworthy allies, then I can survive." Fears being left out, without guidance, unsupported. Desires security, belonging and leadership from affiliate groups.

- **Type Seven** (The Enthusiast): optimistic, impulsive, self-indulgent, superficial.
  Strategy: "If I can distract myself with pleasure and avoid thinking about pain, then I can survive." Fears being deprived, loss of options, being trapped or in pain. Desires to "have it all," experience everything and stay energized and happy.

- **Type Eight** (The Challenger): powerful, pragmatic, excessive, vengeful.
  Strategy: "If I can intimidate and dominate others, then I can survive." Fears being vulnerable, weak or controlled by others. Desires to be self-determined, strong and invincible.

• **Type Nine** (The Peacekeeper): accepting, easygoing, distractible, lazy.
Strategy: "If I can keep an open mind about all possible strategies, then I can survive." Fears direct conflict and confrontation, separation from others. Desires inner stability, outer tranquility and the flow of merging with others.

Levels of Psychological Health

The second most important factor (after lovemaps) for predicting the long-term success of love relationships is how healthy each partner is within his or her own personality type. Here the Enneagram can offer us a helpful perspective for the specifics of each style. However, there are many traits that apply universally to all people as indices of maturity and self-actualization and I discuss these in Part III of this book.

In Don Richard Riso's original edition of *Personality Types* he introduced the concept of Levels of Development, which has been especially valuable for my work with couples. (The Levels are also discussed in *The Wisdom of the Enneagram* by Riso and Hudson, which I recommend to my clients seeking a complete description of the Enneagram system.) Riso's detailed explanations of the Core Dynamics for each Enneagram Type are an impressive contribution not only to Enneagram theory and to the personal development of his many readers but also for those of us who work in the trenches with clients. For each of the nine types he lays out nine Levels of Development with their distinctive traits and behavior patterns, ranging from the Healthy Levels (1-3) down through the Average Levels (4-6) to the Unhealthy Levels (7-9). Riso's descriptions of each Level—and of the process of Integration or Disintegration that takes place as a person moves upward or downward between Levels—are detailed and eloquent.

To me as a therapist, it's clear that two individuals who are at the Healthy Levels of Development and who share compatible lovemaps—no matter what their personality type—have a good chance of creating a lasting relationship. (I feel that type matches and mismatches are less relevant to relationship success than lovemaps, psychological health and the other elements in the Five Factors. But, for readers interested in exploring this subject, we have listed several relevant books in our Bibliography.) However, remaining at the healthy levels can be extremely challenging—and might sometimes feel impossible for many of us.

Let's look now at the remaining three of the Five Factors for analyzing relationship success.

Personality Subtypes

Third on my list of factors that can predict long-term relationship success is having the same Enneagram subtype. When I first started working with the Enneagram in the early 90s, I wasn't aware of how important subtypes actually are. But after years of working with couples, I'm convinced that partners who share the same subtype have a better chance of staying together over the long haul than those with different subtypes. If both partners are Self-preservation or both are Sexual or Social, it's much easier for them to establish empathy, set priorities and share common values as a couple.

Here are the three Enneagram subtypes, each reflecting approximately an equal third of the general population:

• **Self-preservation** subtype people focus on personal survival, security and safety. They pay close attention to survival mechanisms such as food, temperature, clothing, comfort, insurance, health, nesting, money, home and scarce resources. People with this subtype have energy that is stable and solid and their body tends to be more grounded and self-contained. Highly conscious of their environment, they expect to have it adjusted to meet their needs. Important questions for this group are: "How can I regulate the environment and my resources to insure my comfort and survival?" "How can I navigate my way through this?" People with this subtype need to feel physically secure before giving to others.

• **Sexual subtype** people focus on intimacy and desire intensity and personal connection with specific individuals. Continually seeking to connect with another person's energy, they fear being rejected or undesirable. With their attention on the processes of mating, dating and forming close friendships, they are like electric plugs and sockets looking for one another. Sexual subtype people have an intense, searching energy that locks in on the eyes of a person they want to converse with. Merging with others is a highly charged activity and people with this subtype are passionate about seeking the "juice" in any relationship. Important questions are: "How do we, united as a couple, as best friends, buddies, partners function?" "Who's worth talking to?" and "Where are the real connections?"

• **Social subtype** people focus on the community, the group and the social environment. They want to belong, desire acceptance and look for recognition. They fear not "fitting in" or not getting approval and so they may seek affiliation with a clan, tribe, gang, professional association, social group or political party. They often compare themselves to other members of the group and are concerned about how they "measure up" to others' standards. Social subtype people have an energy that is more split or scattered. They tend to be inclusive, adaptive, cooperative and less focused than people with the other two subtypes. Aware of power structures, struggles and appropriateness, they tell themselves and each other: "We're all in this together" or "Let's leave a legacy." They focus on the welfare of others and adapt themselves to the environment in order to gain acceptance.

Subtype is unconscious and is probably determined by biological predispositions from birth as well as early childhood experiences. There doesn't seem to be any cultural or social class or even male-female gender variable that makes people more likely to be one subtype over another. So my assumption is that the three subtypes are randomly and equally distributed within all nine of the personality types. If that's generally true, many of us (perhaps two-thirds of the population) are in relationships with someone of a different subtype.

Being of the *same* subtype makes a love relationship easier and smoother; partners feel more compatible. I explain to clients that the subtype is like a set of unrecognized biases and filters inside our mind. It colors everything, but it works in such an unconscious way that we don't even know we're experiencing everything through this lens of our own distortion.

So, if your unconscious biases are the same as your partner's you have fewer conflicts as a couple. In marriage counseling it's easier to deal with couples who have the same subtype (although that fortunate combination is more often the exception than the rule).

I have one client couple who are both extreme Social subtypes. Even though they have some significant problems and fights over child-rearing and her working hours, they invariably come back to discussing when they're giving the next party or who's coming over for the weekend or how they will acquire more networking associates and recognition. Their status within certain groups is extremely important to them and that common goal consistently brings them back together.

In contrast, I'm counseling another couple where the wife is a Self-preservation subtype and the husband a Sexual subtype. He continually complains that all his wife thinks about is her own needs, financial security, their various insurance policies, her health and physical ailments—but she *never* thinks about *him* or *them* as a couple. "I get so lonely at times when I need her attention and some romantic interest," he says. "I love her so much, but she's always absorbed in her own issues and comfort."

Still another couple I'm seeing suffers in a similar manner because the husband is Self-preservation and his wife is a Social subtype. The wife says, "He's never willing to attend parties, a couples' bridge club, dancing lessons or yoga classes, among other things." At the same time, he's angry that "she wastes her time running around between a hundred people and activities—rather than paying attention to what's really important, like making sure the bills are paid on time, dentist appointments are set up and the car gets serviced."

It's easy to see how the way any given subtype sees the world can lead to conflicts with a mate of a different subtype.

Harmonic Group Matches

The fourth factor that is helpful in predicting the long-term success of a relationship is the Harmonic Groups. Since I'm presenting these factors in order of importance, this one is less significant than the compatible lovemaps, the level of health of both partners and sharing the same subtype. This fourth predictor is having both partners in the same Enneagram Harmonic Group, another concept originated by Riso and Hudson.

They write, *"the Harmonic Groups tell us how we cope with conflict and difficulty: how we respond when we do not get what we want."* They define the groups as follows:

The Positive Outlook Group is composed of types Nine, Two and Seven. All three respond to conflict and difficulty by adopting, as much as possible, a 'positive attitude,' reframing disappointment in some positive way....

The Competency Group is composed of types Three, One and Five. These people have learned to deal with difficulty by putting aside their personal feelings and striving to be objective, effective and competent....

The Reactive Group is composed of types Six, Four and Eight. These types react emotionally to conflicts and problems and have difficulties knowing how much to trust other people: "I need you to know how I feel about this."

In my work I have found that the Positive Outlook Group—the Nines, Sevens and Twos—don't really want to fight. In the interest of things going well, they'll generally make concessions. They want to see the sunny side: the "glass as half full."

With the Competency Group—Threes, Ones and Fives—it's often possible in relationship problems to establish common ground, a kind of "contract" between the partners about being competent, getting the job done, doing it right and being accurate.

The Reactive Group—Sixes, Fours and Eights—enjoy big

reactions and strong feelings. They often measure the love of their partner by how vehement his or her reaction is; they see this as a measure of the partner's caring and concern.

It's easy to see how belonging to the same Harmonic Group gives partners a sense of common ground, of having some of the same values and perspective; when conflicts arise these coping similarities can help them work their way through problems and toward solutions.

Complementary Connections

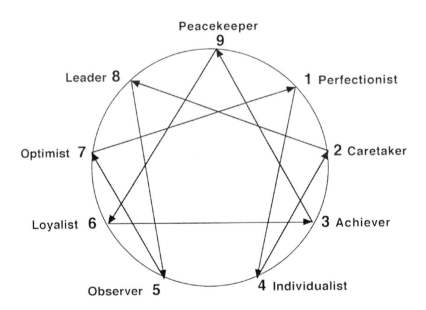

THE ENNEAGRAM

Fifth in importance for predicting the success and durability of romantic relationships is a *shared interior line* between the two partners' types on the Enneagram diagram. I don't know if the divorce rate is any lower with these couples, but I do know that these straight lines inside the Enneagram circle are like underground tunnels through which energy flows, balance is achieved and deep connections and corrections become possible.

The arrows that connect each type with its stress point (moving in the direction of the arrow) and its security point (moving against the direction of the arrow) were originally integrated into the diagram by psychiatrist Claudio Naranjo.

Relationships between two types who have a shared line can be especially provocative and rich. There are complementary elements at work, a deeper kind of internal connection because, though the partners may not share surface things in common, they do exchange certain kinds of "opposite" emotional energies. So an Eight connected to a Two or a Five would have more energy in common than, say, an Eight with a Three; they have greater potential for balancing and correcting one another's blind spots. It's important to recognize that this connection through a straight line is *not* about compatibility, but rather about *opposites complementing* each other so that there is more give and take, more reason for provoking and correcting imbalances, more exchange of energies and agendas between the two. The "opposites attract" concept has some real value when two people have this complementary connection.

Further Enneagram Explorations

The simplified discussion of the Enneagram I've presented above is designed to help readers understand the ways this system is related to the Five Factors I consider predictive of lasting and satisfying relationships. However, my description of the system is by no means comprehensive and this book is not designed either to teach the Enneagram in full or to expand on basic Enneagram theory. Readers interested in a more complete study of the system should consult Riso and Hudson's *The Wisdom of the Enneagram* or one of the other general sources listed in our Bibliography.

In Part II of this book, I'll be looking at each of the Enneagram types in more detail, discussing them in relation to actual cases from my therapy practice that illustrate the special problems of both males and females with each subtype. You can read these chapters in any order.

CHAPTER NOTES: PART I

p. 20: *Lovemaps: Clinical Concepts of Sexual/Erotic Health and Pathology, Paraphilia and Gender Transposition in Childhood, Adolescence and Maturity* by John Money. New York: Irvington Publishers, Inc., 1986.

p. 29: *Personality Types: Using the Enneagram for Self-Discovery*, Revised Edition, by Don Richard Riso with Russ Hudson. Boston: Houghton Mifflin Company, 1996.

p. 29: *The Wisdom of the Enneagram* by Don Richard Riso and Russ Hudson. New York: Bantam Books, 1999.

p. 30: What I call subtypes are referred to as "instinctual variants" by Riso and Hudson in *The Wisdom of the Enneagram, op.cit.*, p. 70ff.

p. 33: *The Wisdom of the Enneagram, op. cit.*, pp. 64-68.

p. 35: *Ennea-type Structures: Self-Analysis for the Seeker* by Claudio Naranjo, M.D. Nevada City, CA: Gateways: IDHHB, Inc., 1990.

Part II

The Enneagram Types
in Intimate Relationships

TYPE ONE: THE PERFECTIONIST IN LOVE

At all levels of psychological health Ones are preoccupied with perfecting themselves. They do this to avoid expressing the powerful feelings that are continually welling up within them—especially anger. The "inner critic" is a powerful goad to Ones, who respond by attempting to avoid mistakes and live impeccable lives. To placate their inner voice Ones must seem right and good not only in themselves but in their chosen work, which explains the driven quality common to people of this temperament.

Average Ones tend to focus strongly on their work—often expending large amounts of energy on details. This focus on tasks makes average-level Ones feel justified in expressing irritation toward others who seem content with lower standards. Quick to criticize others for any moral failings, they reserve their harshest judgments for themselves. Though anger is a common problem for people with this Enneagram style, average Ones are rarely conscious of it in themselves.

Healthy Ones tend to be more conscious of their anger and less rigid in their judgments of themselves and others. They are compassionate toward others' mistakes and may even have a sense of humor about themselves, albeit a dry one. (A sense of humor about personal characteristics and limitations is a sign of health in all Enneagram styles.)

Unhealthy Ones may be self-righteous and cruel in their attempts to punish the guilty. Convinced of their own rightness and goodness, they see the world in terms of good and evil, with no moral gray areas. Any deviation from their rigid ethical code merits harsh punishment. Puritanical, devoid of compassion for themselves and others, unhealthy Ones are invariably grim and unhappy.

Ones with the Self-preservation subtype

Ones are generally focused on improving themselves and the world around them. Self-preservation Ones, whom Oscar Ichazo associates with "anxiety," are preoccupied with physical survival. Ones with this subtype are the most "tightly wound," the most prone to worrying, the most fearful about making mistakes. Often driving themselves to ever-greater productivity, they tend to be extremely task-oriented. They feel guilty about their desires and exert rigorous efforts to control what they see as potentially disastrous self-indulgence.

"The Sanitary Beast"

Gretchen, 59, a Self-preservation One, came to me for help after her husband of 35 years suddenly announced that he wanted a divorce. Before marrying Paul (her second husband), Gretchen had been a highly paid executive secretary to the president of a huge manufacturing company; she was extremely capable and well organized. Since the birth of their daughter 31 years earlier, Gretchen had devoted herself to homemaking.

A tall, strong-looking woman with salt-and-pepper hair and deep vertical lines between her eyes, she looked exhausted as she sank into the chair in my office.

"I can't understand it," she said. "How could anyone do more than I've done? The house is spotless—I even wash the baseboards every week. I do all of Paul's laundry myself—iron his shirts and his underwear. I pay the bills, do the shopping, make all his medical and dental appointments—and our daughter's, too. How could he want a divorce?"

At my suggestion, Paul soon joined our therapy sessions. He had no difficulty answering her question.

"I feel like a piece of furniture," he said. "Gretchen is sterile, anal—compulsive in her perfectionism about the house. In the past two years we've had sex exactly twice—both times when we were away on vacation. I'm 61 years old and I want to have a normal sex life before I die."

Further discussion revealed that Gretchen literally fainted into bed every night, having exhausted herself with cleaning and perfecting everything in their home. It was evident that her self-esteem was based almost entirely on her compulsive housekeeping.

We had many talks that helped Gretchen see that her husband didn't especially value perfect housekeeping and that she was ignoring the things he felt were important—especially affection and a normal sex life.

The choice for Gretchen was clear: *change or divorce*. In our sessions, I helped her see that she had inherent value as a person apart from her excellent cleaning. Since the idea of a divorce appalled her, I pointed out that there were some simple changes she could make. I suggested she try going to bed earlier and commit to a "holding time" ritual with Paul—hugging and kissing, just holding one another for five minutes before going to sleep every night—simply as a way of honoring their marriage. After the first week, Gretchen actually began to enjoy this ritual.

When she finally became open to discussing her personality, survey results confirmed her Type One structure and our conversation revealed her Self-preservation subtype. Subsequent sessions zeroed in on how her One-ish traits—especially her rigidity and perfectionism about cleaning—were suffocating her husband. Over the course of our sessions, she was eventually able to joke a bit about these compulsive patterns and make significant changes.

Paul later took an on-line personality survey and recognized himself as a Type Seven (Social subtype) who got his major validation from friends and work groups.

With both Gretchen and Paul now aware of their own (and their spouse's) personality type, they were in a position to begin more serious work on their marriage. I got them to make "little dates" with each other during the week and "big dates" on the weekend. They would alternate weekly, asking each other for the "big" and "little" dates; the one who did the asking would plan the date, keeping its content a surprise. Both Paul and Gretchen found great benefit in their dates. Each felt more loved and cared for by the other.

I taught them how to do reverse role-playing with each other outside of therapy. To show how this worked, for example, I talked to Paul in the voice of Gretchen's unconscious. Once he became aware of how her childhood had pushed her toward perfectionism, he began to understand her deepest fears and subsequently developed real compassion as he saw what caused her to feel so critical and rigid. After this, it was only a small step to get them to role-play each other (reversing roles so that Gretchen played Paul and vice-versa), reflecting their awareness of the other's inner fears and needs.

All these efforts paid off powerfully. Through our sex therapy sessions, they ended up incorporating many forms of pleasure, sometimes including erotic turn-ons, into their "big" and "little" dates. Gretchen discovered possibilities for receiving sexual pleasure, something she hadn't previously been able to do (though she was orgasmic). Paul stopped talking about wanting a divorce.

Gretchen's difficulties in her marriage were typical of the limitations many Ones have with intimate relationships. Ones can be rigid and controlling—as Gretchen was about cleaning. This was her major focus in life, leaving no room for the pleasures of sexual connection or even the sweetness of simple physical affection.

A common problem with Ones (and certainly with Gretchen) is that even as children they often come to see themselves as little adults, taking pride in being right and good. When a person equates rightness and goodness with "being perfect," as Gretchen did, the resulting obsessive/compulsiveness can devastate a marriage.

In the case of Paul, his wife's compulsiveness and perfectionism were choking off all forms of love and affection that she might have had for him and vice versa. She was suffocating any attempts Paul made toward having fun or creating pleasurable options in the marriage—almost a necessity for any Seven.

It was crucial that Gretchen become healthier in her personality development—this was the most important change that allowed the marriage to endure. Their future together remains unclear, but for now both of them are enjoying a more satisfying relationship than they have had in decades.

Regarding our Five Factors for predicting relationship success, Paul and Gretchen both reported only moderate satisfaction with their spouse's fulfilling of their lovemap criteria. Both are currently at average levels of personality development, with Gretchen sometimes in the unhealthy zone. But both have made significant strides in their personal growth. Gretchen has become more open, relaxed, flexible and pleasure-oriented—difficult transitions for her. Paul has become more patient and compassionate, willing to focus more time and energy on the marriage, with less escapism into his social groups and work.

They do not share the benefits of being the same subtype (Self-preservation versus Social) and are not in the same Harmonic Group. However, they are connected by the direct balancing line between Ones and Sevens, which allows them greater ability to complement each other's shortcomings and differences.

"Enraged and Contaminated"

Mike, 28, a Self-preservation One, set an appointment to see me because he was so angry with his girlfriend, Janice, that he could no longer maintain erections. A tall, well-built fireman, he worried continually about his health, financial security and savings for retirement. How much overtime would he need to work in order to retire by age 55? Should he work a second job in order to purchase a larger home? If he worked too much and then became sick or got injured, would he lose the house? Lose his job? Would it be right to marry Janice, given all his concerns?

Mike had been living with Janice, 34, an ICU nurse, for over two years and had planned on marriage and at least two children with her. Janice, a Self-preservation Six (as we later discovered), had her own concerns over money and the stability and security of their home life. Should she buy a house with Mike prior to their being legally married? What if he left her and she was pregnant or had a child—might she get stuck with all the house payments? She felt great anxiety over Mike's position in the Fire Department. What if he was injured or killed? If they had children, would she ever feel secure enough to stay home with a baby, earning no income of her own?

Sharing the Self-preservation subtype, this couple had many concerns and goals in common. Listening to Mike's catalogue of anxieties, I sensed something more might be involved in his erection problem. When I questioned him directly about this, he acknowledged his anger toward Janice and his shame about expressing it. There were two realities about his relationship with her that especially upset him, he said. The first was the fact that she had given him herpes (unknowingly). The second was her use of sex toys (an electric vibrator).

I asked if he wanted to deal with either of these topics at the moment and he said, "Herpes—it may be the easier of the two." He revealed that Janice had contracted the herpes virus from an ex-boyfriend when she was 19. During the past 15 years she had suffered only three outbreaks that she was aware of—and there had been none in the three years that they had been monogamous sexual partners.

"Janice was completely honest about her herpes from the beginning," Mike told me. "She has her own brand of paranoia and still wishes she could get back at that guy who gave her the virus. She worries incessantly about having a child—that the baby might contract herpes.

"Well, I did get it—through no fault of hers or my own. We used condoms faithfully for over two years. Then her gynecologist said it would be okay to stop the condoms, since we were monogamous and Janet hadn't had any symptoms for at least five years.

"About six months into our non-condom period, I had these warm, tingly sensations on my penis. Janice never had any symptoms at all. We have a great dermatologist who explained the facts about 'asymptomatic shedding'—where the carrier might have some viral cells escape from the skin surface without having any noticeable symptoms. It's unusual, but it does happen.

"When I heard this, I was enraged. I felt hateful and critical toward Janice. I felt betrayed. Her body seemed to me dirty and contaminated. My own penis felt contaminated and I was disgusted with myself as well as her. There really is no cure yet, you know."

"Yes," I said, "I know."

We spoke at length about the nature of herpes, medical treatments and supplements that can help prevent or suppress outbreaks and the possibility of skin-to-skin transmission, especially on the mouth and genital areas without the contagious partner having an outbreak.

I explained to Mike that in the 1970s and 1980s it was standard medical practice to teach people that herpes can be contagious *only* when there is an open sore. Now we know that is not always the case.

Mike seemed to have no trouble comprehending this information, but it was clear that the time had come to deal with his anger. I explained that if he could fully experience his rage he could probably let go of it. Struggling to stay in control while pushing down his fury had not been a successful strategy. If he could let go of his resistance to these feelings and allow himself to fully experience the waves of anger in his body, I suggested, he might gain some relief. Although he seemed uncertain about my recommendation, he promised to think about it for our next meeting.

The following week our session began with his immersion in his rage. I kept encouraging him to let go of his resistance and feel it all. At times he actually shook as he spoke and ultimately cried with great sobs of relief.

He thanked me for encouraging him to work it through. We spent the next few sessions discussing his personality structure and why he held things back emotionally. I explained how Ones naturally resist dealing with their own anger. Mike was eventually able to see the absurdity of his extreme negative judgments of himself for feeling angry. As a child, he remembered being taught that anger was "wrong," and that he could become a good person only if he was always in complete control of his emotions. These are typical messages that Ones remember hearing when they were growing up.

At this point Mike reported that his communication with Janice was slowly improving, now that he had resolved (or at least accepted) the herpes situation. They were expressing more affection with each other and Mike had initiated the five-minute "holding time" that I had recommended for each night when they went to bed.

But there was still no sexual contact, since Mike still felt he would be unable to sustain an erection. He reported a significant lack of sexual desire during the previous six weeks—ever since the "sex-toy incident."

It was time to deal with Mike's second issue: Janice's use of a vibrator. I asked if he still felt that this was a "bigger issue" than the herpes and whether it might be the real reason for his erection problem.

His face became red and I could see that he was holding his breath, obviously trying to swallow his anger once again.

When I encouraged him to again let out his feelings, he began pounding on a pillow, unconsciously.

"Okay, here it is," he said. "This is my biggest issue—probably why I can't get an erection with Janice. I walked in on her masturbating—yes, masturbating, without me there. I got home from work earlier than usual and caught her red-handed, using a *vibrator*—just like they do in porno movies.

"Talk about feeling *wrong*! I felt totally inadequate. This was the worst kind of criticism, the worst put-down anyone has ever laid on me. I'd always prided myself on being a really good lover—the kind of guy no woman would ever have to cheat on—and would certainly have no reason to use a vibrator. That's the angriest, the most *inadequate* I've ever felt, in any situation."

His whole body was shaking. "Janice was stunned when I walked in. She acted terribly embarrassed and paranoid about what I'd discovered. This proved to me how guilty she actually was. We got into a verbal altercation, with her mumbling something about 'normal' or 'natural' or some crap about her own body. I made it clear that *wrong is wrong* and she was clearly cheating on me."

Mike turned to me with a flood of furious questions: "How can any man keep up with a vibrator? What did she expect? I gave her great oral sex, she was very orgasmic—and now she's saying I'm inadequate, I'm not good enough. I'm so enraged by her cheating on me this way that I'm not sure if I can ever have sex with her again."

Throughout Mike's blaming, shaming and accusing, I did extensive active listening, encouraging him to process all his angry feelings. Then I proceeded to ask some standard questions: Did he believe each person was the owner of their own body? Yes. Was there really another man or partner involved? No. Had he ever masturbated himself while he was in this committed relationship with Janice? Well, yes. Had she any malicious or devious intentions? No.

I also gave Mike many case study examples of how and why we use masturbation, especially as a standard part of female sex therapy. It is important for a woman to learn about her own orgasms so that she can, if she chooses, teach her partner what feels good to her. Any woman who had never masturbated or done self-pleasuring would be at a great disadvantage in communicating her sensual/sexual needs to another person. He seemed to understand this and was beginning to reframe his views on masturbation.

In the case of Janice, I explained to Mike that I felt it was a great help to him and to the relationship that Janice was so willing to take full responsibility for her sexuality, then share these feelings with him as her monogamous partner. This could not be described as "cheating."

Janice's use of an electric vibrator for sexual pleasure, I said, was similar to her use of an electric toothbrush. Both appliances maintained her body in a desirable state. Thus, there was no such thing as "competition" between Mike and the vibrator. All such gadgets are designed to facilitate our goals—creating more efficiency and/or health benefits.

By this time I had Mike laughing and his comments took on a different tone. He was willing to admit, at least, that Janice had not committed any form of cheating. His eyes were softer now and his voice had lost its critical quality. His view of sex toys was in the process of changing.

Following many requests on my part, Mike finally invited Janice for a joint session. She struck me as a lovely person—plain, demure and obviously concerned about many of the same issues Mike had discussed, such as the stability of their home, having children, their future together, financial security and retirement.

Mike had mentioned to me earlier that he guessed Janice's personality type was probably a Six. They had expressed an eagerness to take the personality survey, which confirmed his Type One and her Type Six, with both clearly recognizing their mutual Self-preservation subtype. Each of them grew and developed rapidly as a result of their new levels of compassion and insight.

We did some short-term sex therapy, primarily for Mike's sake. This consisted of their moving through a series of intimacy exercises in 15- to 30-minute sessions (two per week). Each time, they were directed to take turns giving and receiving pleasure, with no intent to arouse the partner, for at least five sessions.

During the first session, in which they remained fully clothed, they were permitted to stroke each other's faces and to kiss; in the second session, still fully clothed, they were allowed to stroke each other's faces and non-sexual body parts. The third session, still clothed, allowed stroking of face, body and genitals. In the fourth session, in which they could to be nude, facial stroking and kissing were allowed. Moving on to session five, again unclothed, they were permitted to stroke each other's face and body, avoiding the genitals. Session six, again nude, allowed stroking of face, body and genitals and session seven advanced to genital arousal without penetration (through hand manipulation). In session eight, oral sex was permitted (according to the couple's preference). Finally, in session nine, all activities—including intercourse—were allowed.

The experience of these sessions was extremely positive for Mike and Janice. They were loving and considerate of one another throughout. Mike began to get strong erections and soon felt confident enough to ask Janice for intercourse. Both of them developed much more open communication about their feelings, expectations and sexuality.

In sex therapy of this kind with some couples, I encourage other forms of enrichment, which may include sex toys, sharing verbal fantasies, hard- and soft-core films and DVDs, magazines and books, changes in setting (such as a hotel or motel room), role playing (taking turns being the seducer and orchestrating the whole show) and costumes. Most of these possibilities were not for Mike and Janice, although I did recommend to them Lou Paget's book *365 Days of Sensational Sex.*

During their joint sessions Janice never spoke directly about using a vibrator and she appeared careful about what she said. I understood that she might have a higher sex drive than Mike and thus might need to talk alone with me, but I also sympathized with her need to protect his ego. I openly encouraged her to continue giving herself pleasure in this form when and if she wanted to. Mike seemed to accept my giving her this support and my explanations.

Using our Five Factors for predicting relationship success, Mike and Janice had compatible lovemaps—both were basically satisfied that their partner met their "ideal mate" criteria. On the factor of psychological health, Mike worked diligently to make himself a healthier One, which for him meant greater emotional and psychological freedom to be who he actually is. Janice, who seemed healthy from the beginning, turned out to be a great help to Mike in the final phases of his therapy.

This couple enjoyed the strong bond of their common Self-preservation subtype, which encouraged the same priorities, world-view and concerns. Ones and Sixes are not members of the same Harmonic Group, nor are they connected by a direct line that helps balance their energies, but Mike and Janice's relationship appears to be on strong ground, at least for the moment.

Gretchen and Mike as Self-preservation Ones

Both Gretchen and Mike had high levels of anxiety related to "correct" performance. For Gretchen, driving herself to exhaustion with her compulsive cleaning seemed so essential to her self-esteem that she failed to see the devastating effect it was having on her marriage. When she was able to relax and reconnect with her husband romantically and sexually, the relationship became much more satisfying for them both.

For Mike, the performance problem manifested itself in the sexual area. Although he and his partner, both Self-preservation subtypes, had common concerns about home and financial security, his unexpressed anger at her had led to consistent erection failure. Once his rage was fully vented in a therapeutic setting, he was able to look at his issues with her more objectively, view her with more compassion and use standard sex therapy exercises to help him regain full sexual functioning.

Ones with the Sexual subtype

Sexual Ones, whom Ichazo associates with "jealousy" or "heat," are primarily focused on finding and maintaining the ideal intimate relationship. This vision of a "perfect mate" as someone who will share the One's high standards and who will be completely faithful is central to this subtype. Sexual Ones fear that their partner may fall short of their ideals, thus undermining the relationship. Ones with this subtype often exhibit many qualities of Type Seven: an engaging wit and a magnetic quality that charms potential partners. They are strongly in touch with their desires and may feel deep conflicts about their sexuality. When less healthy, people of this subtype tend to be critical and suspicious of their mates, punishing them in an attempt to purge their own sexual guilt or negative feelings.

"Fatal Flaws"

Vanessa, 34, a tall, elegantly dressed blonde (Type One with a Sexual subtype), settled into our first session and announced: "I really want a long-term relationship and I've dated a lot of men. But every one of them had some fatal flaw."

She had been divorced for ten years after a two-year turbulent marriage to her son's father, who had disappeared seven years earlier. She was the single mother of Billy, an 11-year-old boy. As she talked about Billy, I sensed that she was a perfectionist in her parenting—strict about manners, dress codes and bedtime—but also extremely loving. Her relationship with her son sounded basically healthy.

Smart and independent, Vanessa was in the costume jewelry

making business, the sole owner of a small, successful company. Her one unfulfilled dream was to find a satisfying intimate relationship (an important aspiration for nearly all people, but especially those with a Sexual subtype).

The men she had dated—and even her own parents—had called her "picky," "critical," "demanding" and "difficult to please." Yet Vanessa firmly believed that any fault lay with the other person.

I asked her to tell me about several of the men she had dated recently and why they broke up—to explain these fatal flaws.

She sighed. "Willy was right for me in so many ways. He was five years older than I, had been divorced for twelve years and also owned a small company. He was just great with Billy and they adored each other. But then the whole thing fell apart over racquetball. He insisted on playing every Sunday morning and I couldn't stand that. It showed me how selfish he was—that having a real family life alone with me didn't matter to him. The truth is, no man has ever hung in there for me—they're all pretty selfish, when it comes right down to it."

Under further questioning, it came out that Willy had been playing racquetball on various teams for over 20 years, ever since his high school days and was devoted to the game and to his regular Sunday morning tournaments. From Vanessa's description, he sounded like a Nine with a Self-preservation subtype. Easygoing but self-contained, he wanted their relationship to be smooth and easy. In the face of her insistent demands, he dug in his heels, refused to give up the game he loved and broke up with her.

I asked about the man she had dated before Willy. Greg was a local doctor, an OB/GYN, she told me, a nice man, also divorced, who had just turned 38. But she would get angry every time he was "on call" to deliver a baby in the middle of the night or on the weekend. She realized she couldn't be married to a gynecologist and broke up with him because his bizarre schedule could never allow consistency in their home life and time together. In retrospect, she looked back on Greg and realized she had never felt deeply connected to him. Once she learned about the Enneagram, she thought he might be a Self-preservation Three.

The man before Greg, Sid, 40, was a wonderful guy who owned

an auto body shop—probably a Six with a Sexual subtype, from her description. But his fatal flaw was "bad hair." She was determined to tame his thick, unruly locks by sending him to her own hairdresser, who charged $85 for men's haircuts. Sid was used to paying $8 at the local barber, and the prospect of paying $85 infuriated him. Her offer to pay for his haircut enraged him even more (probably because the subtext he heard behind her words was that the way he looked wasn't good enough, that *he* wasn't good enough). Sid put his foot down and refused the haircut. His response is not uncommon among people subjected to a One's nitpicking. But Vanessa simply couldn't let go of his "bad hair," and eventually they too parted ways.

During the course of our sessions she became aware that the same basic pattern showed up in all her relationships, even some from her childhood—especially with family members. Unwilling at first to take the personality survey, she finally agreed and slowly began to see the reality of her Type One criticalness and inability to accept others at face value. She had previously acknowledged her intensity and strong need for feeling connected as a feature of her Sexual subtype.

Vanessa seemed to enjoy our role-playing with a lot of different situations involving men. I role-played her, demonstrating much softer responses—more open hearted and less critical in nature. Finally I had her read the little book by Richard Carlson entitled *Don't Sweat the Small Stuff* and she agreed that basically "it's all small stuff." Any one of her last three men could have been a real gem, except that she just couldn't tolerate their small specific flaws. She was eventually able to truly understand, accept and then change some of her destructive patterns.

One of the most important lessons for Vanessa was in learning to ask herself the question: "Is it more important to be right or is it more important to be loved?" All her life she had unconsciously believed it was more important to be right—a common principle among people of the One persuasion. But it had now become clear to her, on a heart level, that it was more important to be loved. Considering this question led Vanessa to understand the kind of positioning she was doing with everybody—her employees and business associates, even her parents.

Her need to be right was so entrenched that she automatically made everyone else feel "wrong." I helped her to see that the cost of her being "right" was to put the other person on the defensive. So, in many instances, even when she might be technically correct, it was better not to verbalize this in order to avoid putting the other person in the wrong. When Vanessa saw this clearly she understood why the people she criticized might dislike her—or at least why they might have difficulty sustaining an intimate relationship with her.

As Vanessa gained a new confidence in her ability to relate uncritically to others, she kept thinking about Sid, the man she had rejected because of his "bad hair." Of all the men she had dated, he was the one she felt most connected to. His heart always seemed to be in the right place—not only with her but also with Billy. "Sid took Billy lots of places and they did all kinds of 'guy' stuff together," Vanessa reported. She thought Sid might also be a Sexual subtype and was pleased about his intensity.

Eventually, Vanessa phoned Sid to apologize for her criticality. Humbled by her new self-awareness, she acknowledged what a terrible mistake she'd made in being so critical of his unruly hair and asked for his forgiveness.

Sid accepted her apology but made no move toward renewing their dating relationship. Five months passed and then one day she ran into him at the local car wash. During that conversation Sid observed that Vanessa seemed much softer, less rigid and that she was genuinely sorry for the way she had treated him.

He invited Vanessa and her young son, with whom he had developed a close relationship during the time he was dating Vanessa, to a picnic. Sid, Vanessa and Billy went several places as a threesome over the next month.

When the possibility arose of Sid and Vanessa resuming their former romantic relationship, he insisted they see me before making any decision. Sid was looking for some clear boundaries and proof that Vanessa's attitude had changed.

In our first joint session he used me as a "mirror" to help Vanessa see how her tendencies to be judgmental, controlling and inflexible would not be acceptable if they were to resume their relationship. He was willing, he said, to let Vanessa "pay for all my haircuts for the rest of my life, if she insists. But I don't want her talking to me as if she's the hair police."

Sid turned out to be a healthy, confident, emotionally mature and loving man. He made it clear that dating Vanessa would always be a "three-way street." When she looked at him, uncomprehending, he said, "That's right—you and Billy and me."

Her eyes filled with tears as she realized how deeply Billy had bonded with Sid during the seven months they had previously dated. She knew how happy Billy was to have Sid back in their lives. Sid suggested it might be helpful for him to take the same personality survey that Vanessa had taken. (He already knew he was a Sexual subtype from the worksheets I had given her.) The results confirmed his Type Six structure. As a healthy Six, Sid was a true team player— from the thoughtful and inclusive family values surrounding Vanessa and Billy to the welfare and safety of the employees in his successful auto shop business.

"As for my god-awful hair," Sid said in a later session, "I've decided to turn that problem over to Vanessa. If she thinks an $85 haircut will make any difference, then let her have at it. For 40 years it's been impossible to control—even my barber teases me about it."

Vanessa laughed and took up the challenge. She made it clear that she was "taking over Sid's hair not as a way of criticizing or trying to fix him, but as a way of showing how much I love him. He's such a handsome man—with his thick auburn hair styled right, he'll look even more delicious."

Sid was pleased now to visit Vanessa's hair stylist. He no longer felt she was implying he wasn't good enough. Following Vanessa's splurge on his $85 haircut, he reported that this was the first time in his life he thought his hair looked good. It was satisfying for me to see them settling into a mutually rewarding, non-critical and supportive relationship.

Using our Five Factors for predicting relationship success, it appears that Vanessa and Sid are both deeply satisfied with each other (using their lovemap criteria). Sid is exceptionally healthy in his personality development and Vanessa has made great progress toward becoming conscious and healthy. They have the benefit of both being Sexual subtypes. Although they are not in the same

Harmonic Group and are not connected by a direct line balancing their energies, they are off to a good start, having the three most important elements firmly in place.

"Bisexual Scare"

Dean, 48, a Sexual One, is a psychology professor at a local university. He has a son and a daughter in college (from his first marriage). For the last ten years he has been married to his second wife, Wendy, 42, a Sexual Three with whom he has no children but shares many common values.

"I didn't come to see you," he said, "because of problems in my marriage. I don't want my wife to know I'm even seeing a therapist." The intense blue eyes behind his horn-rimmed glasses held my gaze.

I assured him that all sessions are confidential as he settled into the overstuffed chair opposite mine.

"I love my wife and I know she loves me." He suddenly looked as if he were about to cry. "It's just that I'm so lonely in this marriage."

Wendy, he said, was a high-powered salesperson for an international medical supply company. She made four times the salary he did at the university; both regarded Wendy's salary as an important asset because her income made possible their luxurious lifestyle, including a large home on the beach. But her job required her to travel three out of four weeks every month, often being away from home from Sunday night until Friday night.

"Please don't misunderstand me," Dean said. "I have no evidence that she's been unfaithful, though she's so beautiful I'm sure she's had plenty of opportunities. I came to see you because of my own loneliness. I just need more company, more connection. Sure, I have friends, but I'm not one for going out with the boys and I have no interest in drinking or going to clubs."

As he continued his story, I formed a mental picture of a kind, sensitive man who had been a good dad to his college-age kids. But the kids now lived three hours away, so he could see them only about twice a month for dinner. Dean obviously enjoyed teaching and took a lot of care preparing his classes; I sensed that his students must love him.

As he took a deep breath, I realized he had much more to tell me.

"I have a colleague in the Social Science department," he said, "Barry, a nice guy who happens to be gay and we got into the habit of going to a movie together during the weeks Wendy's traveling. We've become good friends."

I nodded, glad that someone had helped fill the empty space in Dean's lonely life during Wendy's extensive travels.

"Anyway," he went on, "last week Barry and I had dinner and went to a movie, as usual and then as we were saying goodnight he gave me this big bear hug—the way he always does with folks at school. But this time I suddenly didn't want the hug to end. My brain just went blank and I froze there, in the hug position."

I gathered that at this point Barry simply helped Dean into his house, made sure he was okay and then left. Dean, panicked at his response to Barry's hug, immediately found my website and called the next day for an appointment.

"So does this mean I'm gay?" he said. "I've never had a feeling like this in my whole life. It was just such a shock, so powerful—this gay feeling. Maybe I'm bisexual. I don't know what to think."

There were beads of sweat on his high forehead as he waited for my response.

"Anybody—especially a person who's been as lonely as you have—can have a temporary erotic feeling or fantasy about some-one of the same sex," I said. "It doesn't mean you're gay—or even bisexual. It just means that your friend Barry happened to be in the line of fire when you were feeling vulnerable and lonely. A hug from anyone—even Santa Claus—would have been welcome."

We talked about Dean's sexual history and he told me he'd never had a same-sex experience or even a feeling of desire or curiosity in that direction. I explained that most boys explore some kind of erotic play with another boy or a group of boys and that even this kind of activity generally has little or nothing to do with one's ultimate sexual orientation.

It was an advantage in our sessions that Dean was a psychology professor, because I was able to talk to him bluntly, but also academically, about projection, the need for human connection and where his heart was in this situation. I said, "If this were somebody other than you, Dean, would you interpret what happened as a red flag for homosexuality?"

"No," he said, "of course not."

I was able to reason with him and he was able, very quickly, to understand that he simply wasn't getting enough closeness and affection from Wendy. Her traveling most of the time had become too much. I suggested that Wendy might be able to make some schedule changes, but Dean felt doubtful.

After a few sessions, Dean told Wendy about his unhappiness with her travel and she agreed to come in with him during the one week of the month she was in town. She broke down in tears in my office and confessed that she too was tired—so tired—of her go-getter sales career. I suggested that she tell her company she needed a stress leave or simply request a reduced contract.

Knowing that the company would do anything to keep her, since she was their superstar in sales, Wendy decided to tell her boss that, at a minimum, she needed a 75 percent contract. Under this arrangement, she would get 75 percent of her salary, but she would be off work one full week per month and would travel only two weeks per month (every other week). During one of these weeklong trips (which often took her to New York or some other major city), we agreed that Dean would join her so they could have a romantic three-day weekend together about once a month.

After several bumps in the road, this plan worked out beautifully. Dean and Wendy had both resisted taking the personality survey until late in their therapy and finally agreed to it in the interest of "marriage enrichment." Coming to understand each other's Enneagram types ended up producing a tremendous leap in empathy and a powerful bonding experience for them.

The fabric of Dean and Wendy's marriage was good from the start, with four of the Five Factors predicting long-term marital success in their favor: compatible lovemaps, with each feeling deeply satisfied with the other; high levels of psychological health in both partners; an Enneagram subtype match (both were Sexual subtypes) and a Harmonic Group match (Ones and Threes are both in the "Competency Group").

Eventually Dean told Wendy in one of our sessions about his scare with Barry, whom she also knows and likes. She was able to completely understand and they ended up joking about it together. She wasn't at all intimidated and neither was Dean, once he realized that his deep loneliness for Wendy was what had caused him to put himself through hell, questioning his sexual orientation and their marriage.

This case, which was a true success story, illustrates the deep integrity of healthy Ones. It also reveals the pitfalls that can accompany their internal degree of scrupulousness. The "inner critic" in Ones, always alert to possible ethical lapses, can give even healthy Ones like Dean a rough time, especially when their deep emotions are triggered.

Dean's experience also reminds us how useful, in practical terms, the virtue of discernment can be. Even when he was suffering serious self-doubt, he was able, with a little help from me, to see his situation objectively. He understood how his loneliness had clouded his thinking and his ability to be rational. He also came to appreciate and understand his profound—and sometimes obsessive—desire for a flawless relationship.

Vanessa and Dean as Sexual Ones

Both Vanessa and Dean were focused on ideal intimate partnerships. Vanessa initially saw flaws not in herself but in her potential intimate partners. Her perfectionism made her intensely critical of tiny imperfections in them, while at the same time failing to see her own larger failures of compassion and generosity. Eventually, through therapy, she came to understand her own limitations and was able to re-establish a relationship with a fine man whom she had earlier rejected over a trivial flaw.

Dean loved his wife and had no desire for any other partner, but her frequent absences had made him so lonely that he overreacted to an affectionate hug from his gay friend and began having doubts about his own sexual orientation. The "heat" he felt over such an issue is common with Sexual Ones, who tend to be especially intense about anything that might impinge on their treasured ideals for an intimate relationship.

Ones with the Social subtype

Social Ones, whom Ichazo calls "nonadaptable," are often men and women bent on reforming the world around them. They assume that their standards apply to society at large and they have no hesitation in speaking out about whatever they perceive as injustices. Average Social Ones have strong opinions about right and wrong and are often obsessed with rules and procedures. When less healthy, they see the world in black-and-white. Becoming enraged at some injustice or condition, they seek to impose their own narrow brand of righteousness, including drastic punishments for those who deviate from their rules.

"Disillusioned Young Wife"

Liz, 27, a Social One, is a slender woman with curly brown hair. She sat in my office fighting back tears. "I love Zack's daughters," she said, "and I think they love me—the step-mothering part of our marriage is going really well. But Zack himself seems completely uninterested in doing anything together as a family. He's a great dad in so many ways, but he refuses to get involved in any activities outside the home."

A fourth grade teacher, Liz has no children of her own (and no desire for any). For two years she has been married to Zack, 46, a man 19 years her senior with two daughters, ages 13 and 15, from a previous marriage. His daughters were aged 1 and 3 when he divorced their mother, who had become a violent drug addict and was eventually killed in a car accident. Zack, a mild-mannered man who looks young for his years, is a highly sensitive Self-preservation Five, as we later learned.

Liz's lifelong goal was to marry the right man and have an active family life with strong community connections. Seeing what a fine job Zack had done as a single parent and how devoted he was to his daughters, she assumed their visions of family life were similar—and that he would happily join her and the girls in attending a local Presbyterian church, pursuing family hobbies such as skiing and occasionally going to sporting events with groups of teachers from her school. Extroverted and idealistic herself, she has been deeply disillusioned to discover how introverted her husband actually is and how resistant to community involvement of any kind. He's happiest staying home with his girls, pursuing solitary activities in the garage such as woodworking and antique car repairs.

Having realized that her assumptions about their basic compatibility were based more on wishful thinking than on discussion or observation, she came to see me for counseling about what, if anything, she could do to salvage the marriage.

Within a couple of sessions I was able to help her see that Zack's joining her for marriage counseling would increase the chances of success. He did come in with her and he ultimately became more interested in the personality analysis than Liz was. They both took the C-JES survey, and as they learned more about their types they were able to understand each other better and forgive each other for many things.

To Liz's surprise, it turned out that Zack had no objection to her going alone to her group outings; they agreed to pursue separate agendas on this. He was glad to have the girls go with her to the teen church meetings they enjoyed, as long as he wasn't expected to go along. Liz was pleased to have an influence on their spiritual development and was highly invested in her role as stepmother. She bonded strongly with both girls through spending considerable quality time with them.

After several sessions, I was able to help Liz and Zack inject some romance back into their sex life. I suggested they schedule one date with each other every week, alternating which one did the planning. This seemed to work well for them. They're now doing much better, despite serious incompatibilities.

The marriage may or may not last, but their communication has improved radically with their involvement in many of the exercises that I suggested—for example, dyad sentence-completion. Here's how it works: Taking turns, each partner provides five endings for

the following sentences: "The truth about our relationship is...,
"One thing I need from you is...," "One thing I appreciate about you
is...," "One thing I want you to know about me is...," "Our future
depends upon...." The sentence completion is done within a
structured ten-minute period. Partners are *not* allowed to discuss
the issues beyond the completion of their sentences. Instead, they
make notes, and discussions are saved for their sessions with me.

Zack was especially relieved about the ten-minute time limit.
"At least this way," he said, "Liz won't go on and on. I just get too
overwhelmed with all her emotion."

My sense is that Liz and Zack have a good chance of staying
together and enjoying one another in the short term, but the long
term is uncertain. Liz appears to be far more invested in her step-
mothering and social activities than in the marriage. Zack has always
been most invested in his own personal hobbies and interests, which
is typical of Self-preservation Fives.

Like Liz, many Ones are extroverted (especially those of the
Social subtype), while Fives are usually introverted, especially those
with the Self-preservation subtype. This difference was especially
painful and divisive for them.

Liz's idealism, a common trait in Ones, may have led her to
assume that Zack's commitment to quality parenting meant his
values aligned with hers in most other areas of involvement and
relationship. So she never really discussed with him her vision
of what their home life or marriage would be. Thus the couple's
incompatible lovemaps are a serious problem and their differing
visions of what a marriage should be are likely to become more
troubling when Zack's daughters are no longer present as a shared
commitment for the couple and as participants with Liz in many of
the outside activities she loves.

Though both Liz and Zack appear to be in the average range
of psychological health, their lack of truly compatible lovemaps and
the lack of a shared Enneagram subtype are significant limitations.
They do share a Harmonic Group match in the "Competency
Group" (composed of Ones, Threes and Fives). Their focus on
competence is especially strong around parenting issues. Once the
girls leave home, I doubt their values around competency will extend

to other areas. Both girls will be off to college in five years and as Liz and Zack get older she may want more travel, more involvement in organizations and more activity, while he is likely to become even more withdrawn. Ones and Fives share no complementary interior line, so there are no natural "energy tunnels" for balancing each other.

"How Could She?"

Brad, 47, a square-jawed, solidly built Social One, had been married for 16 years to Betty, 46. They have two children, 7 and 10. He'd had two brief previous marriages when he was 19 and 22. About a month before I saw Brad in my office, he had arrived home unexpectedly and discovered Betty having sex in their bedroom with his best friend from high school.

"When I discovered that their affair had been going on for three years, I felt mortified," he said. "How could she do this to me?"

During our early sessions, I learned that Brad had been the CEO of a huge nonprofit corporation in Indiana. I quickly formed a picture of a man who is idealistic almost to the point of naïveté but highly successful in his work. He wants things to be fair and done according to the rules and he's willing to give a great deal of himself in service to a political or social cause.

"I guess you could call me 'Mr. Commitment,'" he said. When I asked for a few adjectives he would use to describe himself, he answered: "Proper, tense, principled, hardworking, quick on the trigger verbally"—a list that confirmed my own impression of him.

When I asked about his marriage to Betty, he said, "I thought I loved her when we got married. But after I discovered her affair, I no longer felt anything for her. I was done, cold, finished."

Betty had told him many times that she felt neglected throughout the marriage. From Brad's description, she sounded like a Two with a Sexual subtype. Brad's friend—her lover, Vern—sounded like an Eight with a Sexual subtype.

Brad, aware of his own political visibility, was especially concerned about how the revelation of his wife's affair would affect his stature in the community. For three days after discovering the lovers together in his bedroom, he stayed in a motel, speaking to no one, unable to decide what to do. Then he called his parents. When he told them what had happened, they urged him to leave Indiana, come to live with them temporarily in Southern California—and to file for divorce. No doubt Brad's parents had a profound influence on his personality and value system. (From his descriptions, it's possible that both parents could be Ones who share the Self-preservation subtype.)

Brad applied for a three-month medical "stress leave of absence" from his job and came to stay temporarily in his parents' home, but was so paralyzed by the social embarrassment of his situation that he was unable to take any further action. When his parents took the initiative and brought him to my office, he told me he believed the disgrace over his wife having an affair with his best friend had made it impossible for him to ever again show his face in their hometown, where he had been such a pillar of this close-knit community.

Since he was obviously deeply depressed (though not suicidal), I believed he might benefit from medication. I referred him to a psychopharmacologist, who prescribed an anti-depressant, and Brad's depression was, in fact, considerably relieved over the next month, which allowed our psychotherapy to become more effective. As I probed into his marriage, Brad confessed that he'd never felt deeply connected to his wife. "Our sex life was pretty hit-and-miss, pretty sporadic—I was generally too tired, with all my committees and volunteer work on top of my regular job." He was out at meetings, men's groups and chamber-of-commerce events at least five nights out of seven. He loved being involved with these community organizations.

The possibility that he had been negligent with his wife was not something he could even consider. "Look," he said, "I'm not the one who had the affair. I never cheated. I never lied. I never did anything wrong. She's the adulteress."

As we got further into the discussion of his marriage, it became clear that he didn't actually miss his wife or the marriage. Although shattered by the damage to his reputation, he had no desire to repair the relationship. His two kids he did miss at times, but felt okay just talking to them regularly on the phone. During these calls he never asked to speak to his wife. He was severely upset and longed for his groups, committees and cronies.

He was shocked and upset with me when I pointed out that, despite his image of himself as a "good man," his performance as a husband really wasn't very good. I believed it was understandable that his wife could have felt neglected. She told Brad after the affair came out that she had already been planning to ask for a divorce during the coming year—because she was so profoundly unhappy.

Brad appeared completely unconscious regarding Betty's feelings and never showed any desire to make amends for his own behavior or choices. He and his parents never wavered from their conclusion that he was right and Betty was wrong. (This is typical black-and-white thinking for Type One individuals when they are unhealthy or under great stress.) In the event that Brad's parents were also Ones, he was receiving enormous reinforcement for his rigid opinions.

When I first broached the subject of Brad making an objective study of his personality type, he strongly resisted, but eventually he agreed to take the survey, which confirmed his Type One structure. (He quickly recognized his own Social subtype). He finally came to see how detached he'd been from his wife. Despite some common values about parenting, it was clear that their lovemaps were highly incompatible and that both Brad and Betty were deeply unhappy with each other as a spouse.

Thus it came as no surprise when Brad hired an attorney and filed for divorce in Indiana, resigned his job there and requested recommendations for companies in Southern California. Seven months later he and Betty were divorced.

Nine months after his discovery of the adulterous scene in his bedroom, Brad still lives with his parents, talks weekly by phone with his kids, though never with Betty and has severed all connection with Vern, his former friend. Though he has not yet settled on a new job in California, I feel sure he will within the next few months. There are few employers who would not welcome a man of Brad's administrative experience and sociability who actually prefers being married to his job!

The Five Factors predicting long-term success in relationships were all-too-accurate in relation to the failure of Brad and Betty's marriage. Their lovemaps had little in common, with the major criteria each preferred in a mate not being met by the other.

Not having met Betty personally, I cannot be certain about her level of psychological health. Brad's level was sometimes in the average range but more often unhealthy. People with the One personality style—especially those in the average and lower levels of health—can be rigid and self-righteous. This lack of adaptability often goes hand-in-hand with limitations of empathy, especially for one's spouse. It seems ironic that Brad, a man so determined to be good and right, could be so blind to the importance of compassion and kindness toward his own wife.

The remaining three predictors of marital satisfaction for this couple were also negative: Brad and Betty did not share the same subtype (his Social versus her probable Sexual); they were not in the same Harmonic Group; and they lacked a shared Enneagram interior line, which would have helped them complement one another.

According to Brad, Betty is "undoubtedly happier with Vern—a warm, burly guy who loves her and the kids and will be a decent stepfather" (and whom Brad believes to be a Type Eight). Betty and Vern's lovemaps are evidently more compatible than hers and Brad's were and they both seem (from Brad's description) average to healthy in their psychological development. The probability of their sharing the Sexual subtype as well as an interior Enneagram line (between Two and Eight) for balancing their differences also bodes well for a long-term satisfying relationship.

Liz and Brad as Social Ones

Both Liz and Brad focused intensely on activities in social groups outside their marriages. For Liz, activities outside the nuclear family are important and likely to become more so, once Zack's daughters leave for college. His aversion to social activities could ultimately be a major problem for this couple, thus putting the marriage on shaky ground. However, we should note that many couples have remained married despite great dissatisfaction, out of pure commitment and principle or because the prospect of divorce and a single lifestyle produces greater fear than remaining in the relationship.

Brad's high degree of "nonadaptability" made him judge his Sexual-subtype wife harshly for seeking affection outside their marriage and he was unable to consider that he might have some responsibility for her affair. His own self-esteem was so strongly linked to his reputation among the townspeople that he could not face ever returning to the same community.

Strengths of Ones in Intimate Relationships

- Integrity
- Fairness
- Industriousness
- Responsibility
- Commitment
- Competency
- Productivity
- Discernment

Limitations of Ones in Intimate Relationships

- Rigidity
- Insistence on control
- Self-righteousness
- Intolerance
- Displaced anger
- Sermonizing
- Criticalness
- Obsessive-compulsive tendencies

Defense Mechanisms of Ones

Many Ones feel resentment, seeing so many people in this world who are less ethical and scrupulous than they are. This resentment—a tamped-down version of anger—can have serious psychological and physiological costs. As one aphorism aptly puts it, "Resentment is like drinking poison and expecting someone else to die."

Often Ones, seeking to maintain their idealized image of themselves as "good" and "right" people, resort to a defense mechanism called *reaction formation* that allows them to oppose their natural human anger, lusty impulses or fallibility by a kind of self-flagellating corrective thinking that may actually be the direct opposite of what they are feeling. Thus the "inner critic" arises—a voice in the head that continually castigates the Type One for any lapse from their impossibly high standard of perfection, creating the fear that they may, in fact, be wrong or even inherently evil.

Another variation on reaction formation can show up in average-level Ones' insistence on their own "goodness" (as opposed to their spouse's "badness"). We saw this in Brad's initial resistance to seeing any flaw in his behavior toward his wife, though it was clear that his neglect was a significant factor in Betty's unfaithfulness. Yet his depression was probably an expression of his repressed anger toward himself, not just Betty. His desperate need to maintain his ego's desire to be "right" ultimately took precedence over everything.

The "Natural Neuroses" of Ones

The first step for Ones, as for all types, is to learn about yourself, your blind spots and "natural neuroses" (a term I coined to describe each type's common dysfunctional patterns, such as Ones' rigidity and perfectionism). It's important to see your own personality clearly and understand what you do and don't want from a relationship.

The second step is to avoid *projecting* your natural neuroses onto your mate. For example, Ones often assume that if someone really loves them, he or she *should want* to be more like them, because that's the right thing to do. Under cover of their own self-righteous-ness, Ones can twist things so that the partner—if he or she is a "good and right" person and really loves the One—must become more like him or her in order to prove this love. We saw this in the case of Vanessa, who assumed that if a man "really loved her" he should become more like her. Strongly aware of the "fatal flaws" in her lovers, she failed to see the serious flaws in her own unreasonable demands. As Ones' level of psychological health grows, they may have less need to hang on to their natural neuroses and may, like Vanessa, move beyond many of their blind spots and projections.

How Ones Blossom in Good Relationships

A loving long-term relationship can give rise to impressive personal growth in Ones. As children, most Ones come to believe that they must be perfect in order to be loved. But they continually observe around them others who break the rules, yet succeed in attracting love.

When Ones do feel unconditionally loved and cherished over time by a partner they love and respect, their sharp edges tend to soften. Their focus is no longer on seeing people and things as right or wrong, good or bad; they find instead the middle ground that characterizes true wisdom, objectivity and fair-mindedness.

Dean, a Sexual One, driven to temporary insecurity about this sexual orientation because of the loneliness in his marriage to a successful saleswoman, was reassured of her love by her effective efforts to cut down her stressful work schedule. Once they were able to have more time together, Dean's basically high level of psychological health allowed him to fully enjoy their already strong relationship and make his own loving contributions to sustain it.

When Ones are encouraged and nurtured in ways that bring about their maturation and growth, they can be the most committed and responsible of all the types. Their discernment about the truth and their ability to bring it out on behalf of themselves, others and their community is a shining gift. Their strength and nobility allow them to embody important principles and resist being caught up in emotionality. Regardless of subtype, evolved Ones as a group have an enormous ability to transcend their ego and do the right thing, without being influenced by personal desires or agendas.

TYPE TWO: THE CARETAKER IN LOVE

Twos at all levels of health seek to win love through serving and helping others. Because average Twos are out of touch with their personal needs and desires, they unconsciously seek to align themselves with people who can fill those needs. But Twos delude themselves into believing that *they* are filling the needs of others, which then becomes a source of pride. Average Twos are continually in search of reassurance that they are loved and valued.

Healthy Twos are altruistic and loving and they nurture others without any expectation of return. They are often deeply humble people who take their greatest satisfaction in seeing others' suffering reduced. Unlike average Twos, they are in touch with their own feelings and have an ability to nurture themselves as well as others.

Unhealthy Twos can be aggressive and manipulative, demanding from others the love they feel they deserve for their selfless devotion. Twos at this level are bitter at what they see as others' ingratitude. They may use their own illnesses—often psychosomatic in origin— as evidence of their self-sacrifice and to punish others. When Twos deteriorate to this degree, they become so unlovable that they drive away the love they crave. In the pathological extreme, an unhealthy Two could become a stalker.

Twos with the Self-preservation subtype

Self-preservation Twos, whom Oscar Ichazo characterizes as "me-first," feel entitled to special treatment because of all they have done for others. These are the caretaker Twos, who can be enormous givers, especially in physical and material ways. They subsequently project their own needs onto others and feel resentful if they do not receive special privileges in return. There is a childish, tender quality to this subtype, especially in the average levels. Since it is difficult for them to ask directly for what they want or need, their feeling that others "owe" them can quickly turn to martyrdom. The "giving to get" motivation is particularly evident in the Self-preservation variant.

"Payback"

Jenny, 29, a Self-preservation Two, is an ample and strikingly beautiful black woman who works as a registered nurse. Married to Jared, 32, a physician, for five years, she told me during our first session: "My husband has asked for a separation. I feel like my life is slipping away."

Answers to my questions about her background revealed that she had immigrated to the United States from Jamaica at age 18 with members of her extended family. She quickly got a job in an uncle's corporation, passed her high-school equivalency exam and put herself through nursing school with the help of student loans.

When she was 23, she met Jared, who was then a medical student, at the hospital where she worked. "He was black, bright and exceptionally handsome," she said. "We were two of a kind!" After dating for a year, they married when Jenny was 24 and Jared 27.

When she came to see me, Jared was serving his residency at a local hospital. Jenny, still working as an R.N., had devoted her life to serving her husband's every need: paying all their bills (including installments on his student loans as well as her own), doing all the shopping and housework, preparing elaborate lunches for him to take to work, making sure all his clothes were clean and pressed. In her obsessive focus on Jared, she had ignored her own needs, gained a significant amount of weight and felt neglected because of his work schedule.

The tension between them had grown increasingly ugly, with her continual demands for appreciation so irritating Jared that he often yelled at her to "get out of my face." This situation had been building for two years before she came to see me. She felt resentful, used and desperate for her husband's appreciation of all she had done. The more bitter she felt, the more she neglected herself, even though Jared encouraged her to be more independent and self-sufficient emotionally. He especially wanted her to join a gym and lose weight. The more insistent she was on his attention, the more he arranged to stay away.

Things came to a crisis when he told Jenny he could no longer stand her constant complaining and asked for a separation. "You no longer need to martyr yourself on my behalf," he told her.

This precipitated her making an appointment to see me. Right after my first session with her, Jared did move out, separated their finances and made it clear that the enmeshment was too much for him. Jenny, heartbroken, was unable to imagine her life without Jared, who had been the center of her life.

Jared agreed to come in for several joint sessions and he struck me as a warm, put-together guy (probably a Social One). He made it clear that he'd had an overdose of Jenny's neediness and determination to be indispensable in his life. He hoped she would go to a weight-loss program, work out at a gym—anything to reduce her dependency on him. No longer having any sexual or romantic feelings toward her, he had increasing difficulty even being civil to her. He was relieved to be living separately and thought it appropriate that he file for divorce.

So distraught that she could hardly look at this reality, Jenny took a two-week leave of absence from her nursing work. Even after her veiled threat of suicide, Jared refused to give in to her demand that he move back home. He expressed a total lack of interest in having children with her and said he no longer trusted her basic attitudes and values. Serious incompatibilities in their lovemaps were being uncovered.

In the face of this, there was nothing for Jenny to do but come to terms with her dependency. I recommended two books that helped set her on the right track: *Codependent No More* by Melody Beattie and *Self Matters: Creating Your Life from the Inside Out* by Phillip C. McGraw. Although completely unaware of her own patterns in the beginning, Jenny was a good student, willing to learn about herself in a profound way and get in touch with aspects of her attitudes that needed changing. Ultimately, she became more self-actualized and less dependent on others' approval, especially Jared's.

The most significant part of her personal growth was her deep understanding of her own Self-preservation Two personality. She read everything she could about Twos. It was rare for me to see changes as enormous as those Jenny made.

Eventually she was able to understand how her martyrdom and sense of entitlement had become such a turn-off for Jared. He had acknowledged himself as a Social subtype and Jenny felt certain he was a Type One. Armed with this new knowledge, Jenny finally realized that he simply did not appreciate all her caretaking. Instead, he wanted someone who would share his political and social standards, a wife he could feel proud of in his many social circles—"certainly not a fat gal who nagged at him for more personal attention," as Jenny summed it up.

Jenny was able to correct many things about her thinking and decision-making. Acknowledging that no matter what she did she would always remain a Two, she was committed to making herself the healthiest Two she could be. In fact, she did learn that she had considerable control over the level of psychological health within her personality type.

Feeling she had made important progress, she tried to re-establish contact with Jared, but he refused her requests to "just be friends" or to date, seeing these overtures as hooks designed to manipulate him into resuming the marriage.

They did divorce and after a year and a half of sessions with me, Jenny felt armed with many tools to begin her life as an independent single woman. She still works as an R.N., lost 30 pounds after joining a weight loss program and recently resumed dating. She is better able now to keep her tendencies toward martyrdom and emotional dependency in check and her self-esteem is much higher.

Dependency is one of the most significant natural neuroses of Twos. In psychological terms, the self-esteem of dependent people is directly correlated with how much they feel needed by significant others in their life. Their sense of purpose in life is often created by what they have to offer their life partner, behind the scenes. Although Jenny can't change her core personality, her level of psychological health is higher now and she can often spot her natural neuroses and catch herself before she acts on them.

In terms of the Five Factors connected with long-term relationship success, it would seem predictable from the outset that Jenny and Jared's marriage would be unlikely to endure. Despite their shared race, intelligence and initial physical attraction, their lovemaps were incompatible in several important ways—especially in how they believed their partner should relate to them. As the marked differences between Jared's and Jenny's lovemaps became conscious, the connection between them began to unravel and these incompatibilities were the main cause of their marriage falling apart.

Although Jared's level of psychological health seemed on the high side of average (from my brief observation of him), Jenny's was on the low side of average to unhealthy—another negative indicator for a long-term connection. Jared's Social subtype in combination with Jenny's Self-preservation was also a deficit, causing their incompatibilities to worsen. Finally, neither of the remaining two predictors of success—a shared Harmonic Group match or a direct connecting line to help them complement one another's differences—was present in this couple.

"Never Enough"

Danny, 26, a Self-preservation Two, had been working in his parents' small Italian restaurant since he was 14. "After my dad died last year," he told me, "I nearly killed myself keeping the place going. I thought after all I did to make a go of it, my mom would at least give me half ownership. But she won't even discuss it—doesn't seem to have any appreciation for everything I've done."

My usual background questions revealed that Danny, whose expressive brown eyes were underlined with dark circles, had not only neglected his own health in his struggle to keep the family restaurant going, he had also neglected his life partner, Tim, 28, a technical engineer with whom he had lived in a committed gay relationship for four years. Tim had been exceptionally supportive of Danny's efforts, even going in to wait tables at the restaurant on evenings when Danny needed extra help. Although I never met Tim in person until late in Danny's therapy, he sounded like a generous man of good heart and spirit, probably a Self-preservation Six, from Danny's description. Danny took the C-JES personality survey immediately and recognized himself as a classic Two, with the Self-preservation subtype. He knew immediately that Tim was also Self-preservation and later confirmed his Type Six.

After his father's fatal heart attack, Danny threw himself into the restaurant, took over his dad's responsibilities and more: ordering food and supplies, hiring and firing personnel, doing much of the cooking and bookkeeping. His mother (possibly a Self-preservation Five) was so depressed by her husband's death that she was unable to continue even the minimal bookkeeping and ordering work she had formerly done. Danny's sisters, ages 17 and 19, occasionally helped out by waiting on tables as a favor to Danny but obviously had little interest in the restaurant business.

Danny, having martyred himself for the sake of the family business, was bitter over his mother's lack of appreciation for his efforts. All his attempts to talk with her about his expectations for being a partner in the restaurant were met with stonewalling. "Yesterday," he told me during our first session, "I just broke down emotionally—gave her two weeks' notice that I was quitting the business altogether."

"And what will you do now?" I asked.

"Tim and I talked it over," he said. "I convinced him that we should move to a different city. He'll have no trouble getting another job—he's a top-notch engineer—and I'll just have to find some new career. I can't survive in this vacuum my mom has created with the restaurant."

Not surprisingly, Danny's resignation finally got his mother's attention and, at Danny's insistence, she agreed to come in to see me. A heavyset woman with a deeply lined face, she seemed panicked at the prospect of her son's departure on top of her husband's death. She refused to take the personality survey: "My personality is none of your business. All I want you to do is what you were hired for— talk some sense into my son!"

It was clear that the last thing she wanted was for Danny to leave the restaurant. After several sessions and many, many tears from both son and mother, she finally agreed to give Danny half legal ownership in the restaurant and to split all profits 50/50 with him on a monthly basis. I suggested that she set up a new will and a living trust to have Danny inherit her half of the business upon her death and she grudgingly agreed. This way the ownership of the restaurant would eventually be his entirely, not shared with his sisters. His mother acknowledged that, given his heroic efforts, this was only fair. She knew that Danny, who has the same basic personality as his dad, was the only reason the restaurant had remained open. I referred Danny to a local attorney and encouraged him to immediately complete all legal work, making it easy for his mother to sign.

Danny, elated at this outcome, readily agreed to remain in the restaurant because he loved the business and the people—both staff and customers. The restaurant, a fixture in their local community, was always busy. Tim, as usual, was on board to help his soul mate with whatever Danny thought was important.

Though Danny still has issues with his mother's inability to connect with him emotionally, her willingness to make him a 50-percent financial partner (and eventual full owner of the restaurant) went a long way toward resolving his need for acknowledgment. Danny had accepted the fact that his mother's inability to express gratitude probably wouldn't change; it would never be enough. But now he could live with this reality. His father, who was probably a Social Two, had been the dominant force in the family and in the business. The mother had always been withdrawn and introverted, so her unresponsiveness was essentially nothing new for her family.

In the meantime, Danny had been suffering from periods of premature ejaculation along with brief periods of impotence in his sexual relationship with Tim. He reported that his anxiety over leaving the business had been as great as his anxiety over staying. Danny's mounting tension and obsessive thinking over his decisions resulted in his becoming detached from his physical and emotional needs. He was so distracted that simple bodily pleasure became impossible.

Although the main reason Danny came to see me did not involve sex therapy, I was able to instruct him and Tim to do a series of "sensate focus" exercises that completely refocused their mutual attention on the process of giving and receiving pleasure—and away from Danny's performance anxiety. I was also able to help Danny understand the point of ejaculatory inevitability—and to practice "peaking" on an arousal scale of zero to ten (with ten being actual ejaculation). He became quite conscious of his level of arousal and learned to control the sensations and return to a lower level of excitement. Repeating this process three or four times, he was eventually able to peak several times at the nine-and-a-half level prior to ejaculation.

Both Tim and Danny were excellent students and they were able within a five-week period to return to their fully functional sex life. Danny had to relearn how to receive pleasure and to ask directly for what felt good to him, beginning with simple face caresses, advancing to non-genital body caresses and eventually incorporating genital massage. During this relearning period, Danny commented several times on how shocked he was that he had become so out of touch with his own body. This is an extremely common problem for Self-preservation Twos.

In the end, he reported feeling completely satisfied in his relationship with Tim and grateful that we were able to resolve his sexual difficulties so quickly.

At the same time, Danny's reading about the Self-preservation Five allowed him to better understand his mother's personality structure. He grew enormously in the course of our sessions—gaining insight into his own deep craving for appreciation and becoming less dependent on his mother's verbal expressions of approval.

Like most Twos, Danny loves serving people, feeling indispensable to their nurturing and meeting their needs even before being asked (he remembers his customers' preferences and often has their drinks on the table before they even sit down). The constant loving support of his partner, Tim and his two younger sisters has also helped fill his need for appreciation.

It's worth noting here that for people with the Self-preservation subtype a connection to the essentials of life is especially important.

Food and money are usually important issues for individuals of this subtype and when we add to this the Two's need to nurture others, the restaurant business seems a perfect career choice for Danny.

Looking at our Five Factors for evaluating relationship success, it appears that Danny and Tim have a solid foundation from the first three criteria. Most important is the high compatibility of their lovemaps, with each of them feeling deeply satisfied with who their partner truly is. As two young gay men, they appear to be genuinely happy with one another.

Secondly, Danny's level of psychological development skyrocketed during the course of our therapy—from average levels, with dips into the unhealthy range as a result of his dad's death, to truly healthy in various respects. Tim seemed healthy, self-accepting and confident from the beginning (although I never knew him as well as I did Danny).

Additionally, they had the advantage of sharing the Self-preservation subtype, which helped align many of their values and priorities. Although they were not in the same Harmonic Group and were not connected by a direct balancing line, they seem to have a strong probability of relationship success.

Jenny and Danny as Self-preservation Twos

Both Jenny and Danny craved appreciation for what they had given to their loved ones and both suffered from what they saw as an insufficient return on their investments of themselves in serving others. Jenny martyred herself in a desperate quest for her husband's love and gratitude and her compulsive caretaking ultimately drove her husband to end the marriage.

Danny sought expressions of appreciation from his mother for his valiant efforts to keep the family restaurant going after his father's death. Only his decision to leave the business and move with his partner to a different city brought his mother to the realization that she would need to give him half the business (a monetary, if not emotional, token of appreciation) in order to change his mind.

Twos with the Sexual Subtype

The Sexual subtype, which Ichazo associates with "seduction/aggression," is characterized by an intense focus on emotional and physical intimacy in one-to-one relationships. Often seductive, Sexual Twos want to be deeply involved in the partner's life and keep him or her entranced through an impressive repertoire of manipulative tricks and sexual gamesmanship. If it appears that the object of the Two's affections is losing interest, the Sexual subtype individual will often pursue the lover relentlessly. Unhealthy Twos with this subtype can be overpowering and even dangerous to those who reject their unwelcome attentions.

"Restraining Order"

Pete, 38, a Sexual Two, a handsome man of French descent, had always been a ladies' man. The veteran of two short marriages in his 20s, he was baffled as to why both his ex-wives had complained that he was "possessive and refused to give them any space." And now Trudy, 36, who had been his fiancée for two years, had just filed a restraining order against him with the same complaint. "Everything I did, I did to show her how much I love her," he told me, in tears. "Why do these women need 'space'?"

"What did you do to show her how much you love her?" I asked him.

In the days since she had broken their engagement, he told me, he had slept all night in his car parked in front of her home; made frequent visits to her workplace to deliver flowers, candy and loving notes; phoned her ten to twenty times a day to express his love. Now she was calling these loving gestures stalking and harassment! He was restrained from having any contact with her except through her attorney.

Pete had been eager to set a wedding date for the following summer, but Trudy had refused. She had sent back the engagement ring he had given her—in an ordinary Express Mail envelope, without even caring enough to insure it.

Although I never met Trudy and she never took the personality survey, she seemed, from Pete's description, to be a Sexual Four. Much as she enjoyed being treated as special in the early days they were together, his insistence on being the primary giver and controller in the relationship filled up all their emotional space, leaving her none in which to reciprocate in her own special way, as Fours often want to do.

He reported that Trudy loved their wonderful sexual relationship and the many common interests they had, but she had told him she could no longer tolerate his continually pushing himself into her life, manipulating how, when and where she did everything.

I invited Pete to give me a few examples.

He produced them with no hesitation. There was the day when a woman who had been Trudy's best friend in high school had come to town on a sudden business trip and called to invite Trudy to lunch. Trudy had accepted and Pete was deeply offended that she would do this without consulting him first. The two of them generally had lunch together and he felt Trudy should have declined the invitation and told her friend she was having lunch with her fiancé. Or, if she really *had* to see her friend, the least she could have done was invite him to join them.

I asked how Trudy felt about his reaction.

"She said I wasn't being fair—that I was acting too possessive, trying to control all her time." He gave me a pained look. "But when you love someone, how can you not want to be with them as much as possible?"

I was beginning to understand why Trudy had felt overwhelmed in this relationship.

"But what she did to me about her parents' Caribbean cruise was even worse," he said. He proceeded to tell me that, when he and Trudy had been together for six months and engaged one month, Trudy's parents had decided, as a 40th wedding anniversary celebration, to take their three daughters with them on a Caribbean cruise. It would be just the family—the three girls and their parents; even Trudy's sisters' husbands were not included. But Pete wanted to go along and saw no reason he shouldn't, since he was prepared to pay his own way. He was willing to sacrifice his one remaining week of vacation time (from the insurance company where he worked as a salesman) in order to get to know Trudy's family.

When Trudy told him she wanted time alone with her parents and sisters, he fought to be allowed to go and was unable to grasp why Trudy refused his request. He wanted to "snuggle up" to her family and was hurt at being excluded, especially when no one had even asked his opinion about the cruise.

We see here how an unhealthy Sexual Two, assuming he is indispensable, can attempt to manipulate a situation into which he has no business inserting himself. In the end, Trudy went on the cruise without him. Their engagement survived, but the cruise was a subject of recurring fierce arguments between them during the eighteen months they remained together.

When Trudy finally called off the engagement, Pete's sorrow and despair lasted for months. Eventually, I was able to help him gain some perspective on how his personality had impacted the situation. He was able to identify himself as a Sexual subtype early on from the outlines I gave him. After taking the C-JES survey, Pete confirmed his personality style. Reading the Type Two profile helped him see his own natural neuroses and understand some of his blind spots. Having viewed himself as "one of the most loving and giving men on the planet," he was finally becoming aware of the dark side of this picture. Trudy had simply overdosed on his guilt trips and attempts to manipulate her.

In the course of our sessions, Pete became aware that people with other personality types have agendas different from his own and he worked on becoming less manipulative, pushy and insinuating. He also made an effort to balance his Sexual subtype with attention to his Social and Self-preservation needs. After four months he ended his therapy with me, having agreed never to contact Trudy again, even after the restraining order expired. Although I knew that Pete needed much more therapy, he insisted on ending our sessions because he needed "the time and money to find someone to replace Trudy," despite all my cautions. I simply invited him to come back to therapy whenever he felt he needed it.

Even though Pete and Trudy had some factors going for them in their relationship—both being Sexual subtypes and sharing the balancing line connecting Twos and Fours—they had some major incompatibilities in their lovemaps and were not in the same Harmonic Group. However, Pete's unhealthy level of psychological development was the major negative factor that ultimately caused Trudy to end the relationship completely.

Twos, male as well as female, have an archetypal parenting quality that sometimes shows up as possessiveness. With an unhealthy Two, such parenting can take on the feeling of smothering. Even for a Sexual Four like Trudy, who certainly had issues around abandonment, the relentless nurturing of her Type Two fiancé eventually became overwhelming. Twos have a natural gift for empathy, but Pete's unhealthy psychological level made it impossible for him to see himself through Trudy's eyes. His own need for attachment, his abandonment issues and his need to control Trudy undermined what might have been some genuine empathy for her needs as his partner. Unfortunately, Pete did not develop a high enough level of health to make it likely that he could avoid making the same mistakes again.

"Marriage Sabbatical"

Edie, 66, a Sexual Two, is a plump, motherly woman who radiates warmth. She has been married for 45 years to Hank, 68, a Social Eight; they have three grown children, all with healthy marriages, children of their own and successful careers. Hank has always been a good provider for his family and Edie has never worked outside the home. A few years earlier he sold his successful electrical supply business, leaving the couple financially comfortable.

During our first session, Edie told me, "I don't understand it. Hank wants a 'sabbatical' from our marriage. He says he's going to move out of our house and rent an apartment so he can live in peace for a year without me butting in on everything he does."

On my questioning, it became clear that she knew Hank was asking only for a separation. He and Edie are devout Catholics, active in their church, so divorce has never been an option. Hank felt that only through living alone could he pursue his political and social causes without his wife's unwelcome involvement.

"Hank has been pushing me away for some time," Edie told me. " He even had the nerve to accuse me of 'horning in' on his projects. I don't know where he gets off, implying that I'm such a pest. I've been carrying him emotionally for the last 45 years."

I suggested that Hank join Edie for her second session with me and he readily agreed. A burly man with a loud voice and strong presence, he was supportive of his wife and aware of the pain his sabbatical plan was causing her. Yet he was determined to do what he could in his community to support animal rescue and gun control laws and to serve as a volunteer in a Marine Corps veterans group. He promised to move back into their five-bedroom family home after one year.

"Before I sold the business," he said, "I wasn't so aware of the way Edie has to have her nose into everything. When the kids were still at home, a lot of her attention got focused on them. But now that I'm no longer working, I'm fed up with being taken care of every minute, even though I know she's just doing it out of the goodness of that great big heart of hers—cooking all my favorite meals, shopping for my clothes, taking care of laundry and dry cleaning, making all my doctor and dentist appointments and giving me lots of great advice, even when I don't need it or want it."

Though Edie was grateful for Hank's willingness to attend joint therapy sessions, she insisted on continuing with individual therapy as well, since "Hank always takes over." Here were two strong personalities, both warm and open and mature, with a lot of love and mutual respect for each other. Yet there was a major problem to be resolved.

Hank's plan for disrupting their shared world had left Edie feeling unimportant and dispensable. She was obviously desperate to maintain her connection with him and he was equally determined to create some space to pursue social causes and activities he valued, apart from her and their home. They were experiencing deep but unconscious conflicts between the clashing dynamics of their personalities.

In the early years of their marriage, both had been extremely busy with their separate tasks—hers revolving around their home and children, his around developing the successful business that sustained them all. He appreciated her being "always there" to problem-solve with him about aspects of his business, even though she sometimes offered more help than he really wanted. Both of them appeared deeply pleased that their children saw them as excellent parents.

Both were eager to do the personality analysis, to learn more about themselves and each other. Both readily took the Enneagram survey. Edie's results confirmed that she was, as I had suspected, a Two. Hank's Type Eight was confirmed not only by the survey but also by two other Enneagram quizzes he had taken. Both agreed that Edie was a Sexual subtype and Hank was Social.

As a Social Eight, Hank was anxious to further develop some of the bonds he had established with other Marine Corps veterans. He loved the socializing and event planning, especially for wounded veterans. During the years he worked full time as the owner of his company, he had felt distressed at not having the time to pursue such endeavors. This was one of the reasons he had sold the company when he did and he was now insisting on having the freedom to serve the causes he believed in.

He also made it clear that he had no desire to hurt his beloved Edie, but needed her to accept that there was little or no part for her to play in some of his present interests.

"All our kids are grown, married and happy," he said, "and this is my time now."

Edie confessed that Hank's new vision of his life made her feel panicky. "It feels like he's abandoning me, abandoning our marriage," she said. "I'm wondering if all this is his way of leading up to something worse. I'm heartbroken beyond words."

"I'm not leading up to anything," Hank said. "I just want a sabbatical from the confines of this marriage—a separation. The idea of divorce never even occurred to me."

Hearing this, Edie seemed to relax a bit. Yet she still wanted to know whether he was dismissing all she had given him over their 45 years of marriage. Now that the kids were gone, did he really think he could navigate his life better without her on board?

Hank appeared stunned as Edie rolled out her questions, never stopping long enough to give him a chance to respond.

I reminded him that these were the questions of a Sexual Two who felt threatened, rejected and discounted. He responded immediately that he loved and treasured Edie as his wife. He had never even fantasized about any other woman and would always remain committed to her and the marriage. "You're my best pal for life," he said.

When I explained that Hank simply wanted the freedom to pursue his own interests and that her place in his heart was in no way threatened by this, Edie's concerns seemed somewhat assuaged. We agreed to meet for more joint sessions before Hank made any move toward renting an apartment or leaving home.

In the course of several joint and individual sessions with me, each of them described what they perceived as the emotional costs of Hank's taking an apartment. They agreed that the upset this would cause for their children, friends and community would not be worth the benefits to Hank. Although he truly needed and wanted a "marriage sabbatical," he was unwilling to go through all the predictable questions, concerns and upheaval that his physically moving out would cause for others.

Following serious consideration of all their options, I suggested that, rather than moving out of the family home, Hank arrange to have his year of separation by remaining in the home—but taking over, for his exclusive use, one of the five bedrooms with a large bath, plus another adjacent room to use as an office. He would be responsible for cleaning and maintaining his space and for his own laundry. Both partners would be respectful roommates with the other. It would be understood that each could do favors for the other only after asking and obtaining permission.

Under this arrangement I was proposing, no one other than Edie and Hank would need to know about their separation. My suggestion brought huge relief to both of them and Edie seemed to immediately gain a new understanding of why Hank needed a space of his own.

We proceeded to work out the details of the plan, including a system for dating: we agreed that Edie could invite Hank to dinner as many as three nights a week, only as it suited her and she would cook for him. Hank would ask Edie out to dinner a maximum of two of the remaining nights, only if and when it was convenient for him. He would have the remaining nights and all daytime hours for his causes or whatever else he wanted to do.

Edie was especially relieved that she would not be faced with having to answer questions from their children and close friends as to why Hank had decided to move out. It felt good to her that he actually preferred to remain in their home, so long as there were definite boundaries and clear expectations about how the "separation" would work.

By now Edie was beginning to look forward to having some open space of her own for things she had wanted to explore. She was considering enrolling in an art class at a local college, something she had never mentioned before this.

The new "separation contract," as Hank called it, was a welcome reprieve for him. He was eventually able to explain, to both Edie and me, the desperation he had felt about needing some space for himself, yet not wanting to hurt Edie or make her feel their marriage was threatened.

The new arrangement worked out so well for this couple, they eventually reported experiencing some new romance. Edie came to realize that her Sexual Two personality had become burdensome for Hank because he felt he couldn't move toward what he wanted to accomplish without making her feel abandoned. She ultimately became able to laugh at herself and catch herself before acting out some of her natural neuroses (such as trying to "help" Hank even when he didn't ask for it or lavishing holiday gifts on everyone, then feeling hurt when her gifts weren't sufficiently appreciated).

Edie achieved much greater levels of consciousness and was able to successfully change so much of her Two-ish behavior that she inquired if she had "become a non-Two." I assured her that her Type Two psychic structure was like her bone structure; it would never change. However, I explained that she had already become much healthier and would most likely continue to grow within that structure.

I'm thrilled, but not really surprised, that the outcome for this couple has been so positive. Using our Five Factors for predicting relationship success, most importantly their lovemaps are highly compatible (both committed to their Catholic values, family life and how they should treat one another). Even though they have different subtypes (her Sexual versus his Social), their high levels of psychological health make it possible for them to bring understanding and kindness to their conflicted situation. Another plus is their sharing the complementary connecting line between Twos and Eights, which enhances their ability to balance one another's differences.

Pete and Edie as Sexual Twos

Both Pete and Edie overwhelmed their partners with their intense focus on the relationship. In the case of Pete, his insistence on participating in every aspect of his fiancée's life eventually became oppressive to her, even though she was also a Sexual subtype, and he was unable to adjust his behavior sufficiently to sustain the relationship.

Edie and her husband both had above-average-to-high levels of health, to begin with and a long and successful marriage that both wanted to maintain. Edie was able, through therapy, to gain considerable empathy for her husband's desire to pursue his social causes and they were able, through love and good will on both sides, to work out a compromise that allowed each of them to have what they most needed, keeping their love relationship and marriage intact.

Twos with the Social subtype

Social Twos, whom Ichazo associates with "ambition," seek to enhance their position in society through making connections with others, matchmaking and hosting social events. Popularity—being noticed as friends of the elite or the hub of social interaction—is to them a sign that they are loved. Adept at social climbing, they maneuver to become indispensable to important people. In unhealthy versions, they can become givers of unwanted advice who become expert at manipulating others to feel indebted to them.

"Knows Everybody"

Ralph, 31, a Two with a Social subtype, is a good-looking, successful headhunter who enjoys "being the center of the wheel," networking and making connections between job seekers and employers. He came to me in distress because his fiancée, Renee (a Self-preservation Five, as we later learned), comptroller of a high-end technical company, had recently broken their engagement. "She said my 'big mouth and personal disclosures' were unacceptable to her," he told me.

I asked him to tell me more about the personal disclosures.

"Look," he said, "I'm an outgoing guy and I might have made a few comments to people about what a great relationship Renee and I have—but I don't see that as any big deal. She's so attractive, so bright and capable—of course I'm proud of her, proud of being with her. We're a great couple—everybody says so. I can't believe she's actually broken our engagement over this."

I asked Ralph to tell me more about himself and his work.

"People feel cared for by me," he said. I could certainly see that his good-hearted, helpful, friendly personality would serve him well in his chosen profession. Hearing his comment about how important it was to him to "talk with every single person in the room" in social as well as work engagements, I had the impression that his sociability might be somewhat superficial.

As I requested, Renee came in for several sessions with Ralph. But she made it clear from the outset that she was there not to repair the relationship but rather to help Ralph and me understand why the relationship was over, from her point of view.

"I'm a private person," she said, "and I found his social behavior revolting. His need to kiss ass with people made me sick and the more he used our relationship to make himself popular, the madder I got."

"How could you think I would ever do something like that?" Ralph said.

"Because several people—you know who they are—made not-too-subtle references to our 'great sex life.' I'm sick and tired of being exposed, analyzed and talked about behind my back."

"I love you," he said. "I'm sorry if I got carried away and said too much to a few people."

"Look, Ralph," Renee said, "why can't you see the truth? I don't like who you are and you don't like who I am." She went on to summarize their profoundly different experiences, even of the same situations.

For example, they had attended several professional banquets and cocktail parties associated with Ralph's work. At one party a female colleague of Ralph's commented to Renee how lucky she and Ralph were to be so sexually compatible. At another work-related event an older woman who had consulted with Ralph for several years put her arm around Renee and commented how good it was that Renee was enjoying such a great connection with Ralph, adding, "You never know when impotence may strike, the way it suddenly did with my husband."

Renee was furious with Ralph after episodes like these. She felt that their private sexual relationship should be off limits as a topic of conversation with any of his professional colleagues. Yet when she confronted him about putting her in an embarrassing position, he would deny having had inappropriate conversations with anyone.

Things became even more strained between them after private information she had shared with Ralph about her younger brother's drug addition also "leaked out, somehow, through Ralph's big mouth." Renee had been stunned when one of Ralph's fellow headhunters, sitting beside her at a dinner party, suddenly offered sympathy for what she and her family were going through. He understood the problems drug addiction could cause in a family, he told her, since he had the same problem with his younger sister. Once again, she felt betrayed by Ralph's sharing confidences that she had assumed were private. At this point she was so uncomfortable accompanying him to his events and parties that she all but refused to attend any more.

Ralph saw his discussing with friends personal things that Renee had shared with him as appropriate communication or simply self-disclosure. He was irritated by her anger at him over what seemed to him trivial matters. He also objected to her withdrawn social behavior. After all, hadn't he made clear to her how important it was for him to be with a woman he could be proud of in social situations? She had been that woman earlier in their relationship, but now her behavior was unresponsive, almost anti-social. Where was "the real Renee," the girl he had fallen so deeply in love with?

"The real Renee is right here," she told him, "and I'm fed up with your blabbering to the whole world about my private life.

"You ought to try writing a new version of *How to Win Friends and Influence People*," she went on. "That's all you seem to care about. It's not about me or any real love you have for me. I'm just a conduit for your social aspirations—not someone you want to spend any quality time alone with.

"Face it, Ralph—it's over. We're just too different: the chasm between us is too big for me to straddle. I don't love you anymore and it's better for me to be out of this relationship than in it. You'll just have to accept that."

Sensing that Renee might be a Five, I suggested she do some reading and consider taking the C-JES survey. She did this and confirmed that Five was indeed her type. We had previously established that Ralph's subtype was Social and hers was Self-preservation. I agreed with her that a marriage between the two of them would most likely have significant problems, especially with their lovemaps being so divergent.

Renee attended only three sessions with Ralph, but he continued with therapy for almost two years after that. His continuing study of the Enneagram confirmed that he was a Two. His Social subtype became increasingly obvious to him, as evidenced by his worry over the rejection he might face from friends and colleagues regarding the breakup with Renee. Now that he was no longer part of a couple, he feared that some of the social invitations would stop. It became clear that he didn't really miss Renee as a person nearly as much as he missed her being an adjunct to his social life.

Eventually, Ralph became willing to look at the blind spots related to his Two personality and Social subtype. I facilitated this by role-playing Renee in some of our sessions and he came to understand what she so vehemently objected to in his behavior and why. He also realized that her personality was not really what he wanted in a wife and that a marriage with her would not have worked.

Their lovemaps were greatly at odds, especially their polar-opposite views about socializing and the need for privacy. This was perhaps the most important cause of the failure of the relationship. Also, Ralph's level of psychological health was about average, often bordering on unhealthy at the beginning of his therapy. Renee's was somewhat higher in the average range. Given the Self-preservation Five's characteristic obsession with privacy, she showed an unusual degree of generosity in her willingness to participate in three therapy sessions *after* she had broken up with Ralph.

Their incompatibility was further confirmed by the remaining predictors of long-term relationship success: their subtypes were different and there was no Harmonic Group match and no complementary connecting line between Twos and Fives to balance "opposite" energies.

An interesting footnote to this case: Ralph's study of the Enneagram allowed him to see what an asset the system could be in his business and he is now using it as a tool for more effective headhunting. He has referred a number of clients to me because he believes "they would do better in their job search if they could understand their personality and correct their blind spots," much the same way he has.

"Madame Butterfly"

Grace, 63, a Social Two, had been married to Maxx, 66, a Self-preservation Six, for five years. Both had been widowed after long and happy first marriages in which each had two children. After being introduced by mutual friends, they had happily embarked on a companionship marriage. Now Maxx was talking about divorce.

Both partners had called me for individual appointments at nearly the same time after a former client recommended me to them. Grace, upon hearing that Maxx had already made an appointment for later in the week, insisted on seeing me the same day she called.

She wanted to make sure I heard her story before I saw Maxx.

There was deep hurt in her wide blue eyes as she told me: "Maxx says it's easier to be lonely being alone than to be lonely married to me. He says I'm so involved with everyone else, there's no time left for him."

"How do you feel about that?" I asked.

She shook her head. "I've done everything I could to get him involved in our country club, the church, my volunteer groups, my bridge club. I do have a lot of friends and I love to do little things for them—see that they meet the right people, get whatever help they need, things like that. I've tried to include Maxx, but it seems like he doesn't really want to be included."

Maxx's side of the story, which I heard a few days later, had a different perspective. "I've never felt emotionally safe with Grace," he said. "She's such a busybody—her energies are so scattered among all her groups and causes—I just can't stand living that way. I thought I was marrying *her*, not her whole social network."

"Do you want a divorce?" I asked him.

He took out a clean handkerchief and wiped his eyes. "Not really. Not if I ever got to spend some quality time with her. Not if she'd stop insisting that everybody in her life has to meet everybody else! I have no interest in spending time with all these people, but I feel as though I'm cramping her style when I ask for some time *alone* with her."

Clearly, Grace's Type Two personality and Social subtype had set her on a collision course with Maxx's Self-preservation Six needs. She was big-hearted, always doing social favors for others, facilitating and networking. People appreciated all this and she loved feeling indispensable behind the scenes.

Maxx had come to feel that his requests for her attention were unworthy and he felt insecure about her feelings for him and his actual value in her life. Furthermore, her scattered Social energies sometimes left his Self-preservation needs for safety and security unfilled. For example, when she frequently took food to serve others but forgot to leave any for him, he felt neglected, even betrayed.

They agreed to have joint sessions with me as well as individual sessions and these proved extremely effective. I was able to persuade them that, even if they did divorce, it would first be helpful to understand themselves and each other, so they wouldn't make the same mistakes again.

Both of them readily took the personality survey and both appeared to be at average levels of psychological health for their types. They were shocked and impressed with the results of the survey and were eager to study their own and each other's type through the reading I provided.

In order to help this couple gain insight into their partner's motives and fears, I used the technique of role-playing each of them while the other listened in. Eventually, I was able to teach them how to do reverse role-playing, with each of them in the role of the other—which worked especially well. Even though this initially caused considerable pain, it gave them insight into their own limitations and taught them much greater empathy for each other.

Through these exercises, Grace realized how lonely and over-looked Maxx felt. She saw how her scattered attention prevented her from focusing on him and their marriage.

Maxx realized that he needed to learn to speak up more on his own behalf, despite his natural introversion. He had assumed Grace could see how he was feeling, but she actually couldn't. At first he was fearful of even describing his true feelings. But after Grace's empathetic response to his revelations, he eventually became more willing to participate in discussions with her about his deepest concerns—things Grace never imagined could be true. He confided to her that he had fantasized her actually having an affair with another man or at least being in love with someone else. He had worried that her true intention might be to dump him, since she was so unwilling to spend any private time with him.

Grace was utterly shocked when she heard Maxx's concerns and realized that her style of loving was completely different from his. She assured him of her love and commitment to their marriage and proposed that they start making plans to do things together, just the two of them.

Once this one-to-one connection with each other was in place, Maxx became willing to go with her to some of her activities—especially in situations where she really wanted his company. When

Grace realized how important issues like food were to a person with a Self-preservation subtype, she arranged nearly all the time to have dinner with him (or at least to leave Maxx's special foods for him whenever she had to attend a meeting).

As they grew in empathy for each other, within a month both were much happier in the marriage. Grace did even more changing than Maxx—planning a romantic getaway weekend for Valentine's Day and arranging many special occasions for just the two of them. By the time he joined her co-ed card club, he felt genuinely included and enjoyed participating with her as a couple.

The partially compatible lovemaps of Grace and Maxx were an important factor in their staying together. Both had been looking for companionship in marriage and there was real affection between them. As they developed deeper empathy for each other and became more aware of the core issues between them, they both became healthier within their own personality structures. This made a big difference in both their lives.

Both Twos and Sixes have needs for contact with others: Twos for enhancing their self-image as helpers and caretakers, Sixes for the safety and security involved in trustworthy alliances. There is some common ground here, with both types having an innate talent for empathy, which was extremely important in the success of their short-term therapy (which lasted only nine weeks).

Their commitment to making the marriage work and their increased levels of psychological health and maturity, once they developed an awareness of each other's issues and needs, was strong enough to overcome their lack of a common subtype as well as their not being in the same Harmonic Group and not having a complementary connecting line for balancing their differences. Their lovemaps, being only somewhat compatible, lacked many of the elements that were present for each of them in their first marriages. Still, the marriage endured and their companionship was significantly enriched by the development of their mutual empathy and caring for one another.

Ralph and Grace as Social Twos

Ralph and Grace both gained a significant portion of their self-esteem from their feeling of importance in their social groups and in both cases their intimate relationships suffered from their primary focus on the community's validation. Ralph saw his fiancée as a social asset and his bragging to his associates about their intimate activities eventually led to her breaking the engagement. His primary concern about losing face with the group over the breakup underlines his Social subtype values.

Grace's focus on enhancing her popularity in her many social groups through networking and participation in various activities left her introverted husband feeling neglected and lonely. However, in contrast to Ralph's case, Grace's development of empathy for her husband's plight led to such a significant shift in her behavior that it helped close the breach between them, so that the marriage became more satisfying for both partners.

Strengths of Twos in Intimate Relationships

- Compassion
- Warmth
- Empathy
- Generosity
- Adaptability
- Supportiveness
- Positive outlook
- High Energy

Limitations of Twos in Intimate Relationships

- Dependency
- Neediness
- Intrusiveness
- Possessiveness

- Controlling
- Manipulativeness
- Entitlement
- Compulsive rescuing

Defense Mechanisms of Twos

As children, Twos often feel that in order to be loved they must make themselves indispensable to others. This frequently involves denying their own needs in order to serve the needs of others—even repressing their personal needs to such an extent that they are no longer consciously aware of them. Then they project outward their own unacknowledged neediness, seeing a world filled with other people's needs and continually striving, through their "helpfulness" and "caring," to get others indebted to them. This projection is often an unconscious defense mechanism.

An important clue to Twos' repression of their own needs is their emotionality when their services to others are, in their view, insufficiently appreciated. Unable to acknowledge their hidden agenda of "giving to get," they can take on an aura of martyrdom, becoming blaming and resentful. Twos are generally poor at using "I" statements in communication.

The defense mechanism of *repression* is evident in many of the cases I've described in this chapter: in Self-preservation Two Jenny's obsessive serving of husband Jared's needs while ignoring her own, in Sexual Two Pete's overwhelming fiancée Trudy with his attentions until she got a restraining order against him and in Sexual Two Edie's butting into husband Hank's activities until he asked for a sabbatical from the marriage. Social Twos are more likely to spread their compulsive helpfulness around a wider social circle, so that their partners may feel neglected, as did Ralph, Grace's husband.

The "Natural Neuroses" of Twos

Blindness to their own neediness and compensatory "giving to get" agenda is one of the central natural neuroses of Twos. For Twos the first step beyond this "blind spot" is to learn more about their dysfunctional behavioral and emotional patterns and come to understand how these patterns relate to the difficulties they perpetuate in relationships.

The second step is to avoid projecting their natural neuroses onto a mate. Twos often assume that making themselves indispensable to others will get them the unconditional love they crave. However, when they dominate all the giving space in an intimate relationship, they may cause the partner to feel smothered, as we saw in Pete's relationship with Trudy. Acknowledging one's own needs and learning to nurture one's self and soothe one's own emotional upsets can be a giant step forward for many Twos.

How Twos Blossom in Good Relationships

Fears of being unloved and unlovable, often entrenched since early childhood, can make less healthy and average-level Twos try so hard to please that they actually *become* unlovable (as we saw in the case of Jenny). However, when Twos have enough confidence in the steadfast love of their mate to acknowledge their real needs (as we saw with Edie), they can grow and mature impressively in the crucible of an intimate relationship. When they are secure enough to do this they automatically create a better balance in the relationship. Twos empowered by a sense of being loved unconditionally often become more inner-directed and able to give unconditionally of themselves, without "hooks" or conditions placed on the partner.

As with healthy individuals of all types, the evolved Two's personality is simply less visible. Twos at this stage of development have a gift for making their mates—and others who cross their paths—feel accepted for *who they are* in their essence. The kindness of healthy Twos has a quality of ease and simplicity, with no sense of strain or expectation. They brighten the lives of everyone around them through their compassion and gentle humor.

TYPE THREE: THE ACHIEVER IN LOVE

Threes make things happen in this world. They are energetic, goal-driven natural salespeople, adept first of all at selling themselves. When Threes think of a solution, they move immediately into action with no moments of hesitation over fears or doubts. This capacity can make a Three successful in the business world but unable to sustain a deep personal relationship. People of this type often find it difficult to connect with feelings, both their own and those of others. They focus instead on creating a public image of themselves as successful and desirable. When they fail to achieve their goals or impress others, their underlying feelings of inadequacy often come to the fore.

Average Threes focus on mastering situations, with a "can-do" attitude, an appetite for hard work and a long list of achievements. They can be stars in the corporate world and hard-driving managers of subordinates. Threes at this level can measure their achievements by the size of their income, beating out competitors and being recognized as super achievers. Because of the importance they place on their image, they usually dress well and appropriately, drive a car that advertises their success, choose housing that reflects their status and select their spouse on the same basis. The "dark" side of their image is often expressed in troubled intimate relationships, personal vanity and an inability to relax. Average Threes are uncomfortable with leisure time; even on vacation they may create demanding schedules and expect others to keep up with them.

Freud was the first of many psychologists to define a healthy individual as one who is able to love and to work. Threes who are healthy manage to find and maintain this balance. They become aware of their feelings and able to empathize with others and achieve real intimacy in personal relationships. Healthy Threes also bring a quality of "heart" to their work that gives their leadership an inspirational quality.

Unhealthy Threes can become entrenched in a heartless, ruthless, competitive stance and show great hostility toward anyone who stands in the way of their success. They generally have inflated opinions of their own abilities and are capable of great deceptiveness. If someone threatens to expose the fraudulence of their public image, unhealthy Threes may concoct elaborate stories to hide their failure and avoid exposing their deterioration. Threes who feel their dark side has been publicly exposed may lose control of their rage and resort to extremes of vengeance against those they hold responsible.

Threes with the Self-preservation Subtype

Self-preservation Threes, whom Oscar Ichazo associates with "security," are the most dedicated to work as a means of survival. More than the other two subtypes, they can be extreme workaholics, driven and focused on money and possessions as their primary source of security.

"Topless Dancer"

Nadia, 28, a Self-preservation Three, is a beautiful, exotic-looking woman who had been working as a topless dancer for three years to pay her tuition at a local university. She kept her work secret from her conservative parents, who had immigrated to the United States from Russia with their two sons just before Nadia was born and have been struggling financially ever since. Nadia was living at home for the current semester to save money, but planned to move out in three months, following graduation.

Two months before Nadia came to see me, her parents found out about her "topless job" from a neighbor who had attended a bachelor party at a local men's club. He recognized Nadia as "one of the cute chicks dancing in only a G-string," and congratulated her father for his liberal-mindedness in allowing his daughter to work at such an establishment.

"They disowned me," Nadia told me through her tears. "My oldest brother was there the day my parents confronted me. My dad kept yelling, 'Are you a prostitute, a whore?' The truth is, I've never had sexual contact with any of the customers at the club. But my family kept accusing me of these awful, degrading things."

In answer to my questions, it became clear that Nadia was anything but promiscuous. She described herself as rather naïve when it came to men and sexuality. She had clearly been over-protected by her fearful and traditional parents. For the past three years she had been in a monogamous relationship with Doug, a fellow-MBA candidate who knew about her dancing job and admired her for being a go-getter who financed her own education (while his own tuition was paid by his parents). Before meeting Doug, she'd had only one sexual partner.

"I make very good money dancing, especially with the tips," she told me. "It's the perfect job for me, because it allows me time to study and attend classes during the day."

Her dream, she said, was to make enough money to provide financial security for everyone in her close-knit family. After she completed her MBA program, she expected to find a high-paying job that would eventually allow her to buy four small houses close together—one for her parents, one for each of her brothers and one for herself and her future husband—possibly Doug. She was interested in the real estate business and seemed to have the potential to make her dream come true.

But now Nadia was deeply disturbed by her family's shock and embarrassment about her dancing, their disowning her—and their demand that she quit her job immediately.
"There isn't any other job that would allow me to go to classes during the day and pay enough to cover my tuition and all living expenses," she said. "But they can't understand that. They just see me as a total disgrace to them and their fundamentalist religious values. My mother said she felt worse than if I had died!"

During our first few sessions, Nadia seemed to be holding the line against her family's pressure. She had strong support from Doug (who she thought was probably a Sexual Six). He respected and loved her, had no objection to her job and urged her to "disown" her "crazy, ignorant family." His expectation, she said, was that they would live together once they both finished graduate school.

But she was emotionally torn by her family's rejection and realized she needed their support and approval in order to feel whole. Their repudiation of her had already taken a toll on her grades and was now taking a huge toll on her relationship with Doug, with whom she had become completely shut down and sexually dysfunctional. Her future looked bleak. She had been brought up to believe that family members should stick together no matter what the circumstances. Now her parents and two brothers were closing ranks against her solely because of a temporary job she had taken to put herself through her M.B.A program.

"It almost feels surreal to me," she said, "as if it couldn't be true. But it is."

Finally, in despair, she quit her job. This plunged her into a black hole of depression so profound that I eventually persuaded her to see a psychopharmacologist for anti-depressant medication. In spite of the medication, her depression worsened. She stopped taking the anti-depressants, dropped a major course at the university (one required for graduation), made up excuses not to see Doug and spent most of her time in bed. Now living on meager savings, she took a job as a bank teller, which she hated.

Suddenly school and the completion of her MBA degree meant nothing. All her material desires were put on hold as she struggled to clarify why it was so important to purchase the four small homes for her family and herself. It seemed bizarre that her family would rather live in poverty than allow her to work temporarily in a topless nightclub.

Her response was to recoil from everything she had formerly valued, including her own beautiful body, especially as it related to any form of sexual functioning. She turned away from Doug completely, eventually refusing even to take his phone calls.
In her sessions with me she kept reiterating how difficult it was to have her dream about buying the homes come to such a bitter end.

How could her parents, her brothers and she herself ever become financially secure without her working as an exotic dancer? How could they ever afford a real home—and stop the dead-end pattern of moving from one cheap rental to another, always searching for a marginally better deal?

I counseled Nadia on many other possibilities for income-producing temporary jobs that might have long-term career advantages, even while she was still in graduate school. Although she listened intently, she seemed unable to appreciate the advantages of any of these alternatives, especially considering the relatively low wages compared to what she had been earning as an exotic dancer. She never went back to dancing, but she never felt happy with her life during the rest of the time I was in contact with her.

Eventually, she had to give up her sessions with me because of money issues. I tried to persuade her to complete her degree and stay in the relationship with Doug—as a friend, if not as a lover. She had to drop her M.B.A. program just one month before she was due to finish, but did keep Doug "just as a casual friend." The flat affect and distance in her eyes the last time I saw her made me fear for her future.

We were in touch by telephone twice after that and, the last I heard, she was still in her bank job—depressed and hating it. She now needed an additional two semesters to complete her degree because of the classes she had dropped. Doug, having graduated on schedule, got a job out of state and begged Nadia to move with him, but she refused. She felt paralyzed and unable to leave her family.

She kept in contact with Doug several times a week, but told me on the phone that she felt "flat" and "passionless" about everything—her degree, Doug, her family, dancing, her sexuality, the real estate. Her spirit had truly been broken.

Part of what Nadia had to deal with in her therapy sessions with me was the issue of "individuation," the ability to evolve her own sense of self and become independent of the nuclear family. During her several months in therapy she came to intellectually understand the concept of individuation, but ultimately she allowed her family to have more power over her life than she herself did. She felt that "no success would be worth it" for her if it negated her position in the family—which defined her sense of feeling secure and being able to survive over time.

Her Self-preservation subtype (seen in her concern about

financial independence and her attempts to train herself for a well-paid career) also has a strong secondary Social element (seen in her dependence on her family's approval). In effect, she could not separate her Self-preservation drive from her Social instinct to preserve the family unit. Any "success" she might have achieved individually would count for nothing if it resulted in damage to the family of which she was an integral part. Ultimately, she found herself at an impasse over her inability to individuate from her nuclear family. She was unable to succeed at her goals and saw herself as a "failure"—a disastrous outcome for a Three.

I felt heartbroken that I was powerless to "fix" this destructive situation and could no longer see Nadia. Although I did what I could to keep the positive aspects of Nadia's spirit alive—helping her combat depression through positive choices, eventually trying another kind of anti-depressant, urging her to stay in touch with Doug and remain in graduate school—I have to acknowledge that at the moment her future looks bleak. She reports feeling stuck. Given her lack of individuation, it's unlikely that she'll move away from her family. Her parents were pleased that Doug moved away; they now hope she will "get some sense knocked into her," meet some "nice Russian boy" and have kids. After all, as they continually remind her, she's "just a girl."

Looking back on Nadia's relationship with her boyfriend, Doug, they seem to have had several elements predictive of potential success. Both of them, according to Nadia, were deeply pleased with who the other really is—and felt satisfied that their lovemap criteria were fulfilled by each other. Both appeared to be at average levels of psychological health, dipping into periods of significant unhealthiness and sometimes rising to impressive levels of personal development.

Although Doug was never tested, from the reading I provided, he and Nadia agreed that he was most likely a Sexual Six. I often questioned whether Nadia might actually be a Social subtype (rather than Self-preservation), but she insisted that she was truly Self-preservation. Either way, the couple did not have the advantage of sharing the same subtype, nor were they members of the same Harmonic Group.

However, the Three and the Six are connected by a direct line that would have allowed Nadia and Doug to balance each other's differences and complement each other's weaknesses.

It's possible that someday they may reunite, but at this point that doesn't look probable.

"An Affair to Forget"

Ted, 46, a Self-preservation Three, is a tall, broad-shouldered man who is part owner of a successful land-development company. He came to see me, devastated, after Pam, his wife of 20 years, told him during one of their recent fights that she'd had an affair with a 29-year-old coach at the tennis club where she played.

"I can't believe Pam would cheat on me," Ted said. "I work my butt off to provide for her and our two sons—she's never had to work a day since she got pregnant with the first one."

He was proud of his good-looking second wife, whom he described as "a doll for age 44," and their sons, 14 and 17. The boys, he said, were both "winners," both lettered in several major sports while maintaining "quite decent grades." Pam, a Self-preservation Seven, he described as adventurous, health-conscious, a serious tennis player and community volunteer who loved staying "on the go." She attended all the boys' sporting events because, as Ted acknowledged, "I'm always gone," working on development projects.

In our first joint therapy session, Pam said she had never sought to have an affair, but felt so lonely in her marriage that she gave in to the seduction of a young tennis coach, flattered that "he couldn't believe I was 44." Immediately after their first sexual encounter, she said, she felt an urge to "scream the bad news in Ted's face," hoping that this would be a wake-up call for him. She had finally done just that, during one of their predictable fights over his frequent absences from home.

Later, when Pam came to see me alone, she told me, "Ted has been having an affair with his job for many years. He had little or no time for the boys or me. We haven't had decent sex for years—and over the last six months even the affection between us has dried up." Pam was exasperated and felt discounted by her husband, who spent virtually no time with his "perfect family." On the rare occasions that Ted was sitting in the living room when the boys came in, Pam said, he would often fall asleep in mid-conversation.

His workaholism was obviously taking a huge toll on all of them.

Fortunately, both Ted and Pam were open to joint counseling and Pam also came to see me alone occasionally. Both of them were eager to do the personality survey. When Ted read the Type Three description, he was shocked that almost every word applied to him and that he "wasn't all that healthy." He also felt "convicted" of being a Self-preservation subtype. Pam was less surprised that the analysis showed her to be a Self-preservation Seven.

Ted, in a classic goal-oriented Three shift, acted immediately to make major changes in his priorities and time schedule. The couple's focus quickly moved from Pam's affair to implementing the positive changes they both wanted. Clearly, both were highly invested in making their marriage work and sustaining their secure home and family life. Within two months their relationship was greatly improved. They were spending much more quality time together as a couple and as a family.

To Pam, Ted seemed like "a new man": he planned "dates" for the two of them, attended some of the boys' athletic events, even cancelled an important meeting to attend one of their basketball games. "Four nights out of seven," Ted decided, the family should have dinner together and he declared himself "damned determined" to reach this goal. Frequently the four of them would meet at a local restaurant near Ted's project, just so he could keep his pledge about four dinners together each week.

The boys found this comical, Pam said, but she herself found it heartwarming. Her sex life with Ted was gradually being restored and ultimately was much improved, as a result of short-term marital enrichment practices. The marriage actually became much stronger and this felt like a "win" for everyone: the couple, their boys and their therapist.

Enrichment for greater intimacy became the key to their success. Although Ted and Pam did not suffer from any sexual dysfunction, per se, their feelings of intimacy had hit rock bottom when they began therapy—to the point where Pam questioned whether Ted would even care about her affair with the young coach. In the end, he did come to care profoundly and essentially blamed himself—which made it easy to forgive Pam.

To enrich their marriage, initially I asked them to commit to three simple, specific practices:

1. *Hug and kiss hello and goodbye:* They would, without fail, kiss and hug "goodbye" in the mornings and "hello" when they first got back together at the end of the day (regardless of what else was going on around them).

2. *Holding time:* They would honor the relationship each night with five minutes of "holding time." This is done mostly at bedtime and it involves only hugging, kissing or perhaps light massage, without any discussion of problems. It has nothing to do with foreplay or initiating sex, but is more in the spirit of a prayer-to-the-marriage. Essentially, it says to the partner: you are important enough to me, for me to devote five minutes of my day to simply "holding you close to me."

Pam and Ted, like many couples, had the problem of not always going to bed at the same time. When this happens, I always have the person who is going to bed first, ask the other to lie down with them on the bed for "holding time." Since Pam frequently went to bed before Ted, it became common for her to request that he tuck her in. This eventually became a valued ritual that both reported as highly satisfying, because it made each of them feel cherished by the other.

3. *Re-entry time:* They would honor the first ten minutes, after getting back together each day, by talking to one another only about positive and personal items. Everything else—problem solving, reading the mail, the boys, changing clothes, answering or returning phone calls—would have to wait until they finished their ten minutes of "re-entry time." I explained that the vast majority of couples' fights start in the first ten

minutes after they re-enter the relationship at the end of the day. (Both partners want the other to "be there," to listen, to meet their needs. Expectations are often unrealistic, with tempers flaring as each person wants their own needs and demands met.) In the practice of "re-entry time," no problems or negative emotions can even be referred to until both partners have the benefit of feeling heard (and nurtured) for those first ten minutes.

Over time, Ted and Pam were able to improve on this, to the point where they would sit and have iced tea or a glass of wine together before jumping into anything else. They couldn't always meet this requirement literally—for example, when Pam took the boys to meet Ted for dinner near his job—but they did do this practice later, when Ted actually got home. Pam later reported that the "re-entry time" was the single most important factor for making her feel close to Ted again.

It seems that almost everyone wants to be heard, seen and honored simply for their presence before having a lot of problems, demands or expectations thrown at them.

Over the next several months, Pam and Ted also grew tremendously in their communication skills—making "I" statements (rather than "you" statements), doing active listening and practicing the rules of "fair fighting." The only major issue left was Ted's workaholism. He eventually got this under control by committing to certain hours and days off, pre-planning family vacations, hiring an assistant who doubled as a personal bookkeeper and saying no to his involvement in the smaller projects that took up 90 percent of his time while producing only 10 percent of his income. Ted was learning to work smarter—not harder.

Among our Five Factors for predicting relationship success, Ted and Pam had the three most important ones. They had highly compatible lovemaps, with both feeling that they had married their ideal mate. Their levels of health increased considerably during the course of therapy as both became more self-aware, pro-active, willing to listen, compromise and nurture each other. Their common Self-preservation subtype was an important factor in their ability to reconnect so quickly—both were primarily concerned with their home, financial security and the physical needs of their family.

Even though they had no Harmonic Group match or complementary Enneagram connecting line, the other three factors were strong enough to allow them to rebuild trust, empathy and the sense of shared values necessary to sustain a healthy marriage. The go-getting attitude they shared energized them to develop both their self-knowledge and knowledge of each other. This was accomplished in large part through their study of the Enneagram and the disciplined practice of their three daily rituals.

Nadia and Ted as Self-preservation Threes

Both Nadia and Ted were powerfully focused on insuring financial security for themselves and their families, a common priority for Threes with a Self-preservation subtype. Nadia saw her job as a topless dancer as a way to put herself through graduate school, an essential step toward her ultimate goal of purchasing homes for herself and her family members. (Housing is another important focus for people with a Self-preservation subtype.) However, pressure from her conservative family ultimately persuaded her to give up her job, her studies and her dreams, including a promising relationship with her boyfriend.

Ted was a workaholic, a classic pitfall for many Threes, especially those with the Self-preservation subtype. His land development work is an especially good fit for a person with this subtype. His single-minded focus on driving himself to make as much money as possible created unhappiness in his marriage and his wife's sexual affair with a younger man led him to seek therapy. Coming to realize his own responsibility in neglecting his wife and sons motivated him to make the changes necessary to strengthen his marriage and family life.

Threes with the Sexual Subtype

Sexual Threes, whom Ichazo associates with "virility/femininity," want above all to be desired by others. They see themselves as extremely sexually attractive and put much effort into maintaining their physical appearance. Average to unhealthy Sexual Threes are generally not aware of what it takes to establish and nurture real intimacy and they may at times be extremely promiscuous as they try to reassure themselves of their desirability. They think of themselves as sexual "stars" and, even in intimate encounters, may stand outside themselves, watching and admiring their own prowess.

"Model Material"

Courtney, 33, a Three with a Sexual subtype, is a stunning blonde beauty who has made top dollar modeling women's sports clothes and shoes. For six years she has been married to Randy, 36, a Self-preservation Six who is a successful screenwriter in Los Angeles. They have a three-year-old son, Josh, who they both feel is healthy.

"There's nothing wrong with me," Courtney told me when she phoned to make an appointment for "marriage counseling." The problem, she said, was Randy's indifference to her concerns about her "weight gain and lost career opportunities." She was certain that the "panic attacks" she'd had recently were caused by him being "such a buffoon and so shut down."

Although they live in Los Angeles, the couple seemed untroubled by the one-hour drive to my Huntington Beach office. I soon realized that they wanted to make sure none of their friends would know they were in marriage counseling. Anonymity was extremely important to Courtney, and Randy seemed to agree. Many of our later sessions were done by phone.

At first, Courtney came to several sessions alone because "Randy had to work late." From my phone conversation with him, I got the impression that he was disgusted with Courtney's "narcissistic concerns" about her body and her "nonexistent modeling career." I sensed that he wanted her to have some sessions alone with me to explore the underlying reasons for her panic attacks.

She told me in these early sessions that she had been sought after her whole life for her looks: "I've always felt fortunate that God gifted me with a healthy, beautiful body." Beginning as a child model, she had until recently taken excellent care of herself, staying in top physical shape and avoiding drugs and alcohol.

But since the birth of her son three years earlier, she had become fearful that her physical desirability and "marketability" had declined significantly. She hadn't had a modeling contract since her pregnancy and now her agent wasn't returning her phone calls. She felt that the final five pounds she'd gained during her pregnancy (and had been unable to lose) were responsible for this situation.

Also because of her five-pound weight gain, she believed, Randy's sexual interest in her had waned; they now had sex much less frequently. Although he said he saw "no difference in her weight" and refused to acknowledge any real problem, once they were in bed he would simply shut down and go to sleep immediately. He refused to discuss her "extra five pounds."

Since Courtney saw those "extra pounds" as the chief obstacle to her happiness, she had been considering the use of illegal drugs for rapid weight loss. Her modeling friends did this a lot, she told me. Even though she and Randy had agreed before they married that she would be a stay-at-home mom after their child was born, she now found their agreement difficult to keep.

"I need just one more big modeling job," she said," to make me feel desirable again and get Randy's sexual interest back." In her fantasy, once she lost the five pounds he would want to make love to her all the time.

Randy felt that he had "stood on his head" to reassure her of his love and his commitment to her and Josh. He made plenty of money, so there was no need for her to find more work. He wanted her to stay home and take care of Josh, as they had agreed.

During Courtney's sessions with me she gradually came to understand some of the real reasons for her panic attacks. She was willing to face her desire to be a status symbol and "trophy wife" (which she perceived as the highest compliment). She eventually saw that she had talked herself into believing that Randy's lack of responsiveness was the cause of her pain. The real issue was her own feeling of worthlessness around her inability to perform as a model; in her own mind, she was a "failure" unless she continually received admiration for presenting the perfect image.

Courtney and Randy were willing to take the personality survey and the results offered them enormous insight. Both com-mented that they had never seen themselves described so accurate-ly. Courtney immediately recognized herself as a Sexual Three and Randy acknowledged his Self-preservation Six structure, once he had time to read about it.

After many tears and attempts at denial, Courtney came to realize that Randy loved her (not her "model image") and that he was simply weary of her self-centered litany about weight issues. He admitted in their joint sessions that he had become shut down, dismissive and cold because of this. A big breakthrough came for Courtney as she realized that her weight obsession had brought about the very situation she feared most—turning off the husband she loved.

During our joint sessions, Randy's deep love for his wife and son was so evident that Courtney's perceptions actually shifted; she became more balanced and focused on the reality produced by our confrontational meetings. And her self-image changed—she came to see herself as having intrinsic worth apart from her external image and performance.

To help her with this process, I suggested that she go for two weeks without wearing any makeup and doing nothing special with her hair (wearing it tied back in her everyday ponytail). We would do an experiment to see if anyone—especially Randy—commented on her appearance.

At the end of our two-week experiment, Courtney was dumbfounded to discover that not one person had noticed her makeup or hair. This included Randy. It was beginning to dawn on Courtney that her "image" was important only in her own mind. She was now better able to accept that Randy was being truthful when he claimed he never even noticed her extra five pounds.

At this point I was able to explain to Courtney in detail my suspicion that Randy was shut down and distant because he could no longer stand her self-obsessed complaining and narcissistic emphasis on her appearance. Her "model image" was of little importance to Randy. He did love and accept her as inherently valuable and lovable—not as a showpiece to be evaluated and criticized.

Being valued for herself, not for the way she looked, was a new experience for Courtney. From her description of her childhood situation, I gathered that her mother was most likely a Three and her father a One. Growing up in this household, where she was praised for her success as a child model, she had never known anything other than her perfect "model image" as the basis for her self-worth.

As therapy progressed, Courtney became able to say no to the drugs offered by her model friends for rapid weight loss. She said to me one day, "If this body's good enough for God and good enough for Randy, then it must be good enough for me."

In the end, the marriage counseling and Courtney's individual therapy were extremely rewarding. Her level of health increased considerably as her perceptions changed and her choices came to reflect a new kind of self-esteem. Randy, though already at a fairly high level of personal development, had little insight, initially, into Courtney's psychological dilemma. However, their lovemaps, the most important of our Five Factors for predicting a relationship's durability, were highly compatible; they were essentially happy with the person they chose to marry. Randy's psychological health, along with Courtney's marked improvement in consciousness, allowed their communication to grow to the point where they achieved new levels of intimacy.

They did not have the advantage of a shared subtype (Courtney's Sexual versus Randy's Self-preservation), nor were they members of the same Harmonic Group. However, they did share the direct line between Threes and Sixes, which was beneficial in helping to balance each other's blind spots and complement their different energies.

Randy, being a healthy Six, was extremely loyal and devoted and his skill in planning for the family's future made Courtney feel secure. Eventually she was able to give Randy useful feedback on his screenplays and valuable advice concerning some of his professional meetings. Their marriage thus became more functional and more satisfying for them both. In the end, Courtney chose to avoid the stress of seeking a "big" modeling contract; she contented herself with doing occasional ads and a few commercials for shoes. More and more, she came to prefer the reality of herself as Randy's "cheerleader" and Josh's mom to her old model image.

"At this point," she said, "I just want to become the best mom and the best wife I humanly can"—a classic Three statement.

"Impotent Again"

Johnny, 62, a Sexual Three, suave and perfectly groomed, is a self-proclaimed "eternal, untouchable bachelor." He had heard from friends that I knew about "sex stuff," and he hoped I would be able to resolve his erection problems in one or two sessions. He made it clear at our first meeting that he didn't believe in psychologists or therapy and had come to see me only because, over the past year, in his last three relationships he had failed to maintain his erection.

His responses to my questions made it apparent that there had also been many other erection difficulties during the past decade. Each of the three women with whom he'd recently had the problem had been patient and compassionate, he said; *he* was the one who got angry. He'd tried various solutions: Viagra, Cialis and other drugs he'd gotten from a doctor friend and "penis shots," also suggested by his friend. Nothing helped.

In response to my inquiries about his relationship history, he told me he'd had two short marriages at the ages of 23 and 26. In both, he was caught having sex with other women and both wives quickly divorced him. His conclusion: "I'm not marriage material." He is relieved that he had no children (that he knows of), though he "wouldn't mind having a few handsome grandkids to show off."

Asked to describe himself, he winked and said: "Smooth, shockingly good looking for age 62." He loves courting and seducing women, prefers short-term relationships of three to six months and told me he can't even count the number of women in their 30s and 40s who have fallen "head over heels in love" with him.

Successful in real estate sales, he also makes a significant income from motivational speeches to other realtors about "Closing the Deal." He enjoys spending a lot of money on clothes, gym memberships, personal trainers and expensive cars in pursuit of his goal of impressing people, holding their "attention, admiration and awe." Even though he could easily afford to buy a house, he chooses to rent an apartment in an upscale singles complex because it makes him feel young—and he meets more women that way.

"I'd rather spend my time working on myself than on a house," he told me.

In response to his concern about shoring up his image through maintaining his erections, I tried to explain that the body is much more than a "screw machine." Like many Threes I've worked with, Johnny had been treating himself as an object—a commodity to be shown off—with no attention to his inner needs or feelings. He was so deeply out of touch with himself, he had lost the ability to relax, to be sensual, to take in genuine physical pleasure with a partner. The very idea of this seemed foreign to him.

I suggested that he begin by getting a series of massages from a *male* masseur—not just "sports massages," but therapeutic sessions designed to reinforce his ability to simply relax and take in pleasure. At first he resented the suggestion, but later he agreed, had the massages and learned to take in pleasure from this non-sexual yet enjoyable contact. However, he insisted on having the sessions with a woman, whom he described as "obese and unattractive," assuming this would satisfy my criteria.

Johnny was so performance-driven and angry about his erection problems, that it would have been impossible for him to be sexually functional. First he had to re-learn basic ways of relaxing, allowing physical sensations to become enjoyable, rather than continually worrying about his performance. I explained that it was impossible to be a spectator evaluating his own performance while at the same time remaining internally focused on the sensual stimuli that actually caused arousal and erection.

This concept was extremely difficult for him to grasp, since anything not involving bottom-line performance was simply not on his radar screen. Using "Three" language, I helped him re-define performance, using sensate focus exercises as a tool for achieving his goal of becoming a "successful lover" and avoiding "sexual failure." The "goal" was to relax and take in pleasure, as opposed to worrying about his performance.

Once he understood this, we were ready to take the next step. I got Johnny to bring Carol, his last girlfriend, to several of our sessions in hopes that she might act as a surrogate partner for him. They had been friends at work before becoming lovers; even though the sexual relationship hadn't worked out, they remained good colleagues and pals. Carol, age 50, was emotionally mature and considerably older than most of Johnny's women and she understood his concerns about erection failure.

I explained to them both how "sensate focus" exercises work and said that if Carol didn't want to do the exercises with Johnny I would arrange for a professional surrogate. Since she was single and had no other boyfriend at the time, she seemed happy to oblige.

Sensate focus exercises, which are designed to help a person relax and focus on sensual pleasure, eventually helped Johnny achieve normal erections. Here is the progression I recommended for his sessions with Carol: Taking turns, each would spend 15 minutes as the giver and 15 minutes as the receiver. These 30-minute sessions were held twice a week, beginning with only the touching of each other's faces while fully clothed, then progressing to full-body touching, still fully clothed (with no focus on genitals). Later sessions included doing these exercises in their underwear, then doing them fully nude. First these nude sessions were without genital contact, then with it, moving eventually into full foreplay and sensual arousal but still without any form of penetration.

The purpose of these exercises was to allow Johnny to explore sensual pleasure while focusing on his internal state of arousal and desire with no pressure to "perform." Although the whole concept was foreign to him, he was willing to try scheduling these sessions twice a week. Eventually the sessions involved penetration, but initially with instructions *not* to ejaculate. Through these exercises Johnny finally learned how to become aware of his own feelings and discover what was pleasurable for him rather than focusing strictly on "performance" (for the woman and for his own ego).

His sessions with Carol went well and within seven weeks he

seemed to be a changed man. He reported that he and Carol finally had "real intercourse," in which he made sure she climaxed; some of the therapy sessions had turned into authentic lovemaking. This experience gave Johnny a whole new paradigm for self-worth.

Throughout his therapy sessions with me, Johnny had been unwilling to take the personality survey or do any reading on personality types. But late in the therapy, he did laugh at himself as he read in my office a description of the Sexual Three at average and unhealthy levels.

"Well, Mona," he said, "I guess you knew me in some ways better than I did."

After several successful intercourse sessions with Carol, he ended his therapy with me. The two of them have remained friends and occasional sex partners (until Carol finds a permanent relationship). Johnny is now happy with himself and pleased to be back in the swing of his life as the "eternal bachelor." Although his impotence may return, he now knows how to use the sensate focus exercises to resolve his difficulties, as opposed to becoming increasingly angry and obsessed.

Johnny's performance orientation is common among Threes and the emotional bankruptcy that often goes with it can interfere with life satisfaction (and certainly fulfillment in love relationships). Image is such a central focus for Threes that they can sabotage their own potential for success in relationships by their continual monitoring of "how am I doing."

If Johnny had been open to reading about his personality, I would have recommended he look at the Type Three chapter in Riso and Hudson's *The Wisdom of the Enneagram*. I might also have recommended some of the classic books in the sex therapy field, such as Bernie Zilbergeld's *Male Sexuality: A Guide to Sexual Fulfillment* or Sam Jultry's *Male Sexual Performance*. However, these would most likely have been too technical for Johnny's more practical goals.

In terms of a committed love relationship, Johnny, as an "eternal bachelor," may always be a poor candidate. His lovemap contains only criteria for "temporary, uncommitted situations with young, great-looking gals." He has no desire to pursue marriage or any form of ongoing "burdens of responsibility." Based on the abandonment he suffered as a child (from both his mother and grandmother), he has no motivation to expand his risk level beyond temporary liaisons. This was as far as Johnny wanted to go in therapy.

However, it was helpful for him to learn about his Type Three and Sexual subtype structure, which gave him some understanding of his real needs and desires. Johnny promised to give me a call if he ever fell "really in love" or "desired anything more permanent with a woman," but he doubted that this would ever come to pass.

Courtney and Johnny as Sexual Threes

Like many Sexual Threes, both Courtney and Johnny assumed that their physical attractiveness and "performance" in their respective sex roles were the key to their value as human beings. When Courtney's husband seemed to lose sexual interest in her, she assumed the cause was the extra five pounds she had gained during her pregnancy and was unable to lose. She became so obsessive about her weight and so fixated on the need to prove her attractiveness by successfully resuming her modeling career that her husband, turned off by her narcissism, sought to distance himself from her still further. Once she became aware of the vicious cycle she had created in their relationship through her obsession with false criteria for her sexual attractiveness, she was able to shift her goals to becoming the most loving and supportive wife and best mother she could be. In pursuit of this new agenda, she found new happiness and fulfillment.

Johnny's pride in being a star sexual performer for the ever-shifting parade of women in his life was brought to a jarring halt by erection problems and he entered therapy hoping for a quick fix. Having had no experience with long-term relationships and no desire to seek one, he learned, through doing sensate-focus exercises with a compassionate partner, to pay attention to his internal sexual feelings rather than continually monitoring his own performance. His basic performance orientation—common in Sexual Threes— remained unchanged by his therapeutic experience. However, the restoration of his virility was his ultimate goal and he was satisfied with his "success."

Threes with the Social Subtype

The Social Three, which Ichazo associates with "prestige," is in search of social status and the trappings of success. Charming and at ease with others, Threes with this subtype look for recognition that they are moving up in the world and are accepted in the social circles they aspire to join.

"Car-Purchase Divorce"

Sally, 47, a chic auburn-haired Social Three in a well-tailored gray suit, sat in my office trembling with rage and frustration. She was ready to file for divorce over the birthday present that Sam, 56, her husband of 12 years, had just given her: a huge bright-yellow Hummer with giant custom chrome wheels.

"He bought that embarrassing monstrosity for himself," she said. "Anything that's bizarre and one-of-a-kind, that's his style. I can't even step up into that thing, wearing a skirt and heels!"

Sam (who is probably a Self-preservation Four) is a successful ophthalmologist in the community where they live, and for years Sally has run his front office. Their marriage is her second and his third. Sam has two grown daughters from his first marriage, which lasted 14 years; both he and Sally are close to the girls. After his first marriage ended, Sam had a short rebound second marriage and then was single for a number of years.

Sally, his super-competent office manager, had been divorced from her first husband for many years and had no children. To thank her for the excellent work she was doing, Sam invited her out to dinner and they developed a romantic interest in one another. After two years of dating they married; that was 14 years ago. Their shared goals for Sam's practice and their common interest in his daughters have formed the basis for a committed, stable marriage, despite their differences in taste and divergent personality styles.

After the appearance of the yellow Hummer in their driveway, Sally was so furious with Sam that she considered making an appointment with a divorce lawyer. But after talking things over with a woman friend, she took her friend's advice and called me instead, frightened at the intensity of her own anger.

Once Sally had vented her rage during our first session, we got down to the facts of the situation. She had needed a new car for some time. Since she liked the black Mercedes she'd been driving, she wanted to replace it with something similar: "an understated vehicle with status and a sense of real power."

When Sam, who was generous, funny and a practical joker known for his unusual gifts, announced that her birthday present was "sitting in the driveway" she felt a rush of pleasure, then one of anxiety. What had he come up with this time?

When she saw the yellow Hummer she burst into tears.

Sam looked like the cat that swallowed the canary. "You'll be the only woman in town with such a hot car," he said.

"How could you buy this without consulting me?" she cried. "If you'd thought about me at all, you would have realized I'd hate this car. You only bought it because *you* like it. I wouldn't be caught dead driving it and I'm embarrassed to even have it parked in our driveway."

Sam, now aware that her tears were not tears of joy, felt mortified. "You're an ungrateful, controlling bitch," he said. "All you care about is being socially appropriate with your big status symbols."

"He's right about that, at least," she said to me. "I do like to be socially appropriate and I want a car that's tasteful, that shows discretion. Why can't he just let me have what I want?"

Since I had counseled Sally and Sam several years earlier on issues such as joint decision making, taste and the inherent value conflicts between a Three and a Four, I was not surprised to see these problems surface again. I knew that, as a Social Three, she needed validation through status symbols (in contrast to Sam, who needed to display his uniqueness through his possessions).

During our following sessions of joint counseling their communication dramatically improved, with a significant increase in compassion for one another's divergent perspectives. Sam returned the Hummer and made an agreement with Sally not to purchase another car without her approval. Sally finally understood where her rage and fear were coming from and realized that she felt unrecognized by Sam. He had never really heard what she had to say. She felt trivialized by his lack of empathy for her needs and desires. Sam was now beginning to understand what she meant.

In our previous counseling, Sally had agreed to take the personality survey and was astounded to see how completely the Social Three description fit her. Sam was unwilling to take the survey, but he did some reading about Type Fours and the Self-preservation subtype and acknowledged these applied to him.

Both of them have had to struggle and stretch to understand the real differences between them. This marriage was never a match made in heaven. Sam and Sally have somewhat compatible lovemaps and both have worked to raise their levels of health over the course of our counseling. (Sally worked especially hard at this.) They have no match in subtypes or Harmonic Groups and do not share a complementary connecting line. Thus the two factors that hold them together are their partially compatible lovemaps and their willingness to move toward higher levels of consciousness and personality development.

Through their growing maturity, their commitment and a lot of counseling, the marriage has endured. Learning to take themselves *less* seriously and take one another *more* seriously has allowed them to stay out of their predictable fights (perfectly exemplified by the Hummer incident). They love their home, their lifestyle and Sam's daughters. Both agree that they want the marriage more than they want out of it and they have worked to become more conscious and more loving regarding their differences. I still see them from time to time for counseling on the situational and personality issues that inevitably arise. While they are not ecstatically happy, they have no desire to end their comfortable relationship.

"Porn Star"

Matt, 25, a Social Three with strong presence and energy, seemed dejected as he sat in my office answering my questions about his background, without immediately telling me why he was seeking my help. He had recently finished his master's degree in economics, he said, just before becoming engaged to Jody, 23, whom he described as "smart, exotic, exciting and down-to-earth, with great joie de vivre."

Recently, he said, he had been employed by a prestigious investment firm, for which he had previously been an intern. He had worked his way up in the company, networking and gradually winning over senior members of the staff. His full-time employment there, for the last two months, happened just before his engagement. Matt and Jody had been dating for a year and a half and he celebrated his great career opportunity by giving her a ring. Their plan was to live together for a year before marriage. His whole family was supportive and everyone loved Jody.

Given this positive life situation, I was wondering what on earth could account for his distraught state. I asked about his family and learned that he had a close relationship with his parents and two younger brothers, who all adored him.

"So why have you come to see me?" I finally asked.

Matt ran his hand through his shiny dark hair, sighed and came out with it. His younger brother, Michael, 23, had recently been viewing a pornographic video and had recognized Jody, his future sister-in-law, as the star of this "scumbag production." Wanting to be absolutely certain that the actress was actually "our Jody," Michael watched the video again. Yes, there was the birthmark on Jody's left arm—it couldn't be anyone else. Uncertain about whether to tell his older brother, Michael consulted with their youngest brother, A.J., 20, who occasionally borrowed Michael's porn videos. After watching the video twice, A.J. agreed that the actress was indeed Jody. The two brothers also agreed to tell Matt and allow him to decide what, if anything, he wanted to do about the situation.

"They showed me the video," Matt said, "and swore they'd never tell our parents—or anyone—if I decided to go ahead and marry Jody anyhow."

"That must have been a difficult experience for you," I said.

There were tears in Matt's eyes now. "I felt betrayed . . . enraged . . . confused . . . heartbroken." Now the whole story came pouring out. Matt was so stunned by this revelation that he stayed in bed for two days—the only days he had ever missed work or school—paralyzed with depression. He saw only one possible course of action: to confront Jody. He knew he could never live with this skeleton in his closet. Eventually someone else would see the porn video and recognize Jody. It was only a matter of time.

Some questions from me revealed that Matt had considered the possibility of a political career later on and the revelation of Jody's porn experience would make this impossible. Furthermore, he couldn't trust his youngest brother not to tell their mother, since A.J. was especially close to her.

Finally, after two days Matt confronted Jody, who wept hysterically and apologized profusely for her "stupid mistake." She had performed in the video four years ago, when she was only 19, she told him—"silly, reckless, impressionable, seeking to make some quick money." She reported doing a total of only two videos.

No matter how much she tried to win back Matt's trust and respect, he could not integrate the reality of what she had done into his lovemap or into his plans for his future and his possible political career. He and Jody talked all night and into the next day. There was no doubt about their love for one another, but Matt could not conceive of himself being married to a "porno actress." He suddenly felt impotent, drained, as if the life force had left his body.

Jody tried to reconnect with him through reason, a plea for forgiveness, a plan for starting over, a suggestion that they share the truth with everyone—or with no one. But for Matt there was no workable solution. Finally, Jody offered to return his ring. He accepted it and broke the engagement. As far as I know, they never spoke again.

Matt continued to see me for some time, to deal with the trauma of his loss. Like most Threes (and especially those with a Social subtype), he was deeply concerned with his image among his peers and with how the community would judge him. His ambition to "make it big" in his career (and perhaps in politics) allowed for no possibility of surmounting the criticism he might face if he married Jody. In the course of our therapy sessions, he worked through and accepted the traumatic loss of Jody—the woman he truly loved but could not remain involved with.

Though Jody never took the personality survey, I feel confident from Matt's description that she is most likely a Sexual Seven. The couple's lovemaps were compatible until Matt discovered Jody's history with pornography. Then everything changed. Their levels of psychological health seemed about average, though Matt's level of development increased markedly during the next few months in therapy. They had no matching subtype, Harmonic Group match or direct connecting line to balance their differences and blind spots. Had they married, it remains uncertain whether the relationship would have endured.

The deal-breaker for Matt as a Social Three was image-related. As he had anticipated, A.J., his youngest brother, did eventually tell their mother why Matt broke the engagement. But Mom had become quite fond of Jody and, even knowing about the two porn videos, was critical of Matt for breaking up with her. Both of Matt's parents thought he should still consider marrying Jody, but Matt refused to reconsider his decision.

Matt's mother is perhaps a Sexual Seven herself. (In a sense, Matt may have been "marrying Mom," in a healthy way). Matt told me he had never been as close to his mother as his two younger brothers were and thought his mom might have seen his marriage to Jody as a way of getting closer to him. This may well be true; Jody had evidently bonded deeply with Matt's mom.

Since the whole family thought the idea of a career in politics for Matt was ridiculous, they could not understand why two porn videos had to be the crucial factor in his decision to break the engagement. Everyone missed Jody, especially Matt—but no one in the family ever saw her again. Even though Matt still thinks about her constantly and fantasizes about getting back together, he refuses to contact her.

Sally and Matt as Social Threes

Both Sally and Matt were strongly conscious of their social status and their conflicts and choices reflected their focus on these issues. Sally needed a car that reflected the image she wanted to project. When her husband gave her a flashy car that created the opposite image, resentment and conflict arose between them. Once he realized how distressed Sally was about the prospect of driving the wrong car, he agreed to return the vehicle and allow her to have a say in its replacement.

For Matt, the conflict was considerably more serious. The revelation that his fiancée had acted in two pornographic videos created, for him, an insurmountable impediment to their marriage—especially since he had ambitions for a political career. Even though he still loved the young woman and his family urged him to marry her anyway, he considered the potential loss of social status, if the videos should ever come to light, an unacceptable risk. He broke the engagement and ended all connection with her.

Strengths of Threes in Intimate Relationships

- Productivity
- Confidence
- Clarity about goals
- Charm
- Motivation
- Practicality
- Attractive image
- Assertiveness

Limitations of Threes in Intimate Relationships

- Workaholism
- Arrogance
- Deceptiveness
- Exploitation
- Impatience
- Aggressiveness
- Vanity
- Competitiveness

Defense Mechanisms of Threes

In childhood, Threes are often rewarded for their achievements and for reaching goals set by their parents. This pattern can set them up in adulthood to regard themselves as "human doings" rather than human beings. More than people of any other Enneagram type, Threes have a tendency to see themselves as objects, even machines. Johnny, for example, approached his erection problem much as he might handle a problem with his car: I was the "sex mechanic," and he expected me to do a quick fix and get him back on the road again immediately.

The primary defense mechanism for Threes is *identification*: creating a public image of themselves as high achievers in a particular area and then buying into that image as being their core self. In the cases of Nadia and Ted (both Self-preservation subtypes), their ability to make money was the basis for their sense of self-worth; with Courtney (a Sexual subtype), her perfect model appearance was the basis for hers; for Johnny (also a Sexual subtype), his ability to achieve reliable erections and gain the adoration of many women was what he identified with; for Sally (a Social subtype), driving a certain kind of car was a key to gaining the admiration and approval of people she valued; and for Matt (another Social subtype), having a wife who would reflect his spotless public image was essential. In each of these individuals, therapy involved looking at the real person beneath the image and helping that often-insecure being to see his or her self-worth as unrelated to money, physical beauty, sexual prowess or the trappings of success (cars and "trophy" spouses, for example).

The admiration Threes often receive in childhood, especially from their mothers, may have a connection to the narcissism that I see in many less-than-healthy Type Three adults. This narcissism may show up as an arrogant attitude reflecting the belief of some Threes that they are the gold standard—that others should appropriately acknowledge their success and achievements.

The "Natural Neuroses" of Threes

Being unaware of their identification with the public image they have worked to create and maintain is the major blind spot of Threes. If you are a Three, you will probably need to get in touch with the real person under the trappings of your public "image" and learn to value that vulnerable being.

Threes' natural neuroses are often fueled by a strong appetite for competition, demanding of themselves that they "win" at their chosen game, whatever it is: the good provider for the family (Nadia and Ted); the physically perfect model (Courtney); the handsome stud (Johnny); the woman who drives "an understated vehicle with a sense of real power" (Sally); the man with a beautiful and virtuous wife (Matt).

This goal-driven, image-obsessed worldview can present major problems for developing and maintaining long-term love relationships. Some Threes (like Johnny) are simply incapable of this. Others (like Ted and Courtney) can be helped through therapy to adjust their "ideal image" to include deep connection with a spouse. Still others (like Matt) might have to face tough choices in order to maintain what is to them an acceptable public image.

How Threes Blossom in Good Relationships

Threes can be one of the more difficult types for a therapist to work with, partly because they're often so impatient to get to the "bottom line." But in this case the process really is the product (as we saw with Johnny).

When Threes become aware of their own psychic structure and become able to invest some of the energy they formerly devoted to shoring up their image into taking in other worldviews, they can be extraordinary human beings. Allowing yourself to be vulnerable to a partner who truly loves you is the key to this transformation. When Threes feel loved unconditionally for their natural and real self, they become less narcissistic, less needy of recognition, less invested in image. They become more invested in the reality of feelings, the quality of relationships and what they truly care about (not just how things look).

This step for a Three requires enormous courage. If you are willing to release what you thought was important for the sake of discovering what's *really* important, your potential for a deeper and more satisfying life experience can be unlimited. Threes who have succeeded in this challenging quest lose none of their gifts for making things happen in the world. In fact, their achievements are enhanced by their appreciation of others' abilities, their capacity to acknowledge their own vulnerabilities and limitations and their devotion to tasks that serve larger purposes than mere personal success.

TYPE FOUR: THE INDIVIDUALIST IN LOVE

Fours at all levels of psychological health are preoccupied with their own idiosyncratic feelings and are aware of themselves as lacking something—love, talent, money, advantages, a sense of self—that they believe others have. Fours feel their very identity is linked to their emotional depth—which for them is the capacity for suffering. Even when they are not professional artists, Fours at an average level see themselves as artistic and romantic, people passionately absorbed with creating beauty in their lives. They use their imaginations to heighten their already intense feelings and sometimes feel overwhelmed by their own emotionality. Even though their inner life is intense, they often present a withdrawn image to the outside world because of their self-absorption. In relationships with others, they are hypersensitive, emotionally vulnerable and quick to feel victimized. Feeling like outsiders, they suffer intensely while longing to break free of this tape-loop of melancholy. They see themselves as "special" and are disdainful of lesser mortals, yet their willfulness and lack of practicality often make them unproductive.

When Fours are healthy they may use their sensitivity and imagination to express themselves in some form of art. Or they may use their acute self-awareness to explore their inner workings and express their individuality through authentic, emotionally honest lives and a distinctive personal style. Even though their primary focus is internal and they enjoy solitude, they are compassionate and respectful toward others. They manage to transmute their personal suffering into a gift for the world in some form.

Unhealthy Fours are deeply depressed, overwhelmed with personal shame and often bitterly angry with themselves and others. Unable to function, they are alienated from society, wracked with despair and preoccupied with death. They may turn to drugs or alcohol to mask their self-hatred and they are the most likely of all the temperaments to resort to suicide.

Fours with the Self-preservation subtype

All Fours focus on what is missing in their lives and suffer from a sense of dissatisfaction with themselves and their situation. Individuals of the Self-preservation subtype, which Oscar Ichazo describes as "dauntless, reckless," are less conscious than the other two subtypes of the envy that underlies their character. They are characterized by tenacity and a strong drive to acquire material possessions and create an elegant personal lifestyle. This may involve financial profligacy and even recklessness. Having a need, like all Fours, for strong emotion, Self-preservation Fours generate it by putting themselves at risk. They have a capacity to endure through extremes of emotion and to find stimulation in dangerous situations.

"Suicide Drama"

Emma, 43, a Self-preservation Four, came to see me three months after her parents, both age 67, were killed in a car accident. An only child who had never been married, Emma now saw herself as "an orphan, with no one to love me." She felt desperate, she told me, alienated from everyone and everything, all alone in the world.

Since her parents' death she had become attached to the symbolism of everything they ever owned: for example, her mother's lingerie and old ski clothing.

Emma's father had built a successful motel chain and she had long been accustomed to the finer things in life. Now, with her huge inheritance, she would never need to work. "Money," she said, "means nothing to me." Yet, in the months since her parents' deaths, she had become, by her own report, "increasingly reckless with money," making purchases that included several cars and a huge yacht that she had never seen.

After acknowledging that she had been irresponsible about her eating habits and personal routines, she added, "It's great to eat when you're hungry and sleep when you're tired." When I questioned her further about her eating habits and routines, concerned about the unhealthy look of her, she admitted she had gained 30 pounds in the three months since her parents' fatal accident. Her sleep patterns were disrupted by her habit of staying up until 3 or 4 a.m. watching high drama films on TV or old family videos because she didn't want to go to sleep.

Her life had no meaning, she said, and she had no sense of self. At times, she didn't even want her life to go on, independent of her parents. Not surprisingly, this way of thinking had led her to overdose several times on the numerous medications that she took simultaneously. Prior to losing consciousness, she always mustered enough instinct for Self-preservation to call her Aunt Pat (probably an Eight), who she knew would come to her rescue.

Aunt Pat, Emma's mother's sister, was the person who brought Emma to see me, made her therapy appointments and set me straight about various aspects of her niece's life. She wanted me to know that "Emma would never have done anything positive for herself."

Emma, she said, had always been "spoiled rotten and had a sense of entitlement to everything she ever wanted or demanded." Her niece, she continued, "loves attention and drama and scared her parents out of their wits with her absurd risk-taking, threats and numerous veiled attempts at suicide." All this, she told me, reflected Emma's attempt to elicit proof that her parents really loved her. And now, it seemed, Aunt Pat—who described herself as Emma's "ambulance driver"—had inherited this unhappy pattern.

When I questioned Pat about Emma's parents, she said her sister was a "horrible mother," overindulgent and undisciplined, who had failed to set good boundaries with Emma since the girl's birth.

Aunt Pat, though trying to help her niece, was fed up with Emma's endless dramas and felt overburdened with her own duties as executor for her late sister's estate. Emma, she said, refused to lift a finger to help settle her parents' affairs. "All she wants to do is eat, sleep, watch TV, bitch and whine."

I could see that Aunt Pat, exhausted by her responsibilities, would have preferred not to have to drive Emma to her appointments with me (which she did for a number of months), but the likelihood that her niece would drop out of therapy without her "ambulance driver" made her continue.

From the outset, Emma was a difficult client. Like many Fours, she was certain she was the only person in the world who had ever felt the way she did; she was so much "deeper" than others that there was no possibility I could ever comprehend what she was really about.

During our sessions it came out that she had isolated herself from Tom, the one man she had occasionally dated during the past year. From Emma's description, Tom sounded like a good and loving man in whom she saw some qualities of her late father. Like Aunt Pat, Tom had become exasperated with Emma's self-centered antics and told her it would be impossible for any man to maintain a relationship with her unless she was willing to change.

On questioning Emma about this relationship, I learned that she would consistently panic in the midst of foreplay or intercourse. Tom was always respectful of her requests, she said, but it was clear that there was no joy or satisfaction for either of them in the sexual connection. Though I never met or tested Tom, it seems to me most likely that he is a Sexual Two, simply because he hung in for more than a year, genuinely trying to help a woman as troubled as Emma.

There is a story told about Fritz Perls, the pioneer Gestalt therapist, that, while conducting a session with a Four at an Esalen Institute workshop, he said to her, "Tell me, how many therapists have you defeated?" I, too, can testify to the difficulties of working with Fours in therapy and I suspect that one important reason is that therapists generally have a strong commitment to reduce the suffering of our clients. This can be a losing game with Fours, who often hang on to their suffering because they see it as a key element in their identity.

After much active listening and compassionate validation of Emma's feelings, I was able finally to tell her that she was heading down a path of self-destruction. I suggested that she would have a better chance of unearthing her true identity if she could normalize her life and become involved in outside relationships and activities.

Something I said must have gotten through to her, because she began eating in more healthy ways and sleeping most of the night.

Emma remained in therapy with me for some time, with the continuing help of Aunt Pat and several extended family members. Eventually she reached some emotional closure about her parents' death. Sessions of deep hypnosis gave her the opportunity to hold an internal dialogue with her inner child and helped set her on the road to self-parenting. For a long while she was preparing to "re-enter the world"—an action she felt was risky because she was never sure who she was or what would have "sustained value" for her. Though she now has more confidence, she is still searching for her "true, authentic self."

Eventually she was able to join a gourmet cooking group and a liberal non-traditional church; these connections made her feel more comfortable. Her extreme emotional intensity moderated as she focused in these groups on becoming more productive and less self-absorbed.

Still too frightened to become involved in any romantic or sexual relationship, she now says that she is at least "holding the door open to the possibility."

As a result of long-term therapy, Emma has come to trust herself more. Though she no longer feels "exempt from ordinary life," her resistance to hearing me refer to her as a "Four" or a "Self-preservation subtype" shows how highly invested she still is in not being put into any category that might include anyone else.

She took the C-JES survey (which confirmed her Four type) and did some reading about Fours, in which she recognized herself, but she insisted that she was different from any Four I had ever talked to. Despite her increase in self-knowledge, it's clear that she remains highly invested in not being understood by anyone.

Emma never tried to restore her relationship with Tom and I believe it's unlikely that this relationship—or any intimate connection with a man—would work for her at this time or in the immediate future. In her match with Tom, there was little compatibility, in any case. Their lovemaps were mostly incompatible, the only positive factors being a few qualities Tom had in common with Emma's father. Tom is a probable Sexual Two and there is a complementary connecting line between Fours and Twos, but this couple has no Harmonic Group match and no common subtype. Most problematic of all is Emma's low level of psychological health, even with the improvements that therapy has helped to bring.

Although I have never felt completely successful in my work with Emma, I can see that there have been significant improvements in her life: she no longer makes veiled suicide threats, she drives herself to her own appointments, she no longer overdoses on her medications and she has been able to connect with several groups with whom she has common interests. Aunt Pat remains a strong positive factor in her life.

"Hong Kong Babe"

Charles, 59, a Self-preservation Four, a balding heavyset man with intense brown eyes, told me during our first session that he was "in trouble again" with his wife, to whom he had been married for "14 long, rocky years." Linda (probably a Social Eight), his third wife and first love from high school, is an attorney who has no children from her earlier marriage or with Charles. She described herself to me as "strong, competent, powerful, usually able to keep Charles in line with his business ventures and his sporadic marijuana abuse."

He said, "My pot smoking never did any harm to anyone. After 40 years of smoking, why would I want to quit now?"

His lavish gifts to female business associates outside the country had also been a continuing issue between him and Linda. Recently she had inadvertently discovered a series of e-mails between Charles and a female wholesaler from Japan whom he had met through his textile company, which imported exotic fabrics for furniture and clothing. The e-mails were heavy with flirtation and seduction and they revealed Charles's plan for a rendezvous with this woman while he was on his semi-annual buying trip to Hong Kong.

In our first session Charles admitted that he had taken his company through great ups and downs, based on his personal mood swings. He had made and lost millions in the course of his depressions, dramas and pot smoking. As he critically assessed the fabrics I had used to re-cover my office furniture, I could see that he was a man of great intensity, refined taste and a thirst for self-indulgence.

Charles seemed, at first, quite defensive as he tried to con-vince me that his company's huge upswings and downturns were marks of his great risk-taking ability. "If you want to win, you have to take risks," he said.

I asked what percentage of the downturns he considered a result of the mood swings and depressions he had previously described.

"Well," he said, avoiding eye contact with me, "that depends on a lot of things. But most of the low periods in my business are the result of my turning down high-end customers because I'm too depressed to talk with them. Sometimes I can't stand the thought of working on certain projects or with certain people—so I don't. I escape, fantasize, numb out. Some customers are just too stupid to appreciate the uniqueness of the fabrics I acquire. They don't deserve to work with someone as creative as I am. That's the truth, plain and simple."

What about the big upswings in his business? Did these result from more deserving customers who were capable of recognizing his value and creativity?

"No," he said, "the upswings come when I decide to really work and stick with it. The big profit cycles show up when I'm out to win, to make my mark in the world."

Then what would cause the change of gears, going into the downturn cycle?

"It's probably when I start feeling cocky," Charles said. "Then I justify celebrating, enjoying my profits. That's when the shit usually hits the fan with Linda. She won't celebrate my successes with me—won't even get drunk or high for one night. She's so intent on being proper and socially acceptable and I'm just some low-life drug abuser. As if I didn't even have a job or earn any money.

"That's when I *really* rebel," he went on, "get high on pot and alcohol, just blow it all out for a week or two. Those are the times when I lose the big clients and get into the downturns."

I commented that it seemed he was caught in a vicious cycle. On the one hand, he wanted to celebrate his big financial wins with his wife, but her refusal to drink much or consume any marijuana ruined the party. This made him feel judged and left him with no one to unwind with.

"Exactly," he said. "That's the only reason I flirt with women on my business trips. It makes me feel desirable and not subject to criticism for just being myself."

I inquired about the previous two marriages he had mentioned.

His first wife, Laurie, he said, "got to be too much of a pain in the ass" after 16 years of marriage. However, he is extremely proud of his two daughters, whom Laurie raised during their teenage years after Charles dumped her. His second marriage, a "nine-month rebound fiasco" with a much younger woman, he described as "merely a pimple on my life's journey—nothing worth noting."

For a man of 59, he was unusually reckless and dismissive in his attitude toward all three of his wives. For example, he described Linda, his current wife, as a hard-working attorney in a small law firm, but didn't think she did "many important cases."

At the moment Linda—who, according to Charles, was "always confrontational anyhow"—was on the warpath over his e-mails. Not only that, but last month she had discovered that he was again secretly using high-grade marijuana. "It's no big deal," he told me. "I know my limits."

In my first joint session with Charles and Linda, it became evident the he had no clear boundaries around marijuana and did *not* know his limits. Linda was enraged over both his pot smoking and the "Hong Kong babe" with whom he had arranged an assignation. Finding Charles's e-mails had been the last straw for her and she was "ready to cut his balls off."

"This is not marriage counseling," she told me. "This is *divorce* counseling. She quickly decided that my approach was "too soft," especially on the issue of financial sanctions for Charles and said she saw no reason to continue with my services. Unwilling to listen to Charles's pleas for more understanding, she had a lawyer friend file her divorce petition.

They did divorce in the end and I continued to see Charles for several years of therapy and intermittent sessions after that, during which he became significantly healthier.

Though I never saw Linda again, I learned she was angry that

I had not persuaded Charles to give her a huge financial settlement because of the "Hong Kong babe e-mails." (In the end, Charles went to Hong Kong, discovered he had no chemistry with the woman and the relationship was never consummated.)

After the divorce Charles moved out of the house he had shared with Linda into a condo, which he decorated elaborately. He adopted two parakeets, began a collection of Chinese porcelain and tried his hand at gourmet dessert preparation. However, none of these activities resolved his irritation and unrest with himself.

Finally, after much explaining and prodding from me, it dawned on Charles that he might find real meaning in his life if he:

• Became more self-disciplined, incorporating more routines, goals and commitments into his daily schedule. (This decreased his binge eating, his bouts of promiscuous sex and some of his sporadic pot smoking.)

• Used his creative talent and business ability in more disciplined ways (as opposed to merely fantasizing). Doing this gave him a greater sense of self-worth and measurable financial profits.

• Developed a small circle of friends, mostly from his gourmet met dinner club and among the fabric importers he knew, who he could trust to call him on his self-destructive behavior, such as marijuana smoking.

Charles later explained to me that the biggest breakthrough of his life was discovering what it meant to be a Four. He had previously looked for an identity through material things—an approach not uncommon to individuals with a Self-preservation subtype—but this had not worked for him. Now he felt he had a workable framework for finding himself.

Charles and Linda's marriage had little going for it, from the outset. Their lovemaps were seriously incompatible and both were at unhealthy levels of psychological development. They had different subtypes and no connecting Enneagram line to balance their differences. With Linda being an Eight, they did have a Harmonic Group connection, since Eights and Fours are both "Reactive" types.

Given how little these two had in common, it's a miracle that their marriage endured for 14 years. The factor that probably kept them together this long was his need for Linda's protection and the sense of structure and boundaries she provided—which, in turn, gave Linda some emotional satisfaction.

In recent times, his pot smoking has become less frequent and he has stopped having promiscuous sex with women he meets in bars. Now seeking a healthy relationship, he says that, when he finds the right woman, "I'll give away my parakeets."

Emma and Charles as Self-preservation Fours

The recklessness typical of Self-preservation Fours is evident in both of the above cases. Emma's recklessness in spending her parents' money on possessions she didn't even care about (such as the yacht she'd never seen) and her need to place herself continually in danger through overeating, unhealthy sleep patterns and overdosing on medications exemplifies the Self-preservation Four's need to ratchet up the intensity of her situation through profligacy with money and compulsive risk-taking.

Charles's continually putting his company at risk because of his bad financial decisions based on his mood swings is also characteristic of the Self-preservation subtype of Four, as is his recklessness about sexual entanglements with women other than his wife.

Fours with the Sexual subtype

The Sexual subtype, which Ichazo associates with "competition," is the most aggressive of the Four subtypes. Individuals in this group develop intense attractions to people and their relationships are generally stormy. Jealous and possessive, they often have ambivalent feelings toward their lovers: hatred mixed with love and admiration.

They tend to become competitive with their lovers, envying the lovers' good qualities, then rejecting them for tiny imperfections. In unhealthy individuals of this subtype, crimes of passion are not uncommon.

"Bigamy"

Natasha, 32, a Sexual Four, after an intense and volatile marriage of just under one year to Carlos, 35, contacted me for a phone appointment after being referred by previous clients who now live near the couple in Arizona. Natasha told me during this first conversation that she was "fit to be tied" over the recent revelation that the love of her life, her "fabulous, hot Carlos" had been previously married to a woman in Mexico and had two children with her.

Though Carlos never took the survey, he is probably a Sexual Nine—warm, easygoing, concerned with avoiding conflict, keeping the peace and making Natasha happy. This has not always been easy, since she would become hysterical over any reference to women who had previously been important in his life.

Natasha was of Russian descent and Carlos of Mexican descent. They had been together for three years, including two stormy years of dating: breaking up, having verbally violent arguments, getting engaged, breaking the engagement, going through periods of not speaking. Both agreed that most of the emotional turmoil was Natasha's doing. Carlos would respond with his duck-and-cover act.

She was the manager of an artists' boutique in Phoenix that sold unusual art objects and paintings, some of which Natasha had created herself. She had met Carlos when he was hired to paint the boutique's storefront signs. Even though a sign-painting career was somewhat boring for Carlos, he seemed content with the easy work and stable income. The two fell in love immediately and, after only two months of dating, Carlos moved into Natasha's apartment.

During their many tumultuous fights, Carlos would simply leave and stay with members of his extended family (aunts, uncles, cousins) who lived in the area. Natasha resented this and accused Carlos's relatives of pitting him against her. She herself had insisted on moving far away from her "dull, white working-class family" in Ohio, who "never understood" her, anyway. But she felt envious of Carlos's "close-knit Hispanic tribe." Natasha desperately wanted to be on the inside, yet always positioned herself on the outside of Carlos's heart and family.

At the beginning of our sessions, Natasha mailed me a picture of the two of them, clearly proud of their unique look as a couple. She was a buxom, green-eyed blonde, Carlos a handsome, well-built Hispanic male. Natasha lived in constant fear that "some conniving, seductive vamp" might snatch Carlos away from her, because he was so easygoing and impressionable. From our phone sessions, it seemed clear that Carlos sincerely loved his wife and wanted only for her "to remain calm and not go ballistic" on him.

Although Carlos and his three siblings were born in the United States, with citizenship, their parents were still Mexican citizens. The family had moved to Phoenix from Mexico City so that the father could work in one of his brothers' businesses before Carlos was born. When Carlos was 15, his father moved the family back to Mexico City, where Carlos lived until age 25.

The part of Carlos's life that he had omitted telling Natasha about (for fear of her jealousy, possessiveness and possible rejection) is that, at age 20, he had married Maria, his Catholic Mexican girl-friend, when she became pregnant. They quickly produced two daughters. Carlos, who had never wanted children to begin with, soon grew tired of the Mexican culture, the religion and the traditional family lifestyle that were so different from what he had known in America.

By the time he was 25, Carlos had become so withdrawn, so depressed, so out of love with his strident, hard-working, tradition-ally religious wife that they decided to divorce. Carlos left Maria everything they had, in exchange for his freedom. She and the girls quickly moved in with her parents and two brothers, who were ex-tremely protective of the little girls. Maria agreed that she would take care of all the divorce papers, since Carlos had already signed all his possessions over to her and she promised to mail copies of the final papers to Carlos at his uncle's address in Phoenix.

Apparently she never completed this task—and the final

papers were never filed. Carlos had essentially forgotten all of this over the past 10 years, seeing this period as "a bad dream."

So it was a stunning surprise to both Carlos and Natasha when they suddenly received a letter from a Spanish-speaking attorney in Phoenix, asking Carlos to come to his office to "sign divorce papers." Carlos felt betrayed, blind-sided and confused. Natasha felt enraged, betrayed and vengeful. This event was what precipitated their initial call to me. They had needed marriage counseling even before this, but the attorney's call had made everything so much worse.

On the phone, Natasha was screaming that their marriage "was not valid, not a legal marriage" if Carlos was in fact legally married to someone else. Which of course was technically true. On top of all this, she had just confirmed with blood tests that she was now two months pregnant, due to an unforeseen contraceptive failure with condoms and foam. Now their "unwanted child" would also be illegitimate.

In response to her hysteria, I could feel Carlos sinking back into the same dark depression he had probably experienced in his early 20s with Maria. I had to work extremely hard to convince him to become proactive, to take charge of the situation rather than continuing his usual nice-guy passive behavior, avoiding conflict. (This is classic Nine behavior and he later acknowledged himself as a Sexual Nine.)

In this extremely stressful situation, it was heartening to see Carlos's positive response to my recommendations. I encouraged him to contact Maria's attorney immediately and he did. Apparently Maria herself had not understood that their divorce was never completed. Their attorney in Mexico City had evidently died without filing the final papers. Now Maria, wanting to remarry, could not get a marriage license in Mexico City because she was listed as still married to Carlos.

Carlos quickly signed all the necessary paperwork to expedite the completion of their divorce, even offering to pay all attorney fees (since he knew Maria couldn't afford them). Since Maria spoke no English, Carlos also wrote a sweet letter to her in Spanish, congratulating her on her new marriage and expressing his pleasure that her husband-to-be would be a loving father figure for his two daughters. He asked the attorney to enclose his letter with the completed divorce papers. Carlos elected not to tell Natasha about the letter, out of concern for her volatile emotional state.

Carlos remained consistently loving and supportive of Natasha. Early in our sessions, I had them both make a "No Exit" commitment agreement (that they would remain together for the duration of our counseling). This was also helpful in making her more emotionally stable. After four weeks of counseling by phone, it was clear that she wanted an abortion. Here she, too, became proactive and received a 14-week abortion through a clinic that a girlfriend of hers had used. Although she considered herself "an emotional mess," she was "sane enough to know that neither of us ever planned to have children."

As I continued the counseling, Natasha wanted to take the personality survey and "absolutely agreed" that she is a Sexual Four. I gently confronted them on the issue of contraception and found that Natasha was unable to tolerate any form of hormone-based prevention (pills, patch, shots), so they were doing the best they could with condoms and contraceptive foam.

I suggested they might do better—if they had absolutely reached a decision not to have children—if Carlos would consider a vasectomy. Within three weeks, he again was proactive and got a vasectomy. This way, their wonderful sexual connection would be even better—with no concern over a possible pregnancy and greater freedom. Both were extremely happy and relieved.

Eventually, Carlos received his final divorce papers. Whether or not their initial marriage was "legal," both of them knew they were married in their hearts. Just as a cross check, I suggested they have a second wedding ceremony (exchange vows and file another marriage license) as a way of celebrating their second anniversary, so there could never be any question about the legality of their union. Natasha loved this idea, because it was such a creative way of both honoring their anniversary and legalizing their marriage. As I write these words, plans for that event are in the making.

The outcome of this case resulted in greatly increased happiness for both Natasha and Carlos. Both were willing to work diligently on their marriage, which already benefited from several of the Five Factors for predicting marital success.

First, they had highly compatible lovemaps (with many unconscious traits in common). Secondly, as they became more conscious, they chose to work extremely hard on their personal growth and this resulted in both becoming much healthier within their personality style. Thirdly, they had the great advantage of sharing the Sexual subtype.

"Nobody Understands"

Calvin, 66, a Sexual Four, a distinguished-looking diminutive gay man with a full head of snow-white hair, was referred to me by one of his fellow musicians. A highly educated, slightly arrogant man who spoke clearly and with great emotion and confidence, Calvin was a classically trained pianist, a graduate of the Juilliard School. He had performed with well-known orchestras in concert halls throughout the United States and Europe and obviously enjoyed the applause of large and varied audiences.

Although he "never made much money as a musician," he told me, he had the good fortune to be the "only child of wonderfully wealthy, now-deceased parents." His father, who had been a successful stockbroker and financial adviser, made sure that Calvin had all the money he could ever want. "Dad always said," Calvin told me, "that it was hard enough being gay, I didn't need to be poor on top of it."

There was only one real problem in Calvin's life and that was his now ex-lover, Jimmy. Jimmy was 15 years younger (now age 51) and had broken up with Calvin ten years earlier, following a 21-year committed relationship. (From Calvin's description, Jimmy is most likely a Sexual Seven.)

Calvin, at age 35, met Jimmy (who was then 20) at a formal holiday party in San Francisco for gay men. Their eyes "locked on," they fell instantly in love and were living together in Calvin's beautiful San Francisco home within four months. Calvin's parents, who were liberal, warm and totally accepting of their son's sexual orientation, treated Jimmy as a second son.

Calvin described himself at the time he met Jimmy as "immature for my age, volatile, exciting, creative and basically depressive." He described Jimmy as "mature for age 20, street smart, energetic, always positive and willing to take risks." Jimmy made Calvin laugh, forced him out of his self-obsessed depressions into real happiness.

Jimmy, Calvin told me, was hard working. Despite all of Calvin's lavish gifts (for example, a $100,000 certificate of deposit and a Mercedes) and frequent pleas to "give up his store so we could spend more quality time together," Jimmy never quit working. He maintained his small video rental store in the city for two reasons, according to Calvin: 1) He never wanted Calvin to think he was a gold-digger and 2) his own freedom—a sense of having options—was essential for his own mental health. In telling me all this, Calvin seemed to have great clarity about Jimmy's motives and pride in his partner's stance.

What, I wondered, could have gone wrong with what sounded like such a happy and healthy relationship? Through much prodding and questioning on my part and many fits of tears on Calvin's, he finally was ready to talk about the real issues: the conditions and reasons surrounding his break-up with Jimmy.

After 21 years of a totally committed relationship, why did Jimmy choose to leave? This was a potent and painful question for Calvin. An even more important question was: Why, after 10 years, was Calvin still so stuck in his rage and pain, unable to move on with his life?

Calvin, after continually testing me to be sure I was a trust-worthy confidante, eventually admitted that he had deteriorated into a "sniveling, self-absorbed, jealous, hateful, sabotaging idiot whom Jimmy grew to despise." The last two years they were living together were miserable, he said and he himself was "the problem, the pill, the jackass—not Jimmy." Jimmy had pleaded with him to get help—from a therapist, a psychiatrist, a priest—anyone who could intervene in Calvin's narcissistic antics. Calvin refused. Jimmy even offered to go jointly for marriage counseling. Calvin still refused.

Slowly, painfully, Calvin was now gaining some objectivity about his own behavior during the period leading up to the breakup. During periods when Jimmy had to work at the store himself—

because a manager quit or someone was on vacation—Calvin would make up accusations about Jimmy "finding a young stud," not really loving him, choosing the store over him. Even admitting how much he admired Jimmy's hard work, positive attitude and independence, Calvin acknowledged that he "hated Jimmy for those same qualities." The love/hate dilemma he had created can be summed up in a phrase Oscar Ichazo used to describe the Sexual Four subtype: "hateful envy."

Calvin further confessed his deep desire, during the last year of their "marriage," to make Jimmy miserable—as miserable as Calvin himself felt. When I asked why, he said he thought it was because he felt Jimmy pulling away, sensed Jimmy's utter exasperation, saw Jimmy struggling to coax, beg or trick him into therapy. Nothing worked, Calvin said, because he was "fearful of all forms of intervention. I was afraid of being found out."

Looking back now, Calvin wishes he had gone for therapy much earlier and had actually been "found out." Perhaps then he might have corrected his "bizarre thinking" and made some changes in his treatment of Jimmy. He remembers with chagrin some of the "stupid schemes" he devised "to get Jimmy's undivided attention"— such as the time he got one of Jimmy's employees to tell him that Calvin had called and sounded suicidal, that perhaps Jimmy should go on home for the night. "Really childish stuff," as Calvin characterized it now.

At this point, Calvin was suffering from a great deal of self disgust, a profound longing to again be with his soul mate and an idealized fantasy version of what their life together would be.

From Calvin's descriptions, it was clear that Jimmy was forever finished with any romantic notions surrounding their relationship. Near the end, Jimmy felt emotionally abused, double-crossed and rejected. Since then he has sustained a respectful but distant style of communication with his former lover: they talk by phone about once a month, but Jimmy insists that he is better off not seeing Calvin in person.

Five years after the breakup, Calvin, in one of his fits of despair and depression, moved from San Francisco to Orange County, where he purchased an elaborate home, thinking this would help his rage and "stuckness" in depression. The move assuaged the intensity of his feeling for almost a year while he devoted himself to decorating the mansion in his own lavish, outrageous fashion. He was also distracted from time to time by his participation in various concerts. Additionally, he made some new friends and began attending functions in the local gay community.

Yet his longing for contact with Jimmy eventually returned and led to his seeking therapy with me. Now, ten years after their breakup, he knew he needed to make some major life changes. What could he do now?

I explained to Calvin that one of the reasons his heart had never fully healed was that he never fully owned up to his own shortcomings and blind spots. Also, he had never made amends to Jimmy for his actions. As required in the 12-Step Programs, Calvin needed to take a full inventory of his life and actions and then figure out to whom and for what, he needed to make amends.

This proved to be an excruciating process for Calvin, yet he hung in there, doing therapy for almost two years. Now, having done his "inventory" and truly having made amends, he is a changed man. At last, he is able to get outside himself and to make positive contributions to other people, causes and organizations. He now has occasional dinner dates with various men, has become involved with several musicians' groups and a political rights organization for gays.

He still talks with Jimmy once or twice a month by phone. Although there is clearly no hope of any romantic reconciliation, Jimmy was so impressed with the detail and sincerity of Calvin's "amends" that he wrote a deeply moving letter of response, allowing "total forgiveness" to flood their "memories of the relationship."

Calvin still sees me from time to time for a "check up from the neck up," as he calls it. He seems much happier and better adjusted. He has trained himself to respond more rationally and less emotionally (and "never hysterically").

This is in stark contrast to the behavior that brought his romantic relationship with Jimmy to a halt. Like many Sexual Fours, Calvin became increasingly obsessed with his love object, possessive and jealous. Further deterioration brought attempts to undermine and sabotage his partner, while rejecting the very traits that he simultaneously found so attractive (Jimmy's work ethic and independence).

The relationship was sustained for 21 years because of their highly compatible lovemaps, Jimmy's relatively high level of psychological health and the fact that both were Sexual subtypes.

Natasha and Calvin as Sexual Fours

The two cases described above show how different levels of psychological health can bring about strongly contrasting outcomes for Type Four individuals of the Sexual subtype. For Natasha, who was certainly jealous and possessive about her relationship with Carlos, the ability to accept her husband's deep love for her was a factor that tempered her histrionic tendencies and resulted ultimately in a happy marriage, despite serious situational difficulties (the revelation of his earlier marriage and her pregnancy).

In the case of Calvin, his love-hate feelings for Jimmy were expressed so venomously that there was no way of salvaging his long-term and potentially lifetime relationship. Calvin's growth through therapy and his ability to make amends to his former partner open up the possibility that he might eventually sustain another intimate partnership more successfully.

Fours with the Social subtype

People with the Social Four subtype, which Ichazo associates with "shame," are driven by a strong sense of inner defectiveness and an expectation that others will see their flaws and reject them. Bottomless pits of longing, they are powerfully aware of what is missing in their lives, intensely envious of those who have it and ashamed of their envy. They have low self-esteem and fear their defects make them unable to function in society.

"My Own Slow Suicide"

Elizabeth, a spry 73-year-old Social Four, is a former beauty queen who played competitive tennis in college and took pride in her non-conformity. Still a handsome, well-dressed, somewhat eccentric sporty type, she insists on being called E-liz-a-BETH. "Don't ever fall into the trap of calling me 'Betty,'" she told me. "I really hate that."

Referred to me by a friend who was a previous client of mine, she came to me for one *big* reason, she said: she was so lonely that she periodically fantasized about death and "how good the relief, the peace of it all might feel." She said she wasn't "normal" and knew she had never fit in with social groups. Yet she took a certain pride in her one-of-a-kind status. Now, feeling lonelier than ever, she wanted to clarify her sense of self and her place in the world, wanted to understand why she always felt on the outside, looking in.

She reported feeling well adjusted to widowhood after six years alone. But she acknowledged this was probably because she had felt alone throughout her married life. Though her husband, Bill, bonded deeply with their two boys, the three of them always left her out.

About her sons, now 42 and 44, she said, "To this day, I rarely see them, because we have almost nothing to talk about." The sons, John and Jeff, own an auto parts business together. Both are divorced and have girlfriends, but neither has any children. "I resent never having been a grandmother," Elizabeth said, "but I have no clue what I ever would have done with a grandchild in tow."

She continued her catalogue of frustrations: "I want to be part of our local country club—especially in the women's tennis doubles. But I can't stand some of the loud-mouthed, uncouth women who play, so I shy away. I never show up to play because I'm so uncomfortable with that group." After a dramatic pause she continued, "I know I'm one weird old bird, but please, Mona, oh please, help me change before I die."

While she readily admitted her "many faults," Elizabeth evidently enjoyed being labeled complicated and mysterious—a woman to be reckoned with.

The friend who had recommended she call me had told her

how helpful the personality survey had been, so Elizabeth was eager to take it herself. She seemed awed by the results and acknowledged that she was indeed "a classic Four, a true-blue Social Four."

This gave me the opening I needed to discuss what was happening in her mind, including her active imagination and vivid fantasy life. She needed to learn how to separate fact from fantasy.

First we thoroughly discussed her "nothing of a marriage" with Bill (who was most likely a Self-preservation Five, from her description). In a literal sense, Elizabeth was correct about their having nothing in common. She revealed how totally incompatible their lovemaps were and that both were average-to-unhealthy in their levels of psychological development. They had different sub-types, no Harmonic Group match and no connecting line to balance or complement one another.

As all this unfolded, Elizabeth wept profusely and ached over the reality of her "wasted, empty life," which had been devoid of any real love. Even her own parents, who were good and decent working-class people, she said, "didn't have a clue who I was." Since she was the fourth of six children on an Iowa farm until the age of 19, when she "escaped into college" as a Physical Education major, there was little opportunity for her hard-working parents to offer any kind of individualized attention. What she had failed to examine was her own unconscious conclusion about this situation: namely, that she was so defective, so shameful, so odd that even her own parents couldn't validate her, claim her or love her.

I saw an opportunity here for a further opening into the therapeutic process. I invited Elizabeth, just for our next three sessions, to deal only with the facts of her situation. She agreed, during that period, to omit all interpretation, fantasy, projection and imagination in discussing her situation. Holding to this agreement was exceptionally difficult for her emotionally, but it shed great light on her thought processes. Here are some of the things she discovered:

1. Her parents did the best they could, raising six children on a rural farm. They were good, honest people who emphasized values, integrity and commitment. Elizabeth realized that she

had benefited greatly from their parenting.

2. Bill was a solid, reliable person who had been a good provider and father, although not an appropriate mate for Elizabeth. He had never betrayed her, never tried to control her, never stood in her way.

3. Her two sons, John and Jeff, had both turned out to be healthy, rather successful businessmen—primarily because Bill had taken so much time with them and taught them so much about cars, mechanics and business practices.

4. Her sons had never rejected her. They were always respectful and moderately open to Elizabeth's feelings and opinions.

Thus, when we got down to the actual *facts*, Elizabeth began to see that her life was objectively different from what she had created in her dark imagination.

I encouraged her to set at least three objective goals for herself—things she deeply wanted. After much introspection, she committed to the following:

1. To improve her relationship with her two sons. In behavioral terms, this meant having two telephone conversations per month with each of them and visiting them in person about every three months (approximately four times a year). They lived about three hours' drive from her home in Laguna Beach. I suggested that she could invite each son, separately, to bring his girlfriend and stay with her in Laguna for the weekend—a possibility that had never occurred to her. She took action on this immediately.

2. To participate in the women's tennis division of her country club. Since she had no doubt about her ability as a player, only her sense of "misfit" with the other women stood in her way. The initial strategy we devised was for her to simply watch several games while cheering on the other players. Her only

goal, at first, was to be the cheerleader, with no negative judgments about the players. She was such a good support that several of the women introduced themselves, explained that they were not very good at tennis and invited Elizabeth to join them for lunch after the match to give them some tennis pointers. This made her feel wonderful.

It was important at this point that Elizabeth learn the technique of Negative Thought Stopping. I referred her to a book entitled *The 30-Day Mental Diet* by Willis Kinnear and she quic kly learned Kinnear's three basic steps: a) *acknowledge* any negative thought immediately; b) *release* it; c) *replace* it with a positive thought. For example: a) *acknowledge* "I can't stand that woman's loud mouth." [negative thought]; b) release this thought; c) *replace* it with: "Everyone's here to have a good time and we're all unique." [positive thought].

3. Elizabeth's third goal was to accept herself just as she is and stop making comparisons of herself and other people. She had become aware of how miserable she had made herself over many years of drawing hateful comparisons between herself and others. She was continually feeling inferior or superior— never at ease with her own internal self.

She became increasingly interested in the spiritual/philoso-phical aspects of her growth following the reading of Neal Walsh's *Conversations with God*. From another book, *A Course In Miracles*, I extracted a phrase that has had a powerful influence on Elizabeth's life ever since: "All human misery is caused by making comparisons."
Elizabeth still has therapy sessions with me twice a month and she remains "determined to conquer the demons within." She now reports "feeling 500 percent happier than I've ever been before."

"The Hidden Designer"

Devon, 19, a Social Four, came to his first session with his parents, who were desperate to find help for their "fragile, moody, lost-as-hell son." A tall, willowy young man, Devon was dressed entirely in black, accessorized with striking silver-studded black leather jewelry.

Wondering whether his attire signified an interest in sadomasochism, I remarked that I had recently seen similar bracelets and pocket chains on several of my guest speakers on the topic of S & M in my Human Sexuality classes.

Devon laughed and told me that he had no interest in S & M, but that, as a designer on his way to world renown, it was essential that he wear the clothes and jewelry he had personally created.

My questions about his background and current situation brought out that he still lived at home, by choice, and had twice dropped out of college because he couldn't stand "the grossness, the insensitivity, the lack of taste among most of the students." Yet he had requested to see me as a therapist because some of the students at the college where I taught Human Sexuality told him I was "cool." Hearing this, I wondered whether his problem might be of a sexual nature. Was he gay? A transvestite? Perhaps a transsexual? Involved in some bizarre sexual rituals or some cult?

His parents were eager to tell me about Devon's two older sisters—one in medical school, the other pursuing a Ph.D. in geophysics. As for Devon, what were they to do with this "odd-ball son" who had requested a sophisticated sewing machine for his 16th birthday? Recognizing the unlikelihood that he would suddenly take an interest in sports (as his father had hoped), both parents were supportive of his goals and prepared to finance his art and design education at the school of his choice.

It was Devon himself who felt "unprepared, defective, unable to face the physical reality of moving out and competing with other creative students." There were indications that he wanted to hide: from others, from college, from the demands of a career and—most of all—from himself. He looked emaciated, possibly anorexic.

At the end of our initial visit, Devon's parents made it clear that they would attend his therapy sessions only if invited. Obviously devoted to their son and ready to help in any way they could, they were sensitive about not interfering.

During our first session alone, Devon burst into uncontrollable tears. Between sobs, he told me how ashamed he felt, how fearful and confused. He'd been avoiding his friends, refusing even to see his long-term girlfriend on weekends. His stomach was in knots and the thought of swallowing food made him sick. He was tired of people asking him if he was gay—he wasn't. He was tired of people teasing him about his sewing. He loved designing and making clothes and jewelry and had sewn most of the clothes he'd worn for the past three years.

He'd even designed and sewn his girlfriend Sue's dress for their high school senior prom. Now Sue was beginning her sophomore year at the University of Southern California, majoring in journalism. Even though he missed her, he felt it was futile to contact her. Besides, he didn't like "the way she laughed" and detested the insensitivity and lack of refinement among many of her "slop-along friends." This had been the basis of one of their "bad arguments" before she had gone away to college. Yes, he was lonely, but he felt she wasn't the right girl for him, anyway.

"I know," he said, "that the real problem is *me*."

"What is there about you that is such a problem?" I asked.

Devon shook his head. "I'm totally confident, but also totally intimidated." He knew he was a great designer, yet couldn't stop comparing himself and his talents with famous designers from Europe and New York. One day, he imagined, everyone who had ever called him "weird, antisocial or gay" would have to acknowledge what a brilliant and creative designer he had become.

So what was stopping him from attending the Fashion Institute of Technology, the design school in New York that he and his mom had visited at the end of his senior year?

He had loved FIT's campus and the curriculum, yet felt he could never "be the best designer there." Comparing his own portfolio to those of seniors and graduate students, he suddenly feared being ridiculed by other students and professors. At times he spoke as if he considered his designs "too good for most people." Yet he also longed for the approval and fame that "mass culture" acceptance could bring. He continually fought within himself over whether to confine his work to elite circles or to court wider acceptance by lowering himself into the "pits of mass production."

Although I could see that his dilemma was sincere, I gently pointed out that he didn't yet have a line of clothing or jewelry—or even a basic design education. It was time to stop hiding out and take steps toward getting what he really wanted.

He didn't like my pointing out that he had more love, more emotional and financial support than 99 percent of the college students I had known in my 37 years of teaching. Yet he finally admitted this was true. It was clear that he needed to decide, once and for all, how to deal with his fears, his stuckness, his disdain and his compulsive comparisons of himself with others (which always led to the conclusion that if he couldn't be as good as the most famous designers in the world, then he was *nothing*).

I assured Devon that we could move slowly, but we needed also to move surely. It was not acceptable for him to remain in this dilemma if he wanted to continue therapy with me. By this point he had done some brief reading I had given him on Type Four, had acknowledged that he is a Social Four and had expressed some relief that I seemed to "understand" him.

In this positive frame of mind, he was willing to devise a behavioral plan (not based on feelings, moods or fantasy). As a first step, he would give himself one more school year, continuing to live at home, to prepare himself for admission to the Fashion Institute. This would involve taking 6 to 9 units per semester in art.

One of the many assignments I prescribed gave Devon some significant insights into his psychological patterns. For one full week his job was to record all his negative reactions and judgments about others (only the negatives, skipping all positive responses). After only five days, he was horrified. His list had gotten so long and "so tediously disgusting" that he spent the last two days of the assignment trying to avoid making any negative judgments about others. He shared this assignment with his parents and on the last two days all three of them tried to stop all forms of negative judgments in their home. The exercise was difficult for them all and they laughed as they shared experiences. In the end Devon felt deeply appreciated by his mom and dad for his "therapy efforts" and resulting changes.

However, the biggest personal insight for Devon—thanks to

this and other exercises I prescribed—was how much of his life he had wasted by making himself the "judge and jury" of others' responses, tastes and personalities. He felt heartsick about this stark reality, yet also humbled and anxious to change his ways. Ultimately, he concluded that everyone has personal tastes and preferences and these differences allow everyone to be unique. Even though his own tastes might be at variance with others', he concluded that he is better off dealing with "other weird people" than isolating in self-absorption.

Devon's continuing journey in therapy has been arduous and I applaud him (as well as his parents) for never giving up. He is doing well in his art classes and prides himself on helping explain techniques to other students less gifted than he. Without my ever mentioning his weight, he gradually began eating better and has now gained at least 15 pounds. He has even started wearing some colors. He has held on to his new philosophy: "We are *all* unique. That's what makes it so great."

He has also been accepted at the Fashion Institute in New York for the coming fall. And he has begun dating a new girl, Debbie (probably a Social Two, from his description), who he feels nurtures and complements him in ways that Sue never did.

Elizabeth and Devon as Social Fours

What do 73-year-old Elizabeth and 19-year-old Devon have in common? As Social Fours, they both needed to acquire some objectivity about themselves, thus separating the external facts of their lives from their internal feelings and fantasies. Both were able to make objective commitments to changing their behavior, based on principles and values rather than on transient mood swings and emotions. Both were able, finally, to stop comparing themselves with others in order to support their feelings of inferiority or superiority. Both replaced their self-absorption with real involvement with others and the outside world. In the process, both realized that they are no more "personally defective" or "flawed" than anyone else.

Strengths of Fours in Intimate Relationships

- Creativity
- Sensitivity
- Devotion to beauty
- Authenticity
- Expressiveness
- Originality
- Refinement
- Profundity

Limitations of Fours in Intimate Relationships

- Mood swings
- Melancholy
- Isolation
- Envy
- Dwelling on memories
- Emotional fragility
- Self-absorption
- Self-dramatization

Defense Mechanisms of Fours

Many Fours do not bond deeply with anyone in childhood. This can give them a strong sense of having been abandoned by their parents because of what they assume is their own inherent defectiveness. Seeing themselves as fundamentally flawed sets them up to make comparisons between themselves and others, which may become a preoccupation, as we saw in Elizabeth and Devon.

The basic defense mechanism of Fours is *introjection*. Because Fours feel so desolate over being abandoned, they take inside themselves the image of the beloved parent, nurturing figure or partner and comfort themselves by continually calling up that image in their fantasies. The problem with this is that the beloved person is *also* the person who they believe abandoned them, so that they feel both attraction to the person and fury at that person's rejection of them. This process can lead to the kind of emotional obsessions we saw in some of the cases described in this chapter: in Emma's feelings toward her parents (who, she felt, had not only abandoned her in childhood but also left her permanently bereft through their untimely deaths); in Calvin's mean-spirited behavior toward Jimmy (who truly loved him, yet was finally driven out of the relationship, thus fulfilling the negative aspects of Calvin's introjected image of his beloved); and in Devon's taking the world-famous designers inside himself (where he could identify with them as role models while at the same time tormenting himself with his own inadequacy in comparison to their accomplishments).

In each of these cases, the negative aspect of the introjected image becomes emotional fact. This "push-pull" aspect of introjection manifests itself in the melodramatic ups and downs Fours often cultivate in their intimate relationships.

The Natural Neuroses of Fours

One of the most obvious of Fours' natural neuroses is their difficulty in sorting out the facts of their lives from their fantasies. The fantasies, which are built into the defense mechanism of introjection, produce unrealistic self-assessments of Fours' abilities and achievements. Their sense of their own fundamental defectiveness can cause them to vacillate wildly between polarities of emotion and to overdramatize situations.

We see different versions of this pattern in each of the Type Four cases I've described. In the case of Natasha, for example, we saw her frenzy of anxiety and sense of betrayal over Carlos's earlier marriage, despite her experience of him being a consistently devoted husband. We saw this problem also in Devon's inflated view of himself as a "great designer" and his equally inappropriate self-denigration as "unprepared and inadequate."

Fours' tendency to rely on the reality of overblown fantasies and hyper-charged emotions (especially feelings of pain and shame) also sets them up for a sense of chronic dissatisfaction with their lives and a belief that the grass must be greener in other pastures. A major trap for Fours is having their sense of self so invested in their own suffering that they come to believe their pain is a measure of their authenticity. Coming to see that pleasure can also be an aspect of authenticity can be a major step forward for Fours.

Giving to others (related to Fours' link with Two) can also help them out of their own self-absorption, as we saw with Elizabeth's offering of support and tennis tips to women at her country club.

How Fours Blossom in Good Relationships

When Fours find themselves truly loved, their journey toward higher levels of health is greatly enhanced. Natasha, for example, despite her dark fantasies about previous and potential "other women" in Carlos's life, has been able at last to recognize that he truly loves her and take realistic steps toward enhancing their marriage (the abortion, the decision for a second wedding ceremony on their second anniversary).

Devon, too, through the consistent support of his loving parents and the beginnings of a new relationship with a more appropriate girlfriend (Debbie), was able to develop his empathy and compassion for others, seeing that everyone is "unique and special" in his or her own way. This willingness to acknowledge others' feelings and personal struggles represents a great leap forward for most Fours.

Through learning to distinguish the realities of their lives from their fantasies (as was the case with Calvin and Elizabeth), Fours may open themselves to the possibility of blossoming as individuals as well as in their love relationships.

TYPE FIVE: THE INVESTIGATOR IN LOVE

Fives at all levels of psychological health seek to maintain their safety by relying on their mental faculties and minimizing contact with others. A large storehouse of precise knowledge gives them a feeling of control over their environment.

Average Fives are preoccupied with their own mental process-es. They enjoy accumulating information and achieving mastery in their fields. Emotionally detached, they resist involvement in intimate relationships. Often tense and intense, they have a tendency toward cynicism and iconoclasm.

When Fives are healthy they are extraordinarily alert and inventive, capable of original insights into the patterns of nature and human life. In love with knowledge, they master whatever subjects interest them and can become world-class experts in their chosen field. Healthy Fives are independent and often display a wry humor.

Unhealthy Fives can become physically and mentally out of touch with reality and people, obsessed with negative thoughts and bizarre ideas, subject to phobias and distortions of reality. When extremely unhealthy, their quest for respite from the torments of their own mind may lead them to extreme isolation and perhaps psychosis.

Fives with the Self-preservation Subtype

All Fives focus on finding ways of preserving their safety and autonomy in the world, but their strategies for doing this vary according to their subtype. Self-preservation Fives, whom Oscar

Ichazo characterizes as preferring to be cloistered in their "castle," tend to be the most fragile, shy and withdrawn. Their basic strategy is to isolate themselves and to minimize personal needs and social contacts. Intent on creating a safe place (a castle or sanctuary) to which they can retreat from a dangerous world, they are easily exhausted by others and need solitary time in familiar surroundings to recoup their energies.

"Restraints, Please!"

Willow, 49, a Self-preservation Five, had been happily married for 23 years to Larry, 51, who is most likely a Social Eight. Their two children—a daughter, 19 and a son, 21— are both in local colleges. Willow expressed dismay that neither child had chosen to go away to school and that both insisted on living at home. She had been looking forward to the empty nest, she told me, so that she could have more privacy, more time to read and study Japanese.

Her marriage to Larry suited her well, she said, because he was gone a lot, running their furniture store, volunteering for various political/social causes and working with the Rotary Club. "I feel tired just listening to him talk about all his activities," she continued. "I'm so grateful that he doesn't insist I go with him to all these things like some husbands do."

By now I was wondering what had brought this self-assured woman to my office. "What do you like most about yourself?" I asked.

Without hesitation, she told me that she liked her capability as a student, her intellectual curiosity, her perceptiveness and independence. "I'm not at all interested in status symbols or creating some kind of public image," she said.

This was clearly a woman with a strong sense of self.

I asked if there was anything she disliked about herself.

She spoke about feeling awkward in various social situations. After a pause she added, "I have a tendency toward certain obsessive thoughts and fantasies."

I invited her to expand on this and after some hemming and

hawing she disclosed that she felt "extremely stuck—obsessed, if you will—on a horrid, pathological sexual fantasy." This fantasy, she said, took up so much of her thinking time and emotional energy that she had exhausted herself. Convinced that she was psychologically sick, she had made an appointment with me in the hope that sex therapy could cure her of this disease.

I explained to Willow that over 90 percent of the adult population, both male and female, regularly engage in all kinds of sexual fantasies. This is perfectly normal, I told her. Even couples married for 50 years might either fantasize individually or verbally share a variety of made-up fantasies as a form of foreplay to enhance their sexual arousal. I asked her to tell me more about the content of her "horrid, pathological fantasy."

My casual explanations and vivid examples from other clients gave Willow the confidence to disclose more. She explained that since she was a teenager she'd had a repetitive, intense fantasy of being tied-up, handcuffed and forced to have sex with a domineering male partner. Having revealed so much, she was overcome with embarrassment, perhaps anticipating that I would judge her harshly or prescribe some form of therapy to cure the "sickness" she was sure she had.

When, instead, she saw me chuckling at her revelations, there was surprise in the blue eyes behind her rimless glasses. I reassured her that her fantasy of being tied up, forced and raped was shared by hundreds of thousands of women. Knowing her intellectual interests, I pointed out some of the traditional studies on women's sexual fantasies, such as *The Hite Report* by Shere Hite and Nancy Friday's classic descriptions of such fantasies in *My Secret Garden*, along with other broad-based national surveys.

The look of relief on Willow's wide face was worth its weight in gold. It had never occurred to her that she could be normal— that such thoughts and sexual turn-ons are not even considered unusual, let alone pathological.

I further explained that having a favorite fantasy is far different from real-life practice. Of course she didn't actually want to be raped! Her fantasy was most likely ingrained by related images that she had stumbled onto as a teenager, at which time she was highly aroused. The same fantasy, over time, became a generic source of arousal. Willow seemed to understand this simple principle of classical conditioning.

She quickly moved to the issue of discussing this with Larry. She had always been rather quiet during their lovemaking, which she reported as satisfying to both of them. Her quietness, she said, was a result of her being so completely absorbed in her own fantasy, as she was during masturbation.

Was she obligated to tell Larry her 35-year-old secret fantasy?

Of course not, I said; it was her private business. But could telling him possibly be helpful? Would it make them feel closer? I shared with her other clients' experiences in similar situations.

Willow said she could never, on her own, bring up the subject with her husband. But with my help, armed with my level of comfort and knowledge, it might be a good thing to share with Larry, she felt.

I assured her that I would support any decision she made—this was her business and hers alone. Eventually she decided to take the risk—but only if I would agree to share with Larry in a joint session all the cases, books and studies I had described to her. She preferred to have me do the talking and I said I would.

When Larry arrived for the joint session, I saw that he was a big, warm, loving, protective guy. (Willow and I had previously discussed how Larry actually fulfilled almost all of her lovemap criteria.) He was clearly grateful that Willow had invited him to share the session with her and concerned about anything he could "do, change or create to help."

I assured him there was nothing Willow needed or wanted him to change and that, in fact, she was deeply satisfied with their relationship.

Then why was he here?

I explained that Willow and I had agreed that I would assist her in sharing an idea—actually a fantasy—with him.

Larry laughed. "What is this, some kind of set-up?"

No, I told him, it was that Willow had felt so awkward, so ashamed about a recurrent sexual fantasy she'd experienced since her mid-teens that she'd enlisted my help in explaining it all to him.

He nodded his acquiescence and I quickly explained that

many—in fact, most—women have fantasies of being restrained, perhaps tied up or handcuffed and forced to have sex. I said that this most likely became part of Willow's lovemap as a teenager masturbating with explicit images.

Larry seemed delighted with this information and quickly volunteered that he'd always had the reverse fantasy—that he would overpower, restrain and force the female to surrender to him sexually. There was unmistakable love in his eyes as he continued, "But I never wanted to offend or turn off Willow. You know she's much more sensitive and private than I am. What a relief!"

Following much laughter, I reassured both of them that fantasy can and often does play a major role in enriching and expanding the sex lives of many couples, especially those in committed long-term relationships.

Larry pronounced himself "ready to roll" and assured Willow that their sex life could only get better and better. "You just need to let me know what specific fantasies turn you on."

I didn't feel they needed much more help from me, at least at this time. I encouraged them to give me call in the future if and when they ran into a "bump in the road."

Willow and Larry had three of the Five Factors that predict successful relationships. First, they had highly compatible lovemaps; second, they were both fairly healthy in their personality structures; third, they shared a complementary balancing line (connecting Fives and Eights on the Enneagram diagram). Though they did not share a common subtype or the same Harmonic Group, the other three factors produced a highly functional and satisfying marriage.

"Wrong Turn?"

Glen, 42, a Self-preservation Five, came to see me because he believed he was having a nervous breakdown. He had recently accepted a full professorship at a well known university and he and his wife, Trish, 41, had moved four weeks earlier to Southern California from Maryland, where he had been teaching at a small private college. It was now July and he was scheduled to assume his new teaching duties in September.

He was in a panic over the prospect of having to "impart massive amounts of historical information to large groups of undergraduates." As his story unfolded, it became clear that his distress was largely based on a misunderstanding about what constituted a large class. In his former college, he had been accustomed to teaching groups of 10 to 15 students, using the Socratic method he favored. Now, faced with the prospect of teaching classes of 35 to 40 undergraduates, he was uncertain whether his time-tested teaching methods could be applied to groups of this size.

He felt deceived by the university about his new working conditions and confessed that he was extremely uncomfortable in front of large groups (larger than 20 students). Yet other faculty members he had met from his new university considered a "large class" one that contained 200 to 300 students. The other professors' ability to cope with such huge classes left him feeling overwhelmed and uninformed about lecturing techniques that could be effective even with a group of 40.

His narrow shoulders shaking with emotion, he said, "At this point, I just want to quit everything—resign my professorship, get a divorce and move to a shack in the woods."

A divorce? I asked him to tell me more about his marriage.

It seemed to Glen that his 12-year marriage to Trish (a Social One) was falling apart. She had made an immense sacrifice by moving with him to California so he could take advantage of his great job offer. Doing this meant leaving behind friends and family and resigning her highly paid position as Executive Secretary/Office Manager of a small Maryland law firm, giving up 20 years seniority. She was currently looking for a top-level management position and had consulted appropriate headhunters—so far, to no avail. Her gallant attempts to meet neighbors, join a local church, sign up for a lecture series and make new friends had produced only resistance on Glen's part. Preoccupied with his anxieties about his teaching and feeling guilty about uprooting her, he found it impossible to get past his resentment over her "shoulds and oughts" and her forcing him into social contacts he wasn't ready for.

Trish, realizing they needed professional help, had actively sought referral to a therapist and had been given my name. As a Self-preservation Five, Glen was resistant to any form of help that might involve revealing his private thoughts and feelings. However, in the face of Trish's persistent urgings, he researched therapists in the area and agreed to see me alone (without Trish). Having discovered from my website that I had extensive college teaching experience, he thought I might be able to offer some useful advice about teaching classes larger than he was accustomed to.

I suggested to him at our first session that he and Trish might benefit from some joint sessions, but he was intent on first dealing with his anxiety about the teaching challenges he was facing. I sensed immediately that he was a Self-preservation Five (which he later confirmed with the personality survey). In our initial sessions, I did extensive active listening, making certain that he felt heard and understood by me, while sharing many of my own college teaching experiences.

Through empathy and rapport, I was able eventually to help Glen reframe some of his fears. After some serious resistance, he began to see himself more clearly—as the competent and popular professor he had always been. He became able, once again, to see what his former students had so appreciated about him and to understand why a top-flight university was eager to offer him a full professorship with research opportunities.

We talked at length about teaching styles and techniques for keeping students interested, including dividing the class into dyads or small groups of 3 to 5 students for certain debates and class exercises. I helped Glen to see that a class of 35 or 40 wasn't so very different from one of 15 or 20.

Over the next weeks his panic and depression seemed to lift. After working out many different classroom activities—such as question-answer formats between students and small group projects—Glen realized that in a 16-week semester he couldn't possibly use all the techniques he had accumulated in our sessions. Now he was feeling competent again and fully prepared. His previous anger at Trish and the university had turned to excitement. We agreed that he would teach the first semester and see how he felt at the end of it before making any decision about continuing in his new position.

It was now time (in Trish's opinion, past time) to begin joint sessions. Hurt as she had been over her husband's emotional withdrawal, she struck me as a psychologically healthy and mature woman, genuinely concerned about Glen's depressed condition. She, too, had felt depressed over all she had given up in an effort to make Glen happy, only to see him more miserable than ever. She also felt betrayed by his unwillingness to "even try to make new friends or become involved in any social activities."

Since both Glen and Trish were exceptionally well read and highly educated, they were able to rapidly comprehend structural differences between a Self-preservation Five and a Social One. As they learned more about their own and each other's type and subtype, they were able to gain a great deal of insight and empathy for one another.

Glen saw that his isolation and unwillingness to reach out or communicate were aspects he needed to drastically improve in himself. Trish for the first time was able to objectively see what Glen meant by her preaching and spewing out self-righteous "shoulds." They were both willing to change and strive to become healthier within themselves.

By September, Trish had found an acceptable job and persuaded Glen to attend a lecture series on art history with her and join a local non-denominational church, where they met several other couples in their age group. She was beginning to feel more socially connected and also emotionally closer to Glen.

After only four weeks of teaching, Glen reported feeling confident in the classroom, thanks to the students' responsiveness and his ability to create dialogue and debate between them. He had successfully experimented with several of the dyad and small group exercises we had discussed. After class one day he overheard several of his students discussing how much they enjoyed him and his student-oriented discussion/debate style. This seemed to increase his confidence even beyond what it had been during his years teaching in Maryland.

Glen and Trish's marriage continues to grow and their communication has achieved much greater levels of intimacy. Trish received a major promotion in her job after working for just over one month and she no longer makes veiled threats about moving back East.

Their marriage stands a good chance of becoming more satisfying if both of them remain committed to conscious growth within their personality structures. In addition, their lovemaps are somewhat compatible, with several significant differences. Although they do not share a common subtype or a complementary line to balance opposite energies, they do have the benefit of being in the same Harmonic Group. Both belong to the Competency Group (composed of Ones, Threes and Fives), where all the types emphasize being experts in their field, being prepared and professional and focusing on career objectives.

At the moment, as I continue periodic marriage counseling with them, it appears that they most likely made the right turn by moving to the left side of the country, California.

Willow and Glen as Self-preservation Fives

For both Willow and Glen, the "castle" of individual isolation and resistance to change was a distinct factor. Willow's "castle" was the secret fantasies that allowed her to achieve sexual satisfaction with her husband, but her fear of sharing them with him made her so uncomfortable that she began to see herself as "sick." My reassurance about the commonness and value of such fantasies made it possible for her to emerge from her "castle" into a richer, more trusting relationship with her husband.

Glen's "castle," or sanctuary, was the tried-and-true teaching methods that had brought him success in his former college setting and his anxiety about finding ways to apply them to larger classes at his new university was stressful not only to him personally but also to his marriage. As with many Fives, increasing his sense of his own professional mastery was a key factor that allowed him to risk exploring new avenues in his relationship with his wife, as well.

Fives with the Sexual Subtype

Fives with a Sexual subtype, whom Ichazo associates with "confidence," like to share confidences with the few people they trust. Sexual Fives are generally more willing to risk emotional contact than Self-preservation or Social Fives. But the ambivalence Sexual Fives feel about being close to others often gives a love-hate cast to their relationships.

"Sharing vs. Space"

Nan, 37, a Sexual Five of striking natural beauty who earned her living as a CPA, came to see me because the conflict in her 14-year committed lesbian relationship with Bobbi, 35 (a Sexual Two who was a surgical nurse), had reached crisis proportions. "Lately," Nan told me, "I feel scared that Bobbi might just lose it during one of our fights and hit me or push me in a fit of rage."

"How long have you been feeling scared about this?" I asked her.

They hardly ever used to fight, Nan told me, but their conflict over Nan's beloved younger brother, Curt, was now causing serious tensions between them. Curt, a single, footloose man of 32 (probably a Sexual Seven), was in jail, facing charges of cocaine possession and sale that could earn him at least a 5-year prison term. Curt had done a little pot and some drinking in college, but never anything like this. A respected and highly creative photographer working in the local area, he'd "just got caught up with the wrong crowd," Nan said.

I asked how this situation had caused problems between her and Bobbi.

"Bobbi was never all that crazy about him," Nan said, "especially when he'd drink too much and fall asleep on our couch on weekends. She felt he was intruding on our time together. But what got her really mad was what his friends asked me to do."

A group of Curt's photographer friends had asked Nan to participate in a creative project they had devised to earn enough money to pay for a top-flight attorney who might be able to get Curt off with little or no prison time. What they wanted her to do was to pose almost nude for a series of high-gloss shots taken by various professional photographers to make a calendar that they could auction as a "Special Edition" on the Internet to make some quick money.

Every aspect of this project turned Nan's stomach: being the center of attention (which she had always detested), opening herself to the salacious comments of Curt's photographer friends, having her body publicly exposed. Yet she wanted to help her brother.

Having shared all her secrets with Bobbi for the past 14 years—ranging from their teenage shoplifting escapades to their disastrous attempts to have sex with boys, Nan told Bobbi about the calendar proposition. Both Sexual subtypes, they had always been eager to share confidences with each other. But now the deep differences between Bobbi's Type Two and Nan's Type Five came to the fore.

Bobbi was shocked by the "stupid and outlandish scheme" of Nan posing for the calendar. She wanted Nan to tell Curt's colleagues to forget the whole ridiculous idea. When Nan tried to discuss the pros and cons of the proposal from an intellectual point of view, Bobbi became irate.

Nan's response was to turn off emotionally, which only made Bobbi more hysterical. The more Nan shut down, the louder Bobbi yelled, attacking Curt for his promiscuous lifestyle and lack of stability, seemingly jealous of Nan's family bond with her brother, insisting that Nan had no obligation to bail him out.

Now, Nan told me, for the first time in their relationship, she wanted to push her life partner away. Bobbi had always been somewhat invasive and emotionally controlling, but Nan had managed to maintain her own boundaries by insisting on her solitary time for daily meditation. It was essential now, she felt, to take a strong stand, make her own choices regarding her brother and get Bobbi out of her face, even if that meant moving out.

"Is that what you really want to do?" I asked.

Her beautiful blue eyes filled with tears. "I don't know," she said. "Bobbi is the only person in my life I've ever really trusted—the only one who knows what I truly think, the things I'm afraid of." She covered her face with her hands to muffle her sobs.

"Maybe there's a way to get the space you need without doing something that drastic," I said. I suggested that she and Bobbi have a 2-month separation inside their home, with Nan moving into the guest room in order to structure some much-needed privacy. Bobbi reluctantly agreed to this, knowing that the alternative, in Nan's mind, was simply to separate for several months.

Fortunately, both women were anxious to take the personality inventory and Nan finally agreed to allow Bobbi to join her in our sessions. They quickly came to an understanding about Nan's feeling of being "invaded" and trapped by Bobbi's loving help and strong opinions. They learned that a Sexual Five can appear self-contradictory—on the one hand, craving complete intimacy with her trusted mate, yet simultaneously needing time out for private recharging of energies.

Bobbi had often felt this was "crazy," since she, as a Sexual Two, never seemed to need any time out. She loved feeling constantly connected to Nan and sometimes felt unappreciated for the hundreds of favors and caring gestures she provided for her partner. Most other personality types, Bobbi learned, can feel crowded, controlled or manipulated by the unsolicited advice and help a Two is so eager to offer.

It was good to see their insights deepening, forgiveness and empathy between them taking hold. But I still needed to help Nan make some timely decisions about whether—and how—to help Curt.

In a session alone with Nan I confronted her with the realities of the almost-nude photos and the consequences their exposure might have for her Public Accounting career. In the light of this, she saw the wisdom of saying no to Curt's well-intentioned friends. During our discussion it became clear to Nan that they could simply hire a woman who was already comfortable in such situations—perhaps an exotic dancer or stripper from a local nightclub—and offer her cash (perhaps $1,000) to do the calendar photo shoot. If Curt's four friends and Nan each contributed $200, they would have the $1,000 for their calendar girl.

Nan and all four of Curt's friends thought this was a brilliant solution. One of the friends knew several exotic dancers and made the arrangement the following day. Nan made these decisions without discussing them with Bobbi.

In the end, a beautiful, high-gloss erotic calendar was produced and it eventually earned about $6,000 from Internet sales. But before the profits could be realized, Nan needed to move quickly to secure the services of an attorney for her brother. The man several people recommended required a $10,000 retainer. Nan, isolating herself in order to give the matter serious consideration, made the decision to take the $10,000 from her retirement account and hire the attorney on Curt's behalf. This turned out to be the right decision for him as well as for Nan.

Eventually, he was sentenced to probation, many hours of community service and an intensive drug-treatment program, with no prison time (due to this being his first and only offense). The grand total of costs for Curt's defense came to $30,000. Though his colleagues ultimately contributed the $6,000 from calendar profits, Nan's out-of-pocket expenses totaled $24,000. She had not consulted Bobbi about any of this.

Nan felt enormously relieved that her brother did not have to go to prison. Grateful for her help, he promised to pay back the $24,000 she had spent. She wasn't concerned about the repayment, but cared deeply that her actions had solidified her bond with her little brother.

Soon after this, in a joint session with Nan and Bobbi, Bobbi came to realize that "every move Nan makes is not subject to my approval." Bobbi had obviously come to understand that her help and constant pushing for intimacy had sometimes made Nan feel resentful.

Likewise, Nan was learning to communicate more openly about her need for space and privacy. No longer inclined to push Bobbi away, she accepted that Bobbi was her ultimate life partner. Both of them were now better equipped to establish appropriate boundaries yet share everything they both wanted and chose to discuss. As far as I know, Nan has never elected to share with anyone, including Bobbi, her decision to pay for Curt's attorney.

Overall, Nan and Bobbi have a close and committed relationship. Although they are not members of the same Harmonic Group and do not share a complementary connection for balancing opposite energies, they do have three of the Five Factors for relationship success going for them. They have highly compatible lovemaps, they share the same Sexual subtype and they have taken huge steps forward in terms of psychological health. Their mutual willingness to become more aware and accommodating of personality differences has actually turned their crisis into a journey of relationship growth, resulting in deeper levels of intimacy. I still counsel with them periodically for minor problems and both seem highly satisfied with their relationship.

"Internet Complications"

Steven, 17, a Sexual Five, was forced into my office by his irate father, Don, who had discovered that Steven had been not only been buying and selling marijuana online under the cover of his paper products business but also was involved with a 20-year-old girlfriend who had "got him into pornography."

Sitting in my office, Steven was withdrawn, cerebral and filled with rage over the invasion of his "private business" by his dad and stepmother, Sue. Steven's biological mother, whom he seemed most bonded with, had become an extreme drug addict, leaving his father with full custody of Steven and his older sister, who was now away at college.

Steven, who appeared older and more intellectually mature than his 17 years, stated his case quietly but forcefully: "I don't think my life is anyone's business but my own." To which his father retorted, "The fact is you are a minor, living under my roof, at my expense and in my custody. And that *is* my business!"

Surprisingly, Steven was willing to take the C-JES survey, to prove to his dad that he wasn't crazy. Although he was not forthcoming with personal information, he readily acknowledged that he is a Type Five with a Sexual subtype.

Although his dad never took the survey, all three of us agreed that Don is most likely a Self-preservation Six. Don acknowledged that he is "naturally paranoid over most things, but especially over this kid's actions." He clearly had good intentions, loved his son and wanted only the best for him.

To Steven, the best situation would be to live on his own, out from under his father's thumb. He had definite plans for moving out in 5 months to live with his girlfriend, Kate, after he graduated in June and turned 18 in July.

In our second session together—our first without his father—Steven told me he could "outsmart most of my stupid teachers, the school principal, my parents and even you, Mona." He demonstrated this by announcing, "I read that whole *Wisdom of the Enneagram* book this week and I can assure you that Kate's a Sexual Nine."

Impressed and a bit amused, I made no effort to question his abilities or acumen. I said that I was only a paid employee who was still struggling with computer problems. "Maybe I should hire you, Steven, as my computer consultant," I said. We both had a good laugh and I assured him that I was not interested in meddling in his private business, I was only here to be of help.

However, I reminded him, his father had hired me to counsel them because he had three specific concerns about the direction Steven's life was taking and because he felt their communication wasn't good enough to solve these problems without professional help:

1. Steven's relationship with Kate, age 20 and her connection with pornography.
2. Steven's use of online pornography (which Don feared could be an addiction).
3. Don's recent discovery that Steven's online business actually involved the sale of marijuana, not just paper products (unquestionably the most serious issue).

Steven and I agreed that he and I, alone, would discuss these three issues, as he felt ready. First, he wanted to bring Kate in to meet me, so I could see that "she isn't some freak." When he did I saw that Kate is a lovely young woman and that they make an exceptionally attractive couple. The connection between them appeared strong and relatively healthy.

The three of us discussed lovemaps and learned that they both felt exceptionally compatible. Kate expressed her sense of "almost disbelief" that Steven was only 17. "In many ways," she said, "he seems older than I am. He's so knowledgeable."

When I brought up the issue of pornography, Kate was embarrassed and deferred to Steven's explanations. Yes, he said, they had occasionally "used porn as a sexual turn-on," although Kate seemed to have little interest in it. His blue eyes flashed with anger as he described how his dad invaded his computer before he could delete his sent e-mails, found several to Kate that contained some "gory, graphic porn stuff," and assumed that Steven had some kind of addiction going, for which Kate must somehow be the cause. (Steven confided that his dad knew of two male friends, ages 16 and 17, who were clearly addicted to pornography, so Don's assuming that Steven was also addicted was perhaps understandable.)

They had been sexually active for 10 months, according to Kate, who was unassuming and seemed naïve compared to Steven. She explained that she had little interest in porn and that, after about 50 gross images, she actually found it a turn off. But she wanted to please Steven. "Even he," she said, "is losing his interest in the pornography—at least when we're together sexually."

He confirmed this and explained that he occasionally masturbated with porn but found Kate far more interesting and supportive than his websites. He wanted me to reassure his dad that there was no need to be concerned about Steven being addicted to porn the way his two friends were.

I made it clear to Steven that this would only be covered in a joint session with his dad, him and me—that I would never discuss his private affairs without him present. It might even help more, I suggested, if he invited Kate and his dad for a joint session so that Don could see for himself what a lovely person Kate is. Reluctantly, Steven agreed.

I was aware that Steven had kept Kate at a distance from his dad and stepmother. He explained that he'd done this on purpose, since he hated people knowing his business and didn't want any judgments, interference or "feedback,'" as his dad called it.

I explained that, in the absence of real information, one's imagination tends to take over and in the case of a naturally paranoid parent (who had the history with his ex-wife that Don had) it was no wonder that he was concerned about Steven. For the first time,

Steven expressed a bit of empathy for his dad.

Now we came to the topic of marijuana—the frequency of use, the buying and selling and specifically the sale of it through Steven's Internet business. By now we had established good rapport and I sensed Steven wanted my help with his dad, yet greatly resented any invasion of his privacy.

He readily confided in me that he and Kate had smoked pot a number of times since they became sexually active. It was an "occasional turn-on" that allowed Steven to mellow out and Kate to lose her self-consciousness. Yet Steven sheepishly admitted knowing that "pot possession is highly illegal and selling it is even more serious."

The on-line paper business that now served as a cover for his marijuana dealing had been developed by Steven and two male friends to sell note pads headed with cute, sometimes racy sayings such as "Listen Up," "My Shit List," "Do Me," or "Get It Here." The three of them had elaborated on his titles as code words for obtaining and selling marijuana. Steven was the "middle man" whose Internet business allowed him to arrange the deals and thus keep most of the profits without actually touching the pot himself (except for his own little stash, which he didn't care much about).

His main motivation was the income—not because he cared about money, as such. To him it represented freedom—to finance his own apartment with Kate, once he turned 18. He could see no way to make the necessary amount this quickly any other way. His paper products provided only about 25 percent of the profit, while the pot sales amounted to about 75 percent.

After much discussion, Steven agreed that he and Kate could and would stop all use of pot as a first step. At some level, he seemed relieved, being smart enough to see where this could go.

After numerous sessions with Steven alone, with Steven and his dad and with Steven and Kate, I was able to show Steven that his secretiveness, guardedness and unwillingness to share his concerns and plans with his dad had actually damaged his own interests. He had assumed that once he moved out of his dad's home at age 18, he had to be totally independent financially—that his dad would no longer help him with his education or living expenses.

This was certainly not the case. Don said he had every intention of financing Steven's education, just as he had for Steven's older sister, who was doing well in college. Steven appeared shocked and relieved. They had never discussed this before, primarily because of Steven's attitude that his life was "no one else's business."

After much explanation about the "pornography e-mails to Kate" and Don's realization that Steven, not Kate, was the instigator, Steven and Kate came to an agreement (in light of the many examples I presented about the negative effects of pornography) that the continued use of porn images would not be healthy for the growth and intimacy they desired. They agreed to discontinue all use of pornography. Kate was greatly relieved and Don was pleased to have been included for the first time in such intimate discussions with his son.

Don ended up telling Steven that he liked Kate and thought she was a healthy influence on him, an assessment I completely agreed with. Steven always appeared surprised when his dad expressed approval of anything in his personal life.

Following many in-depth discussions, Steven made the decision to get out of all pot possession and sales. Notably relieved that the money pressure was off, he decided to "turn over all the pot sales to my friend, who will jump at the chance," and to devote his own creative efforts to expanding his paper business.

Don expressed his pride in his son's brilliance and industriousness and reiterated his assurances of full financial support during Steven's college years, "so long as you stay within the boundaries of the law."

Don and Sue helped Kate decorate the apartment that she and Steven would be moving into and the four of them, at Steven's suggestion, celebrated his 18th birthday together the weekend he moved in.

Nan and Steven as Sexual Fives

Nan and Steven both exemplified the intense Sexual Five focus on sharing confidences with an intimate partner, while still requiring private time for their own purposes and projects. For Nan, the strongest need was to create a personal space for herself in her committed relationship with a Sexual Two, whose tendency commonly is to overwhelm an intimate partner with unwanted help and advice. Through joint counseling, these two partners were able to understand and empathize with one another's contradictory needs and create a situation in which they could maintain their loving relationship while creating this essential breathing space for Nan.

Steven's intimate relationship with his Sexual Nine partner had few actual problems. Their lovemaps were extremely compatible and as a Sexual Nine, Kate was comfortable merging with the agenda of her partner. The primary problem for Steven was expanding his small circle of confidants to include his father, who genuinely cared for him but, as a Self-preservation Six, often appeared more judgmental than supportive. Individual and joint counseling sessions helped the whole family achieve new levels of communication and mutual acceptance.

Fives with the Social Subtype

Fives with a Social subtype, whom Ichazo associates with "totems," seek to become part of society's intellectual elite through mastery of special knowledge. Social Fives are often scientists and academics who enjoy analyzing trends and exchanging complex ideas with their peers. They find safety and validation in the social status that accompanies their affiliations.

"Indispensable but Dispensable"

Shannon, 47, a Social Five, a solidly built woman with close-cropped gray hair, sat in my office distraught about the "double-whammy" she had just received: Will, 49, her husband, had filed for divorce and the small law firm where she had felt indispensable for almost two decades had asked for her resignation. "I just want to disappear," she told me. "I never want to speak to anyone again."

She described her marriage of 24 years as "long and difficult, but stable." The strongest bond between her and Will seemed to be their mutual pride in their only child, Dottie, 21, who was currently doing well at an East Coast university.

According to Shannon, Will was a quiet, rather withdrawn mechanical engineer who was conscious of his lack of interpersonal skills. Although he was never willing to join his wife for any joint counseling and never took the personality survey, Shannon later described him as probably a Sexual Six. He obviously wanted many things from the marriage that Shannon wouldn't or couldn't provide and vice-versa.

Will's most basic need in the marriage, Shannon told me, was a sense of loyalty and security, a home that provided warmth and a marriage that created a safe haven. Contributing the affection and attention he needed was not possible for Shannon, who saw her husband as needy, dull, nervous and insecure. Will saw her, she said, as arrogant, self-sufficient, controlling and cold.

Although repetitive fights and arguments were standard procedure in their home, they had agreed to stay together for Dottie's sake. However, with Dottie close to finishing her Bachelor's degree, tensions between husband and wife had been mounting rapidly. It was clear that neither partner filled the other's expectations or even most of the basic elements of their partner's lovemap. Each had longed for something distinctly different from what their spouse actually was.

Shannon's chief desire, she told me, was to "feel indispensable because of my knowledge and expertise." She had read many books on childrearing when Dottie was born and had mastered all the information necessary to manage the family's finances. She had also set up a complex computer system for her employers that they had become totally dependent on. Bright and focused as she was, she was utterly unaware of others' emotional needs. All her efforts were devoted to becoming the "resident genius" in both her household and her workplace. Her mastery of pertinent information gave her a sense of being powerful and secure in the world.

Over nearly 19 years of employment, she had become the

Office Manager and resident computer expert who had set up the law firm's accounting, billing, filing and documents system. However, when her employers demanded that she share with them her knowledge about the computer system she had devised, she balked. Since Shannon was planning her first vacation in over 6 years, it was now crucial that she record passwords and train a new woman the firm had hired—things she never got around to doing. In fact, she told me, she felt fiercely resentful about being asked to give away her skills, her information and her hard work. The new employee, she felt, could learn on her own, the same way Shannon had done.

Shannon enjoyed feeling like the "secret agent," the only person who had enough information to make things work. As a Social Five, her self-esteem was clearly built around her intellectual prowess and her ability to wield power through her expertise. She harbored the delusion that she was indispensable, both in her career and in her marriage.

So it was a major shock for her to discover, within just a few days' time, that she was dispensable to both her husband and her employer. Her two bosses were willing to pay the price of creating an entirely new system, so that Shannon would no longer have such direct control over their law practice. Her career with them was over. She was summarily escorted from the building with her personal effects.

Receiving divorce papers from Will a few days earlier had also been a shock, though not nearly as devastating as her forced resignation. Shannon reported that Will had told her he was sick of her talking down to him and trying to embarrass him with her "arrogant, obnoxious sense of secret 'know-how' and intellectual B.S." His resentment had been building from the time of her insistence on certain child-rearing practices when Dottie was a baby to the establishment of her present management system for the family's finances. Because she tried to control most of their bill paying online, with a system she made certain Will would never learn, he didn't even know where she kept the checkbook. He was tired of fighting and simply wanted out. All he requested was half of their savings, retirement accounts and equity in their home. Shannon could have all the furniture, the better car, both computers and the cat.

Shannon's unhealthy beliefs had blown up in her face and she now realized how dispensable she actually was. All of her knowledge, expertise and guru-like advice suddenly meant nothing to her husband or her employer. It had never meant anything to her daughter (who, Shannon told me, brushed off her mom as "quirky").

Over the next several months I was able to assist Shannon in learning to see certain problems and conditions from others' perspectives. The C-JES survey confirmed that she is a Type Five with a Social subtype. Once she had enough information about her own personality style, she began to change, slowly and painfully. Empathy seemed exceptionally difficult for her, but the use of intense role-playing seemed especially helpful in her efforts to learn it.

Shannon decided to take a six-month sabbatical from all work and to focus her efforts on increasing her level of psychological health. One significant realization she had in the course of our sessions was that her marriage had never been truly satisfying for either her or Will. Their lovemaps were incompatible in many respects, with each having ideals and expectations that were impossible for the other to fulfill. Both were fairly unconscious and unhealthy in their personality structures. Not only were these two major factors for predicting marital success lacking in their marriage, the remaining factors were also absent: Shannon and Will didn't share the same subtype or Harmonic Group, nor were their personalities connected by a complementary line to balance their different energies. There had been no real emotional glue to hold their marriage together.

Now determined to create a whole new life for herself as a more self-aware, mature human being, Shannon continued long-term therapy in order to realize her goals. As a Social Five, she longed for the validation of her skills and expertise and it did not surprise me that within three months she found employment as Office Manger for a small manufacturing company.

"Passing On"

Leon, 81, a Social Five, a distinguished looking man with white hair and a white mustache, had been widowed for five years when he was invited by his daughter and her husband to take part in family counseling sessions with me on behalf of their drug-abusing son, Jebb. A highly regarded emeritus university Professor, Leon was familiar with the Enneagram and already knew himself to be a Social Five.

He had always been deeply bonded with both his grandsons— Vance, 22 and Jebb, 19—and was deeply distressed about the current crisis over Jebb's cocaine addiction. Historically, Jebb had always turned to his grandfather when in difficulties. He would go over to Leon's house to talk, eat, argue, laugh and spend the night. Every time Jebb had a run-in with his parents, Grandpa was on board to offer insight and advice.

Unlike his straight-A older brother, Vance, who never got in trouble, Jebb was more of a free spirit—not truly defiant, but rebellious against the dictates of society in a creative and intellectual way, seeking to establish his own path in life. According to Leon, Jebb was probably a Social Seven.

Grandpa Leon and Jebb had related to one another emotionally at many levels all through Jebb's life—especially during his teenage years. They spent countless hours together debating, exploring and criticizing most of society's practices and ideals.

Leon had been a Professor of Philosophy and Religious Studies at a local university for most of his academic career. He had retired at 66 to spend more time with his wife, best pal and soul mate, Helen (a Social One), who had died five years earlier after a long and difficult battle with breast cancer.

I had several family counseling sessions with Leon, his daughter and his son-in-law, strategizing about how best to intervene with Jebb's blatant use of cocaine. Our sessions were highly successful and the family worked well together as a group, including Jeff's older brother, Vance. The only family member that Jebb had ever confided in was Grandpa Leon, who always understood, accepted and rationally discussed Jebb's options—a skill his parents were not as proficient in.

Now Jebb was refusing to honestly disclose his behavior around cocaine and suddenly seemed to be escaping from everything, even his relationship with Grandpa. Leon, clearly heartbroken about the situation, requested a session alone with me.

In our first private session Leon cried uncontrollably, experiencing a profound emptiness that had been building for years. This was about much more than Jebb's cocaine experiments. Leon admitted that Jebb's failure to consult him on the cocaine use was the last straw. It made him feel worthless, he said, "done for" in life's journey—as if no one wanted his wisdom and philosophical insights. Ever since he had stopped teaching, 15 years earlier, he had lacked a significant public audience for his most important ideas. He missed the student contact, especially his small seminars with graduate students. Now he was wondering whether he should have kept teaching longer.

However, there was his beloved Helen. His life, apart from the university, had revolved mainly around her. Leon was still "passionately in love" with Helen, whom he had always found "irresistible, beautiful, incredibly intelligent, filled with grace, social poise and love." Helen adored her husband's intellect and cared deeply about his profound ideas and theories. She was his best "sounding board."

Now Helen had "passed on," like his teaching, his friends, his students and his work. "Everything in my life seems to have passed on," Leon said in a shaky voice. It seemed that the closest person in his life—Jebb—was also preparing to "pass" on Grandpa and Leon had grown increasingly depressed over the past month as he felt his grandson quietly pulling away.

Jebb knew that illegal drugs were the wrong way to go. This time there really wasn't anything to debate, morally or philosophically, with Grandpa, as he had done with so many other topics. Jebb, feeling guilty and embarrassed, wanted to hide his actions from everyone except his fellow drug-using daredevil Type Seven friends. However, as he discovered later, his family knew much more about his drug use than he gave them credit for.

We planned an intervention, led by Leon—a surprise meeting

where all his loved ones would individually confront Jebb about his behavior, their feelings and requests for change. In the end, Jebb was profoundly moved by the comments of all who participated (his mother and father, brother Vance, Grandpa Leon, his favorite aunt and uncle and two of his best male friends from high school). Though all eight people said much the same thing, it was probably Leon's tears and his deep level of self-disclosure that shook Jebb most.

As a result of the intervention, Jebb agreed to no further cocaine use and willingly began attending CA (Cocaine Anonymous) 12-step meetings, as well as short-term therapy with me. Leon, clearly relieved, told me Jebb's maturation and growth seemed to be taking place before his very eyes.

Jebb was normally a highly affectionate young man who routinely hugged friends and family. At the end of this 5-hour intervention in their home, Jebb hugged and thanked each person individually for caring enough to spend so much time and effort to help him make the "right choices."

Above all, he hugged and cried, then hugged and cried even more with Grandpa Leon long after everyone else had left. He asked if he could, once again, spend the night at Grandpa's—the way he had always done when he had a problem to work out. His mom and dad were deeply pleased with the entire outcome.

Leon later realized that "getting out of my mind and into my feelings" actually helped lift his depression. He also developed a more objective appreciation for the incredible 50 years of marriage he had shared with Helen and chose to celebrate this gift rather than dwelling on the loss.

He and Helen shared the four most important factors for predicting relationship success: 1) Each of them felt the other was a perfect match for their lovemap. 2) They shared a fairly high level of psychological health throughout the marriage. 3) They shared the Social subtype. 4) Within the Harmonic Group, they were both part of the Competency Group (composed of Ones, Threes and Fives).

Leon later commented that his expectations for a relationship with a grandson were fulfilled by both Jebb and Vance, but especially by Jebb. Leon realized that Jebb's becoming healthier in his personality structure also allowed them to be closer, just as Leon's own new levels of development facilitated greater intimacy. In addition, Leon shared the Social subtype with Jebb (as he did with his wife), as well as benefiting from the connecting line between Fives and Sevens that created a natural balancing of his and Jebb's energies.

Leon also came to understand that having an audience for sharing some of his "bigger ideas" and social debates would be a welcome outlet. This led him to volunteer as a community guest speaker, both on campus and for outside organizations. Leon seemed especially excited about a lecture series that was being developed through the local community college on "Creating Manhood." He was exploring outlets for sharing ideas and connecting with people who appreciated his expertise. This was clearly meeting his need for validation of his wisdom and expertise as a Social Five.

He was also preparing himself for the following year, when Jebb would most likely be transferring to a university out of state, at which time they planned to continue their frequent phone calls, e-mails and vacation visits. Leon was "passing on" profound appreciation, skills, leadership and some of his knowledge and expertise, but primarily living his life as an incredible role model for younger men in the community. As far as I know, Leon no longer falls into his old ruts of depression.

At age 81, he observed that "old dogs *do* learn new tricks."

Shannon and Leon as Social Fives

Both Shannon and Leon offer examples of the deep craving Social Fives have for validation of their knowledge and skills by others. Shannon's use of her technical expertise to keep control of her employers ended up backfiring when her desire for power so undermined the efficiency of her workplace that she was fired from her job. Using the same tactic with her husband ultimately destroyed all emotional connection between them and led to his filing for divorce.

Leon, a much healthier Social Five, faced up to his depression at the possible loss of an important intellectual and emotional connection with his favorite grandson and took steps to salvage the relationship. He also came to terms with the death of his beloved wife and found a way to gain validation of his ideas, even in retirement, through service to the wider community.

Strengths of Fives in Intimate Relationships

- Observation
- Logic
- Curiosity
- Insight
- Non-Intrusiveness
- Objectivity
- Independence
- Intellect

Limitations of Fives in Intimate Relationships

- Withdrawing
- Stinginess
- Paranoia
- Negativity
- Emotional Detachment
- Defensiveness
- Mistrust
- Secretiveness

Defense Mechanisms of Fives

As children, many Fives felt invaded and the family environment seemed unsafe to them. It's possible that with Five individuals an inborn sensitivity creates a low psycho-physiological threshold for tolerating the imposition of others' energies.

Thus it is not surprising that the primary psychological

defense mechanism used by Fives is *isolation of affect*—a deliberate tamping down of emotions that protects their fragile core from violation. Focused on issues of safety and security, Fives commonly see others as more intrusive than helpful. Often highly introverted, Fives recharge their batteries by isolating themselves from others and frequently have issues around privacy.

Willow's need to keep her sexual fantasies private even from her husband and Glen's withdrawal from his wife because of his fears about his new teaching situation offer examples of this. Nan's decision to keep her financial help for her brother secret from her life partner also shows a preoccupation with privacy and fear of conflict. Steven's insistence on keeping private his concerns about paying for college led him to seek a way of earning money that put him at risk for serious legal repercussions. Shannon's single-minded focus on hoarding her expertise both in the workplace and in the home ended up destroying both her job and her marriage. Leon's healthy ability, despite his depression and loneliness, to reach out to his family and to the wider community was the saving grace of his life.

An important aspect of Fives' *isolation of affect* is compartmentalization—the need to keep different aspects of life in distinct compartments as a way of maintaining control and keeping themselves from becoming overwhelmed. We see this in Willow's longtime strategy of keeping her sexual fantasies walled off from her marriage and in Nan's compartmentalizing of her financial help for her brother in an attempt to avoid conflict with her life partner. It is also evident in Shannon's strategy of using her impenetrable computer system to keep her bosses from having any control over her. She thought she had others boxed out, but she actually had herself boxed in.

The "Natural Neuroses" of Fives

A tendency to hoard—physically, mentally, emotionally and financially—is one of the central natural neuroses of Fives. This arises out of Fives' scarcity thinking—seeing their physical energies, store of knowledge, emotional stamina and financial resources as finite and easily exhausted. If Five is your type, a first step beyond this "blind spot" would be to take steps to objectively test each of these perceived limitations against some objective measure in the real world.

Fives often assume that retreating inside their own intellect will provide a refuge from the emotional and physical demands of others that might be too draining. Embracing this strategy can result in Fives becoming crammed with data, using their knowledge as a buffer zone between their fragile selves and a dangerous world.

Fives commonly see themselves as less vulnerable to others' expectations and intrusions if their physical and emotional needs are kept to a minimum. At an extreme, this may result in physical neglect of their bodies (which they may see as simply a vehicle for carrying their minds around) and deep loneliness due to their unwillingness to risk intimate connection with another human being. Learning compassion for themselves and others can be a huge step forward for many Fives.

How Fives Blossom in Good Relationships

When Fives are truly loved by a person they trust and respect—as Leon was in his 50-year marriage—they lose much of their natural anxiety and reframe the closeness of a beloved partner as their own preference (rather than a potential invasion). The loss of connection with a loved one may plunge the Five into serious depression, as Leon experienced with his wife's death and the distancing from his beloved grandson. But a healthy Five can regain his balance, as Leon did, repair a troubled relationship and make a generous contribution to his community.

A positive experience with a therapist can often help Fives test the boundaries of trust and arrive eventually at an understanding that not every relationship is destined to become invasive. Even with the most skittish of Self-preservation Fives, a therapeutic intervention can be effective. In Willow's case, for example, I was able to facilitate a deeper connection between her and her husband by validating her sexual fantasies as normal and even desirable. A therapist may also be able to help a Five deal with competency issues that can be a serious threat to his self-esteem, as we saw in the case of Glen. Once his fears about teaching were laid to rest, his relationship issues with his wife became much less pressing.

Fives with a Sexual subtype, who have a longing to exchange secrets and confidences, may be more inclined to trust a carefully selected intimate partner, and for them personal growth through relationship is often less problematic, as we saw with Nan.

For all Fives, however, the journey toward self-actualization is more likely than not to be a mental journey. For healthy Fives, detachment from the world's cravings and follies may go hand-in-hand with deep compassion for suffering fellow humans.

TYPE SIX: THE LOYALIST IN LOVE

More than with any other personality style, the variations and contradictions within Type Six are enormous. Sixes are often immobilized by fear, which they manifest in two contrasting ways: through aggressiveness or through visible anxiety. Psychologists commonly call this the "fight or flight" syndrome. Aggressive or "counterphobic" Sixes, who are often unaware of their fear, seem eager to pick a fight, in order to avoid being attacked first by someone else. "Phobic" Sixes, who are more aware of their fear, tend to flee from the dangers they perceive. All Type Six individuals are mixtures of these two aspects, in different proportions.

Average Sixes tend to be wary, insecure, preoccupied with safety issues, confused in their thinking, loyal to those they trust, pessimistic, complex and contradictory. Many long for an authority they can rely on and may seek to ally themselves with people or institutions that seem confident and trustworthy. Others may be rebellious and resistant to alliances with any kind of authority.

Healthy Sixes make strong reciprocal bonds with others. They are courageous, affectionate and reliable in their relationships and responsible in their service to the larger community. Notable for their persistence and hard work, they have a gift for cooperative problem solving and can exhibit leadership ability.

Unhealthy Sixes may become paranoid or violently reactive, but are fundamentally irrational in their actions. They may be delusional, guilt-ridden and panicky as they strike out against perceived enemies. Suicide attempts as a cry for rescue are also possible in this state.

Sixes with the Self-preservation Subtype

In Sixes, the subtypes are especially distinct. The Self-preservation variant, which Oscar Ichazo associates with "warmth," is more phobic. People with this subtype seek security through winning the support of stronger people or groups. The most obviously dependent of the Six subtypes, they fear taking risks and often resist moving beyond familiar patterns.

"HIV and Herpes"

Sandy, 27, a Self-preservation Six, is a slender, petite woman with a pixie-like cap of auburn hair. When she came to see me, she had been living with her fiancé, Jay, 29, for about a year. Over the course of their three-year relationship, Sandy explained, they'd had only one serious area of conflict—her chronic worrying about Sexually Transmitted Diseases (STDs). Now Jay was threatening to break off their engagement if she couldn't find some way to control her anxiety.

In taking a brief history of Sandy's concerns, I established that the only verifiable health condition she or Jay had actually suffered was a mild case of Type 1 oral herpes. Perhaps once a year (or less often), Sandy would have a cold sore outbreak on her bottom lip, usually following extended sun exposure. Jay, who had most likely contracted the condition from Sandy through ordinary mouth-to-mouth kissing, had experienced only two herpes outbreaks on his upper lip during the entire three years they had been together. He seemed unconcerned about the incidences and begged Sandy to stop her "silly paranoia."

She seemed hyper-vigilant and panicky over possible future ramifications of their shared herpes condition—including fantasies of genital herpes and the possibility of weekly outbreaks.

I explained repeatedly to Sandy that her form of oral herpes, although highly contagious, was exactly what her doctor had told her—a mild viral condition, caused by the herpes simplex virus type 1 (HSV-1). An estimated eighty percent of the American population over age 12 has some form of HSV-1 in their biological system. I also explained that various remedies are available to reduce the probability of an outbreak and new medications are available to reduce the intensity and duration of the sores, when and if they occur. HSV-1 is distinctly different from HSV-2 (which causes most cases of genital herpes), although the HSV-1 virus is contagious from mouth to genitals.

But Sandy's worry button had been truly pushed. The information I provided seemed to have little effect on her. She continued to describe worst-case scenarios that preoccupied her. Her mind quickly jumped from herpes to HIV and then to AIDS, her skewed logic connecting these conditions on the basis that all were viruses and all were transmitted sexually. I began to understand why Jay had demanded that Sandy make an appointment with me.

More than ten years earlier I had been Jay's instructor in a college course in Human Sexuality. He remembered the lectures on sexually transmitted diseases and trusted that I would, as he later told me, "talk some sense into Sandy."

But it was evidently not the technical information about STD transmission and treatment that Sandy needed. Rather, she was literally stuck in her habit of needing to worry incessantly in order to forestall greater anxiety. She explained to me that she saw her worrying as a "gift" that actually helped prevent bad things from happening.

Through intense active listening during our sessions, I was able to help Sandy arrive at the conclusion that her worry, per se, was not capable of influencing external events, for good or bad outcomes. Instead, her worrying had become a mental strategy for coping with ambiguity and uncertainty. Dealing with her negative fears and projections, dire as they were, was easier than having to tolerate the unknown.

Jay attended several sessions with Sandy and explained that, although he loved her deeply, her paranoia about STDs had exhausted him. Both of them had been tested for HIV (and other communicable diseases) three different times throughout their completely monogamous relationship. Jay had decided that if I couldn't find a way to "fix" Sandy he would seek to extricate himself from the relationship.

Sandy was already feeling anxious over the possibility that Jay might break their engagement. She truly loved him, trusted him completely and felt guilty about her negative thinking.

It was clear to me that traditional therapy techniques such as negative thought stopping (described in the Type Four chapter) would only exacerbate Sandy's negative thinking. It was essential that she learn greater tolerance for uncertainty and the unknown. She also needed to accept the fact that human beings do have anxieties and discomfort over many issues, that emotional conflicts are normal and that she could take positive action in spite of her worrying.

My first step was to devise a plan for Sandy to set aside a 15-minute period every day, during which she could pay attention to her most pressing worries—and write them in a journal. This way, there would be no forgetting or loss of control over her specific concerns. It would all be set down in black and white. I specifically encouraged her to describe her deepest fears—even exaggerate them—in her writings.

Writing her concerns during the 15-minute period, I sensed, might help release Sandy for the remainder of the day—so she wouldn't feel the need to do any more worry-prevention until the following day.

At first, she reported feeling much better after her writing sessions. However, during the second week, she reported becoming bored and resenting the stupidity of continually going over the same old garbage. She realized that this was the same thing she had been doing to herself mentally—and to Jay verbally—every single day.

In short, she was beginning to gain some insight into her own natural neuroses—the structural pitfalls in the thinking patterns of the Type Six personality. At my suggestion, Sandy bought Riso and Hudson's *The Wisdom of the Enneagram* and used the surveys in the book to diagnose herself as a Six with a Self-preservation subtype and Jay as a Self-preservation Three. Jay later confirmed that this was his type.

Sandy was beginning to notice that certain actions were rational and helpful for reducing her anxiety, while others were not.

It became clear that much of her worrying led only to exhaustion, more avoidance and conflicts with Jay.

I assisted Sandy in inventing her own concepts of "good" worrying—where she could or should take some action to avoid or resolve a possible problem—as opposed to "bad" worrying. She began to see that "bad" worrying had no positive results, wasted her time and now caused her to feel bored. She generalized this insight to all areas of her worrying, not just STDs.

She continued to see her structured 15-minute journal writing sessions as an option whenever she needed to get control of the "bad" worrying. However, by this point, she was able to tolerate greater degrees of ambiguity than she had imagined possible. While recognizing that human beings rarely know anything for certain, she was determined to make her "good" worrying count in ways that had positive, measurable results and would be constructive for her future with Jay.

After a month or so, Jay was becoming increasingly pleased with her progress. Eventually, Sandy invited Jay to help her distinguish "good" worrying from "bad" (but only when *she* requested it). I encouraged Jay to be patient and to do a great deal of active listening. He could especially help, I suggested, by *asking* Sandy how her specific worrying might be productive (or not), rather than *telling* her how she should think.

Jay and Sandy continue to thrive, feeling more closeness and empathy than ever before. Considering my Five Factors for predicting relationship success, this increased intimacy is no surprise. These two share deeply compatible lovemaps. Jay is exceptionally healthy in his personality development and Sandy has been willing to move quickly to higher levels. Although they are not in the same Harmonic Group, they do share the Self-preservation subtype and enjoy the benefits of a complementary energy connection (the line connecting Sixes and Threes), which allows them to balance each other's differences.

"House on Fire"

Stan, a Self-preservation Six, is a well-built 40-year-old fireman in the throes of a complicated divorce. Although he was noticeably anxious, even panicky, during our first session, he was obviously proud of his recent promotion to Captain after 18 years in a local Fire Department. He had been referred to me by a fellow fireman who was my client during a recent divorce.

From Stan's description of his history, it was obvious that he was well liked and respected by the men in his department, though he seemed weighed down by his responsibilities to them and to his home and family. He struck me as warm, loyal, frugal and much more concerned about financial matters than his soon-to-be ex-wife, Becky.

Becky, 39 and Stan had two beautiful but highly rebellious daughters, one a high school senior, the other a sophomore. The two girls appeared to be the major focus of Stan and Becky's almost 20-year marriage. According to Stan, both girls had recently been acting out—ditching their classes and earning poor grades, in contrast to their formerly excellent records. Jen, 17, was openly defiant and disrespectful, having sex with her boyfriend and staying out all night. Beth, 15, had become sneaky and so headstrong that punishments for her actions had little or no effect.

Having spent a lot of time thinking through worst-case possibilities, Stan believed that if he and Becky could not reconcile, the girls' future would be disastrous. He firmly believed that the stability of the family's home life and their physical and financial security were of paramount importance for getting the girls back on track.

Their marriage had never been easy, he explained, especially for Becky. They had married too young, when Becky had just turned 19 and he was 20. Even though they waited almost two years to have children, Becky felt trapped by her pregnancy and parenthood. Unhappy with motherhood, she sold cosmetics in department stores and worked for a perfume manufacturer but never felt satisfied with her life. Although Stan worked hard and believed he was an excellent provider, Becky always felt he was unable to produce enough income for them to live "comfortably" in Southern California. She openly criticized her husband for not earning more money.

Now the girls, following their mother's example, were treating their dad just as disrespectfully as Becky did.

Several months before coming to see me, Stan had gone into emotional shock the day Becky announced she had fallen in love with another man and was filing for divorce. She was practical and matter-of-fact about their situation and had obviously consulted an attorney. Stan could keep the house and the girls, she said. She was planning to move out with a minimum of stress, in order to maintain the girls' stability in school. She would accept whatever the courts awarded her in alimony and was willing to wait seven years to sell their home and split the equity after Beth had finished four years of college.

Stan reacted as if he'd been stabbed in the back. The very foundation of his family, for whom he had given his life, was being destroyed.

After speaking with me several times by phone, Becky agreed to join Stan for several sessions of "divorce counseling." She quickly acknowledged herself as a Sexual Seven, based on the reading material I had given Stan (who had taken the personality survey, which confirmed his Six type and Self-preservation subtype).

Becky made it clear from the beginning that she was not open to any kind of reconciliation. She confirmed what Stan had told me—that she'd been unhappy with the marriage since the time they had children and felt she was never cut out for parenthood. Nor could she ever be satisfied with a good, kind, loyal, salt-of-the-earth, hardworking, *boring* husband like Stan. The way she saw it, now was *her* chance to be happy. Over the past year, through her work, she had met and fallen deeply in love with an exciting 50-year-old man who traveled a great deal internationally for his sales job, had been divorced for 20 years and had three grown children.

She just wanted *out*—out from under the burden of her marriage to Stan, the house (which always had something wrong with it) and their two girls, who continually created conflict and drama. On the basis of her reading about the Enneagram, she suspected that both daughters were "probably Type Eights." Too bad, but Stan would have to deal with them, because she was out of the picture.

For the past two months Becky had been living alone in a small studio apartment, happier than she'd been in the past 18 years. She had been generous with Stan on all financial matters, knowing he would have (and want) the responsibility of the house and raising the girls as a single father.

My next few sessions with Stan were extremely difficult. He was unable to accept the reality that Becky was already divorced from him emotionally and had moved on with another man. His disbelief prompted him to try everything possible to change her mind. Eventually, however, when the truth about her betrayal and abandonment became inescapable, Stan's hurt turned to rage.

Believing that he could no longer trust Becky, he decided to cut her out of their life completely and secure full legal custody of the girls. He was successful with the full custody because Becky did not contest it. The girls were able to see their mother on a regular basis because of her visitation rights. The visitations, however, were irregular, since the girls' reactions bounced from total rejection of Becky (on their discovery of her affair) to begging her tearfully to "go back with Dad and be our mom again."

Over the next several months, the divorce became final, Becky moved out of state with her new love and Stan's hours at the Fire Department became more regular with his promotion into administration. He continues counseling with me, sometimes in family sessions with his two defiant daughters.

I have been able to structure weekly Sunday night "Freedom of Speech" family meetings for the three of them. In these sessions all three of them are allowed to express their views, concerns and anger without judgment. They vote on appropriate topics (such a food choices, family trips and household chores). These sessions have been effective in empowering the girls. However, Stan holds the reins on rules and boundaries that are not negotiable. When these are violated, consequences are enforced. The girls appear much happier with such clear guidelines.

A new bonding between Jen and Beth has evolved—something that never existed when they were competing for their mother's attention. Though they appear more responsive and appreciative of their dad's efforts to hold the family together, they still plot ways to ditch school, see their boyfriends and have sex every chance they get, without their dad's knowledge. I hear about these schemes during the 15-minute segments of our family therapy sessions that I spend with each girl alone.

Stan reports feeling relieved that Jen will be attending community college next year and he hopes this will help her mature. His friends and the men at the fire department have been extremely supportive. Several of their wives have invited him and his daughters for dinner and offered to take the girls shopping for school clothes and prom dresses.

Although friends have made efforts to introduce Stan to suitable women, he still cannot bring himself to date. "It's going to be a long, long time before I trust anyone again," he says. Although he is becoming healthier in his own personality, he continues to suffer bouts of rage and depression, for which he rejects any form of medication, preferring to handle his problems through therapy.

He now feels it's better to have no relationship than to have a wife who lies, cheats and sleeps with another man. Since Becky moved out, he has not missed a single day of work. Aware that he has been preoccupied with financial issues such as the girls' college tuition and their medical insurance, I referred Stan to a financial planner, who has helped him deal directly with his money worries.

Although still unwilling to explore the possibility of a new relationship, Stan is doing extremely well in two important areas—his single parenting and his new administrative position. He does less catastrophizing—envisioning worst-case scenarios—and more proactive planning. He is also growing in insight, thanks to various books I've recommended, such as Harville Hendrix's *Getting the Love You Want.*

As hard as Stan tried, his marriage with Becky was never a strong one. Both of them had been unconscious about their lovemaps, never thinking about specific qualities they desired in a mate. In fact, Becky had never even considered the option of not having children. Stan's lovemap was more fulfilled by parenthood (and, at first, by Becky as a wife) than her lovemap ever was. Although he has made great strides in psychological health since their divorce, both he and Becky were average to significantly unhealthy at times during their marriage. The combination of his Self-preservation subtype and her Sexual subtype did not encourage compatibility. They did not share the same Harmonic Group, nor were they connected by a complementary line that might have helped balance their differences.

Sandy and Stan as Self-preservation Sixes

Sandy and Stan, like most Self-preservation Sixes, were both concerned about survival issues. In Sandy's case, the focus was on health and her catastrophic thinking around what is essentially a minor problem. So obsessive was her worrying, that her fiancé threatened to break off their engagement. With therapy, she learned to control her anxieties and the relationship has become stronger.

After the breakup and during his marriage, Stan became preoccupied with financial issues—providing for his daughters' support and planning for their college education. Following my advice to consult with a financial planner helped assuage some of Stan's anxieties. While currently unwilling to risk involvement in another intimate relationship, he is doing well with his work and single-parenting and has a more balanced life.

Sixes with the Sexual Subtype

The Sexual subtype of Six, which Ichazo associates with "strength" and "beauty," shows more bravado than the other two subtypes, attempting to compensate for fears by looking powerful and/or seductive. In their belligerence, contrariness and counterphobia, "strength" Sexual Sixes often resemble Eights. The "beauty" group, somewhat more phobic and tentative, uses their sexual allure to attract support.

"Going Crazy"

Yvonne, 34, a Sexual Six, a tall, exotic-looking brunette with piercing dark eyes, came in for her first appointment looking haggard and upset. Through tears, she told me she had considered "homicide, divorce, mass murder and suicide" as ways of coping with her impossible dilemma. She had two young sons, ages 5 and 3, both autistic and a husband who was passive and unhelpful. Much as she loved them all, she felt unable to deal with the daily stress and overwhelming complications by herself.

Her husband, Ken, 38, is a tall, good-looking airline pilot with an engaging smile. He was sweet and loving, Yvonne said, but avoidant and ineffectual with his two boys. Always fearful of doing the wrong thing with the boys, Ken was incapable of administering any form of discipline or meaningful assistance.

Yvonne took the C-JES personality survey, which confirmed my sense that she was a Six with a Sexual subtype. In later sessions, when Ken joined Yvonne, he was also eager to take the survey, which validated his Sexual Nine type. He seemed stunned by the accuracy of this depth analysis. "It explains," he said, "why I numb out, go unconscious and avoid conflict—especially with Yvonne."

Yvonne had grown increasingly enraged over Ken's neglectful parenting, especially in contrast to her fierce, single-handed battle with the county school system to get maximum hours of instruction for her two autistic preschoolers. I had encouraged her to press even further and her confrontations with school administrators paid off handsomely in procuring direct supervision for the boys. This seemed to lighten Yvonne's daily burden.

Ken had never been of any significant help with the boys. Early on, he was avoidant and decided that his role was to earn money to support the family while Yvonne stayed home and handled the kids and the house. He was adept at compartmentalizing his thoughts, actions and responsibilities. In his way of thinking, he had no need to be involved in securing programs for the boys, since Yvonne had "all day to do it."

When he made comments along these lines during joint sessions, Yvonne would fly into fits of rage, accusing him of having affairs with women at work and never truly loving her. During these episodes, Ken would sit silently for long periods as Yvonne's dramatics played out.

However, he was growing weary of her paranoia and rage attacks as well as her continual questioning of his loyalty. He never planned to leave her or the boys, he told her. He would keep his commitments. Yet he was clearly fed up with her continual pushing and pulling, her outbursts of venom and her appetite for conflict. He desperately wanted Yvonne to get a grip on herself.

During the first few years of their relationship she had been his perfect lovemap partner. When they met and married, she too had worked for the airlines; she was the svelte, luscious, loyal yet flirtatious vamp that Ken had always dreamed of. Strong, aggressive and far less fearful of controversy and conflict than Ken was, she never hesitated to distinguish the "good guys" from the "bad guys." He admired her spirit and felt she complemented him perfectly as a wife. Now, however, under the stress of her role as keeper of their two autistic sons, she seemed a completely different person.

Ken came close to Yvonne's ideal as a mate, except that he was never assertive or responsive enough to fully satisfy her need for a strong, unconditional connection. Yet, through it all, he did remain totally committed to Yvonne as her lover and breadwinner for the family. This connection was their strong suit and I was able to build on their solid lovemap foundation.

I had them both visualize and describe in detail the feelings they had for one another during those first two years of falling in love and living together and the following three years as a married couple. It was exciting to see the sparkle, the exchange of sexy glances, the hugs and hand holding as they described their attraction to one another. Their love and commitment to each other and the boys was profound. This was something Ken had previously never been able to fully verbalize because he felt so incompetent as a father.

Eventually I was able to confront Ken about hiding out in his role as provider and neglecting his responsibilities as co-parent. He responded by revealing his feelings of incompetence and fear of somehow damaging the boys even further. He had no training about autism and no real understanding of it. Feeling trapped in his ignorance, he made little proactive effort to educate himself. He had numbed out.

After several sessions, Ken became willing to read several short books and attend two group lectures with Yvonne for parents of autistic children. Also, he committed to assuming several household chores, which took some of the burden off Yvonne.

His involvement with the boys also increased. I encouraged him to make use of the teaching skills he had learned through the lectures by visiting the boys' special classes on days when he was not flying. At first he remained an observer, but after only two visits he began asking questions about how he could most constructively respond to the boys. The teachers were openly grateful for his interest and were generous with show-and-tell examples, giving Ken and Yvonne specific skills and disciplined responses to maximize positive learning for the boys.

At first, Ken was reluctant to give up his time for golf, which he enjoyed and felt he deserved. Yvonne and I both agreed that he deserved his hobby and time off. This support allowed Ken to take another look at the big picture and realize that he also had other priorities—the most important of which he now recognized as Yvonne and the boys.

On his own, Ken made the decision to play golf only once or twice a month and devote the remainder of his days off to co-parenting, helping Yvonne and, whenever possible, creating late-morning dates for lovemaking while the boys were still at school. After all, I pointed out, why not spend the private hours on sex and intimacy, while keeping chores, grocery shopping and laundry for when the boys were home from school?

Simultaneously, I felt the necessity to confront Yvonne with her excessive wine drinking—a topic she avoided every time Ken brought it up. She had been in the habit of drinking not only one glass with dinner but also two or three before going to bed, to insure she slept well. I encouraged her to do some research on her own regarding wine consumption. Knowing how common it is for a Sexual Six to challenge a therapist's authority, I was wary about suggesting specific limits for Yvonne.

After several weeks of research on the Internet, Yvonne

concluded that, while six ounces of red wine with food could be health enhancing, further consumption produced no added value and, over the long term, could be detrimental. She decided, for herself, that she would limit her wine to one glass per day. Given the change in Ken's behavior, she no longer needed to evade the reality of his previous non-involvement with the family.

Their marriage now began to feel much more rewarding, as Yvonne and Ken continued disciplined sessions of active listening.

The last big hurdle was dealing with Ken's secret guilt over his marijuana smoking at the time Yvonne conceived. Yvonne had known about his occasional pot smoking when they married; what she didn't know was that it had continued for almost five years after the marriage—mostly during layovers following long flights. Ken's real concern was that his pot smoking had somehow damaged his sperm and that this might have contributed to the boys' autism.

This information did not cause Yvonne any great concern. From her reading and research, she already knew there was unlikely to be any connection between sporadic marijuana use and autism.

Since such technical medical information is outside my scope of practice, I insisted that Ken and Yvonne talk with a physician who specializes in pediatrics. They arranged the consultation and the doctor confirmed there was no correlation. He went on to assure them that there was nothing either or them had done or failed to do that could have caused the autism.

From this point on, a new spirit of cooperation, forgiveness and release filled their marriage, which continues to grow and become more fulfilling.

Evaluating this relationship using our Five Factors for long-term success, I'm not surprised that, with counseling, things turned out so well. Yvonne and Ken's lovemaps were extremely compatible. Although both began with average-to-low levels of psychological health, they grew significantly into much higher levels as the counseling progressed.

In addition, they were fortunate in sharing the same Sexual subtype as well as being directly connected by the complementary line between Sixes and Nines that helped balance their different energies.

"Defying Authority"

Joey, 28, single, a Sexual Six who sells sports equipment, was referred to me for anger management through his company's Human Resource administrator. He described himself as explosive, passionate, courageous, defiant and—at times—self-sabotaging due to his violent temper. He also had a contagious smile and boyish charm that were major assets in his sales position.

Joey seemed less than pleased to be in my office. He told me that his sports equipment company had sent him here "to get fixed." "Well," I said, "they must think you're worth saving, if they sent you to me." His response was a snicker and a skeptical look. Having heard that some therapists use hypnosis, he made it clear that he didn't want "any of that crap."

I assured Joey that I would never try to accomplish anything that he didn't instruct me to do. I was *his* employee, for whatever issues he believed were important. There would be no surprises and all of our sessions would be strictly confidential. Even though his company had referred him and they were paying the bill, my professional commitment was to assist him, not his company.

As I attempted to take a short personal/career history and establish what Joey wanted from therapy, he was unusually vigilant and defensive.

He was sick and tired, he said, of people telling him what to do—but not telling him clearly, then changing their minds, playing head trips, making it impossible for him to succeed. Nothing was going right in his life. He sensed that his girlfriend, Kim, 28, was about to break up with him and he feared his boss was about to fire him.

As Joey described his job disappointments, I learned that this was his third major work endeavor. With only two years of college and several short-term jobs in between, he was proud that on his first career path, working for a chain of fitness centers, he had moved up quickly into management. That career ended abruptly, however, when he got into a screaming fight with his immediate boss that nearly became physical.

For his second career effort, his longtime dream had been to become a police officer and he was successful in gaining admission to the Police Academy. About five months into his program at the Academy, Joey got into another verbally abusive altercation, this time with his instructor. Feeling he was absolutely right in his viewpoint, Joey refused to back down. He positioned himself so that either the instructor would be fired or Joey would be dismissed. Thus his dream of becoming a policeman crumbled within the following few hours.

Describing this second career loss, Joey was fighting back tears and I sensed that I needed to proceed cautiously and allow him to determine the course of our conversation. "This police sergeant/instructor," he said, "reminded me of my dad—a real asshole, a drunk and an abuser. I don't want to talk about him."

I assured Joey that there were no requirements for what we talked about. He was free to discuss—or not discuss—whatever was relevant for him. However, I could see that authority figures—especially certain men—posed gigantic challenges for Joey.

Somehow we got back to the reason he came in—his current boss. Joey was struggling to figure out how to handle his present situation as a sales representative for a well-known line of sports equipment. He liked this third career because it allowed him freedom to set his own schedule, a company car with mileage and decent medical benefits. However, he could already feel a buildup of the same rage he had experienced with his police academy instructor.

I told Joey that he was clearly on the right track—being willing to objectively evaluate his feelings and make changes in the way he dealt with them. He briefly mentioned that even the thought of his terrifying father triggered a panicky rage, followed by flashbacks of abuse, uncontrolled violence and then abandonment. I asked what he wanted most at this moment.

"Just to feel safe," he said, "to feel secure in relationships and not give way to panic—which is always what leads to my god-awful temper. I hate it!"

This outburst must have left him feeling extremely vulnerable, for he immediately shut down, informing me that his dad was not why he was here. "All that about my dad is none of your business, anyhow, Mona."

I quickly changed the subject and asked if there had ever been a time in his life when he'd felt truly safe.

After pondering my question, he said, "The only time I've felt really safe was in my Karate classes—and that was after two years of training. Eventually, I got really good at it—and that's where I feel secure, because I know I can handle myself."

I attempted to explain that it was possible to apply some of the Karate principles to his work situation. He could remain rational, use mind control and remain in charge of his own energy without being reactive to others. Joey laughed and said he couldn't see any parallels. Then he abruptly changed the subject and insisted on telling me the latest bad news about his girlfriend.

"I broke up with Kim," he said, "beat her to the draw before she could give *me* the axe. All we've done for the last two months is fight. She wants to get married, I don't. She wants kids, I don't. She's ready for us to live together, I'm not. Plus she's OD'd on my questioning her. She's so pretty I can't trust her not to be with other guys. So I keep asking her where she's been and I never believe what she tells me."

We spent little time analyzing Kim, who sounded like a Self-preservation Four. However, I did point out that Joey always seemed afraid of being abused, hurt, abandoned, misled and unable to trust others. He *never* felt secure or safe except in his Karate class.

It was time to deal with his deepest hurt: his core issues of extreme parental abuse and neglect. In a few unguarded moments, Joey had let it slip that both of his parents were dysfunctional alcoholics. His dad would beat Joey and his two younger sisters with a belt for no reason. His weak and ineffectual mother would stay drunk in order to cope with his dad's violent temper. She never tried to intervene or rescue the three children and was completely absent emotionally.

But Joey had suddenly decided that it was a waste of time and money for us to discuss his childhood, since neither he nor I could change these facts—though he acknowledged that at least I had helped him realize that "men who remind me of my asshole dad trigger my rage." He agreed to work on this, but saw no reason to continue therapy, especially for the discussion of his childhood.

Since this was only our third session, I quickly gave him several techniques for mind control and visualization, along with certain physical practices using acupuncture points to help him control his anger.

Joey again panicked and abruptly closed off the possibility of any further sessions. "I like you a lot, Mona," he said, "but you're getting too close to the bone. I can't take any more of this therapy crap right now. It makes me feel too vulnerable. I'll just do the Dad/male-authority-figure mind control bit you taught me—and see how it goes."

I reassured Joey that I would be available for him when and if he ever wanted to resume therapy. Although I didn't feel that aborting the process after a few sessions was in his best interest, I knew that he had learned to feel safe with at least one other person—me.

Looking at Joey's relationship with Kim from the perspective of our Five Factors for predicting long-term success, I see that, because of their personality differences and their incompatible lovemaps, this couple would have been unlikely to succeed. More importantly, Joey's level of psychological development seemed so unhealthy much of the time that he would be unable to sustain *any* love relationship at this stage.

Recently he left me a phone message saying that our techniques worked; he had been able to redirect his anger and not verbally blow up at his boss in a tense situation. As I write these pages, it has been four weeks since I last saw him. I trust that he will one day feel ready to return to therapy.

Yvonne and Joey as Sexual Sixes

Both Yvonne and Joey are "strength" Sexual subtypes, showing extreme counterphobic tendencies in their aggressiveness and defiance of authority. Yet fear is clearly the motor running both personalities. Yvonne's ability to confront authority and vent her rage has actually served her family well, since she has obtained greater educational benefits for her two autistic sons than a less assertive personality could have. The main problem in her marriage came from her need for greater support from her passive Nine husband and, since the relationship was basically strong, counseling was helpful in obtaining that.

In Joey's case, his abusive family history had contributed to his need to fiercely defy any male authority figure that reminded him of his violent father. His problem with controlling his rage in confrontations with his bosses had become a serious problem for him and his lack of trust, among many other factors, made any relationship with a woman problematic. Some anger management techniques given to him in the few counseling sessions that he would allow might serve as a basis for him to build on, but his fear of therapy (because of the strong emotions it brings up in him) is a major obstacle to his further development.

Sixes with the Social Subtype

In the Social Six subtype, which Ichazo associates with "duty," we find people who are anxious about the social order and who may even be social activists. Social Sixes are sensitive to group norms, conscious of authority issues and fearful of making mistakes. In general, this subtype shows a mixture of phobic and counterphobic behavior.

"Eternal Guilt"

Olivia, 62, quickly recognized herself as a Social Six, based on results from her personality survey. A pretty woman who appeared far younger than her age, she projected a warm, healthy, unpretentious quality and displayed a lively sense of humor. Following a 40-year marriage, Olivia had been widowed for almost two years.

Before she would talk about her marriage (which I sensed had been problematic), she insisted on telling me about the positive aspects of her life—her two beautiful and successful daughters, both happily married with children of their own; her substantial career as Executive Secretary to a demanding corporate president, after whose death she took early retirement from the company; her fundamentalist religious faith and her significant work for both her church and an anti-abortion political group. Being part of a bonded group—family, church, corporate and volunteer organizations—was important to Olivia's feeling of safety and support in the world.

Sensing there was more to her story, I asked why she had come to see me.

She suddenly burst into tears and told me she was a fraud and a sinner who might actually be responsible for her husband's sudden death. It was essential, she said, that I know the truth about her marriage to William.

Now it all came pouring out. They had never been particularly compatible and she had lost all sense of real connection with him in the first years of their 40-year relationship. Both were 20 when they married and by their third year together, when Olivia was pregnant with their first daughter, William had become cold and shut down. Although her loneliness throughout the marriage was excruciating, her religious beliefs forbid divorce. No one she knew had ever been divorced and she could not face the rejection she envisioned—from family, church friends and volunteer group colleagues—if she were to embrace such an option.

I commented that she might now be experiencing some sense of freedom as a result of William's death—and that she might also have some guilt over feeling this way.

"You don't know the half of it," she said. She listed some of their incompatibilities: she was devoutly religious, he was an atheist; she was devoted to having children, he was ambivalent; she was conservative, he was liberal; she was against abortion, he was pro-choice.

They'd had no sexual activity together in over 20 years. She had suspected that William might be addicted to pornography, but never cared enough to investigate further.

As we talked more about William, Olivia concluded that he was probably an unhealthy Self-preservation Five and I agreed. Thinking back on the emotionally bleak years of her marriage, she broke down in tears and blurted out a dark secret—during the last ten years of her marriage, she had been involved in an affair with a married man five years her junior whom she had met through her church.

Alan was stuck in a marriage with circumstances similar to her own. He was a good and decent man of the kind Olivia wished she had married. They spent two years developing a strong friendship that eventually evolved into a monogamous adulterous relationship that was fulfilling for them both. Although I never met Alan and he never took the personality survey, I think he is most likely a Nine.

Olivia was tormented not only by the guilt over her ten-year illicit affair, but also by the fact that she and Alan were making love at the very moment William collapsed in their garage from a fatal heart attack.

In the two years since then, Olivia had convinced herself that "God struck William dead in order to punish me for the affair with Alan. If I'd never allowed anything to start with Alan, William might still be alive."

Eventually, I was able to show Olivia that there could have been no causal connection between her affair with Alan and William's heart attack. We carefully read together the coroner's report, which described the technicalities of how the heart attack occurred. Also, we discussed the impossibility of knowing God's intentions and the likelihood that they might differ considerably from those of human beings.

As Olivia struggled with her conflicted values, she began to show signs of self-forgiveness and a willingness to ask God's forgiveness. Terrified that her daughters or fellow church members might somehow discover her affair, she prayed to be spared rejection from the groups she held most dear.

Now Olivia felt the need to reveal a second shameful secret, for which she was certain I would reject her and cancel all further sessions—a clear projection of what she feared would happen with her significant reference groups and friendships. I explained that my rejecting her was not possible, since I was here only to counsel and support her, not to judge her, regardless of what she had done.

Her terrible secret turned out to be the abortion of her third child. William, who had not wanted their first two children, became enraged when Olivia became pregnant for the third time. He threatened to divorce her, move out of state and leave her financially destitute if she refused to have the abortion. Furthermore, he threatened to destroy her reputation with all her support systems, including their daughters and her church.

Terrified, Olivia agreed and William took her to a medical clinic in Nevada, where she secured a legal medical abortion. Until this moment, 30 years later, she had never shared this secret with anyone. Guilt and remorse overwhelmed her once again. "I'm such a hypocrite," she said, "with all my work for the Right-to-Life movement."

But her suffering over her own abortion had led to some questioning of her absolute anti-abortion position. She reported feeling empathy for several teenage girls in her congregation who confessed to having abortions because they felt trapped and without any workable alternative.

I made no judgments or suggestions, but encouraged Olivia to clarify her own values and follow her own heart. This was a novel idea to Olivia, who had never questioned *any* of her basic values. How could she, being the only daughter of a fundamentalist minister and a cold judgmental mother who instilled the fear of God in her from the moment she was born?

Now, at age 62, Olivia was beginning to take responsibility for her own thoughts and desires, questioning how *she* wanted to live the remainder of her life. Many of these questions involved Alan. Not surprisingly, the shock and guilt surrounding her husband's death had thrown their relationship into a tailspin. Although she continued seeing Alan, she had called a moratorium on all sexual activity. She reasoned that God might look more favorably on her if she could embrace this kind of penance.

During the course of our counseling, Alan's tolerance of his wife's hateful criticism finally broke. He decided he could no longer sustain the way he was living, moved out of the house he and his wife owned, filed for divorce and rented a cozy apartment (which he hoped eventually to share with Olivia). She longed to be with him and share the sweetness of their love once again.

I was able to help Olivia see that she is worthy of love and affection and that, although her choices are hers alone, her need for group validation is still essential to her well being. She agreed. It was an unusual and intuitive suggestion on my part that she invite her dear friend Carolyn, who had referred Olivia to me, to join us for one of her therapy sessions. I knew Carolyn well as my former client and my hope was that, through our session with her close confidante, Olivia could at least experience some group consensus and validation (through Carolyn and me supporting her).

To my surprise, Olivia invited Carolyn to our very next session and poured out her heart about her affair with Alan, the circumstances of William's fatal heart attack and the abortion of her third child. As I had hoped, Carolyn was kind, compassionate and comforting to her friend, validating Olivia's painful feelings as well as her plans for the future.

Olivia planned to start dating Alan openly when his divorce became final, in five more months. After they announced their engagement, they planned to live together. Alan had suggested that they change churches eventually, seeking one that was more liberal and affirming. Although uncertain about this at first, Olivia later agreed that they needed a fresh start.

She had already decided to redirect her volunteer work. Although still personally opposed to abortion, she chose to counsel young girls with unwanted pregnancies, where she might occasionally share her own story and assist them in making the best choice for themselves—whether that involved keeping the child, putting it up for adoption or having an abortion.

Olivia also felt a need to have therapy sessions, similar to the one with Carolyn, with her two daughters. Now 38 and 35, they were mature, interested in their mother's well being and lovingly supportive. They both expressed how much they wanted their mom to get on with her life—to marry Alan whenever she was ready—and to know that she would forever have their unconditional love and approval.

Olivia is, in fact, now moving on with her life, seeing Alan regularly and planning to live with him once his divorce is final. There is a high probability of a successful marriage between Olivia and Alan, considering our Five Factors. Their lovemaps are highly compatible; both are consciously striving to reach greater levels of psychological health; they share the Social subtype; and they have the advantage of being connected by the Enneagram line between Sixes and Nines that helps to balance their differences.

Looking back at Olivia's marriage to William, assuming he was a Self-preservation Five, none of the Five Factors for marital success were present. Their lovemaps were severely incompatible; both were unhealthy in their psychological development (especially William); they had different subtypes, were not in the same Harmonic Group and were not connected by a complementary line. The marriage endured only because Olivia's rigid belief system could not entertain the possibility of divorce.

"Cancer Within"

Henry, 48, currently in the process of his third divorce, is a Social Six. He is also the proud father of a 24-year-old soon-to-be-professional baseball star. Recovering from prostate cancer, Henry looked gaunt after surgery, chemotherapy and radiation. He hated looking emaciated and feared further rejection from women and from people in general. His longtime friend and colleague, Buddy, aware of Henry's depression and fearful that he might do himself harm, had insisted that he see a therapist.

In our first session Henry assured me that he was not a suicide risk, but acknowledged that he had reached an all-time low. Although his cancer treatments had been horrendous, his major issue was his terror of more rejection, of losing his support network—his baseball "family," the group of avid parents of potential professional players; his colleagues in the insurance business; his neighbors who had formerly invited him and his soon-to-be-ex-wife, Trisha, to various parties, plays and holiday celebrations.

Henry saw his cancer as the physical manifestation of his internally troubled state. He felt he no longer belonged anywhere, not even in a family. His first two marriages (one in his mid 20s, the other in his late 20s) had both ended when his wives became involved in sexual affairs with other men. The only positive aspect of this for Henry was that he and his first wife, Tammy, had produced his only child, Jerry, the light of his life, in the first year of their marriage. Jerry was less than two years old when Henry found out about Tammy's affair with one of her childhood boyfriends, whom she later married. He still found it painful to run into her with her husband and two teenage kids at some of Jerry's games.

His second short marriage was equally distressing and Henry's hopes of finding a faithful wife who would be a good stepmother for Jerry were dashed. After that, Henry remained single for almost a decade, looking after Jerry, attending all Jerry's sports events, developing himself in the insurance business and training many other insurance adjustors. He formed important alliances with various male confidantes such as Buddy while becoming ever more deeply involved with Jerry's baseball activities.

By the time Jerry finished high school, he had been recruited by top universities and offered large baseball scholarships. It was clear that he might be professional material and Henry was his son's most loyal fan.

However, Henry's cancer had now forced him to go on a six-month disability leave from work and miss out on almost everything that mattered to him—especially the support network around Jerry's baseball.

All these major losses were capped by the announcement of Henry's third wife, Ellen, 47, that she was divorcing him after eight years of marriage (her second). She wanted to be free to travel the world with a lover, she said and could not face the prospect of being Henry's nursemaid. She felt besieged by the push-pull of his need to pick fights with her in order to test her loyalty. Feeling she had been loyal, she was now fed up with the whole situation and wanted out.

Later in Henry's therapy he begged her to join in our sessions, if only for divorce counseling—to help me help him. She came in, but made it clear during our one joint session that she wanted a clean break and had already applied for a job in London. She was most likely a Self-preservation Four, but was generally hostile and uninterested in taking any "crappy psychological survey" that Henry suggested.

Ellen's decision to leave him during his second round of

chemotherapy confirmed for him that he had lost all support from people who mattered. He was skeptical and pessimistic even about therapy at first. He kept questioning my credentials, my background and why I chose to be a therapist—seemingly determined to pick a fight with me.

I agreed that I couldn't heal his cancer, couldn't make Ellen fall in love with him again and couldn't give him a new body. But there were some kinds of help I might be able to offer that could lead to real change. Certainly nothing would work without his cooperation.

In order to reduce Henry's defiant skepticism and extreme anxiety, I proposed that we make a contract. Both of us would do our best for four sessions. At the end of these, if he didn't feel there had been some significant improvement we would call it quits. Henry agreed.

With our first session already gone and Henry noticeably fatigued, I asked him to dwell on just one thought for our second session. This was the saying, "It is not what happens to us that matters, but rather *how we respond* to what happens." I wrote out this sentence on a sheet of paper and asked Henry to jot down any thoughts he might have about it before our next meeting.

He arrived for the second session still ambivalent and anxious about doing therapy. I inquired about his past week and eventually asked what his thoughts were about our one principle. "What principle?" he asked. He had forgotten all about it.

I reassured him that this was quite normal, especially for someone under great stress. (By this point I suspected Henry might be a Six and was perhaps being passive-aggressive, seeing me as an untested authority figure and unconsciously sabotaging the process, possibly challenging me to be his ally.) Instead of engaging in any form of analysis or confrontation, I offered to be Henry's secretary. He would tell me *what happened* and I would record how he *actually responded* and also an *alternative, healthier response*. We agreed to make no judgments and to offer no analysis regarding his real or alternative responses. It had never occurred to Henry that he could brainstorm alternatives without making judgments.

We began with Henry's biggest concern—his pending divorce from Ellen. *What happened?* Ellen moved out and filed divorce.

Actual response? Panic, betrayal, sense of abandonment, anxiety, fear, hatred. *Alternative response?* Although in great pain, Henry could now see that any wife who would abandon him in his time of greatest need was not the kind of woman he would want to be married to. He had never fully trusted Ellen somehow and was beginning to understand why.

Now Henry asked me to write out his second *What happened.* He has lost contact with all the baseball people and groups he was formerly so close to. *Actual response?* Feeling as though he didn't belong anymore, loneliness, loss of connection, self-pity. *Alternative response:* he could make e-mail contact with most of these people and reveal that he was temporarily undergoing cancer treatment but planned to be back at the games within four months. He could request their assistance in keeping him informed by fax, phone or e-mail.

Henry, now on a roll, asked me to write fast so we could cover more subjects—his first two marriages, increasing his weekly phone contact with Jerry (whose love and loyalty he never questioned), his lack of contact with work colleagues, his inability to attend his monthly card club, his feeling behind on issues in the insurance business since he had been on disability, his inability to drive himself to and from his doctors' appointments and treatments, the falling away of his social life in the neighborhood since his separation from Ellen. For all of these issues, Henry was able to come up with healthier alternatives and actually put them into practice.

In our third session, he was eager to give me the results of his "alternative responses" even before I had a chance to ask. He was noticeably more open, lighter in spirit, even humorous. He now realized that Ellen had never been the right partner for him and was beginning to feel some relief from his depression. Instead of talking only once a week to his son, he had asked Jerry to phone him during the week, which the son was delighted to do.

Henry did reach out to many of his colleagues and friends from work. He requested that the head secretary from his department make a special request bulletin for anyone willing to drive him to his appointments. He also sent a group e-mail to all the men in his card club. Much to his surprise, several of the players who had taken early retirement were not only free but pleased to give Henry rides, as needed.

Five of the families in his neighborhood responded over the next several weeks with invitations for various get-togethers. Henry was gaining strength and confidence. He had become proactive, taking action toward what he wanted to accomplish. I gently reminded him of our first principle: "It is not what happens to you that matters, but rather how you respond to what happens." He chuckled and, for the first time, offered me a big hug as we ended the session.

In our fourth session, I reminded Henry of our contract and asked for his assessment. Did he feel there had been improvement? Was he feeling any better?

Henry laughed. "I don't want to stop therapy now," he said. "We're just getting started. I'm ready to take that personality survey you mentioned."

There were some bumpy times ahead, but Henry eventually came to understand his Type Six personality and his Social subtype. It was difficult at times for him to objectively examine his old beliefs and prejudices. In many instances he decided to table his decisions and not take any action at the moment.

As a therapist I felt deeply rewarded by Henry's continued willingness to grow in several different directions. Now, two years after his first session, his physical strength and mental health are greatly improved and he exemplifies true success as a result of the therapeutic process.

In retrospect, Henry himself was able to see that only one of the Five Factors for predicting marital success was in play with Ellen—both were in the "Reactive" Harmonic Group (Sixes, Fours and Eights). Incompatible lovemaps, their generally low level of psychological development, different subtypes and having no complementary balancing connection—all these contributed to the failure of their marriage.

Olivia and Henry as Social Sixes

Both Olivia and Henry had powerful connections with important groups in their lives, showed a strong sense of duty toward others and relied on these groups to validate them. Olivia, though miserable in her marriage, could not consider divorce for fear of losing the approval of her family, friends, church and volunteer group associates. So great was her sense of guilt and shame over her extramarital affair and the abortion she'd had early in her marriage, that she had never been able to share these secrets with anyone. Coming to understand that she did have the support of her family and friends who counted most was a milestone on her path toward greater psychological health.

Henry, feeling he had lost his support systems after his diagnosis of prostate cancer and third divorce, had become deeply depressed and pessimistic about his future. Through therapy he was able to explore alternative ways of thinking. He was able to become proactive on his own behalf, reconnect with the groups and individuals that were important to him and become reassured of their support.

Strengths of Sixes in Intimate Relationships

- Loyalty
- Commitment
- Strong work ethic
- Reliability
- Friendliness
- Cooperativeness
- Compassion
- Respect for tradition

Limitations of Sixes in Intimate Relationships

- Hyper-vigilance
- Paranoia
- Doubt
- Prejudice
- Anxiety
- Defensiveness
- Blaming
- Issues with Authority

Defense Mechanisms of Sixes

Sixes, suffering deep-seated anxiety and insecurity, are often unaware that this terror is built into their personality structure. Therefore they continually look outside themselves for a "cause" to explain the fear they are feeling. Finding a possible reason for their interior fear, they are able to gain some relief from their inner tension by projecting their fear onto the person or situation that looks threatening. Because their fearfulness is so deeply ingrained, they are hyper-vigilant for something "out there" that might account for it. This defense mechanism of projection, while common in individuals of all types, is especially focused in Sixes on outside threats.

The cases in this chapter illustrate projection in various ways. Sandy, a Self-preservation subtype suffering from a mild form of herpes, projected her fears onto the possibility of more serious diseases caused by viruses (such as AIDS). Joey, projecting onto his bosses the qualities of his abusive father, lost important career opportunities when he was unable to handle the rage that came up in him. Olivia projected onto her friends, family and colleagues the harsh judgments of her behavior that she herself made and personally feared. Learning that these individuals were actually supportive helped her examine and adjust her own value system. Henry, suffering from cancer and abandoned by his wife, projected his fears of losing his support system onto friends and colleagues who were actually compassionate allies. In each of these cases, as well as the others in this book, therapy consisted of giving these Type Six individuals some form of reality check that helped them see the irrationality of their fear-driven projections.

The "Natural Neuroses" of Sixes

The natural neuroses of Sixes are based on a deep-seated suspicion of the motives of others and a strong need for trustworthy allies. Their obsession with safety and security often leads to black-and-white thinking that places others in "us versus them" categories. Sixes generally display a built-in paranoia that is often understandable in light of some of their family histories—many have been betrayed, abandoned or abused early on. It is not uncommon in the history of Sixes to find an alcoholic or mentally ill parent. Many Sixes have also felt unsupported by authority figures on whom they depended for help.

This need and inability to depend on others frequently motivates Sixes to search for dependable authorities and some find security in hierarchical organizations such as corporations, the military or the police force (or, with less healthy individuals, in cults or gangs). The tendency of Sixes toward what Buddhists call "doubting mind" means that they require significant support and validation in order to feel confident about their choices and decisions.

How Sixes Blossom in Good Relationships

When Sixes find they can trust their partner or group, they can blossom. Once they feel secure, they are able to relax their paranoia. This allows them to become open to sharing their lives with a partner and healing their defective thought process, which was shaped by fears that most likely had a basis in reality. Sixes are preoccupied with loyalty because it is the quality they most need from others and have been most conscious of lacking in their life.

For example, once Yvonne was able to trust that her husband would help her with the overwhelming task of parenting their two autistic sons, she found a renewal of the love and trust that had been so strong during the first years of their marriage. Olivia, once she understood that revealing the truth about her abortion and extramarital affair would not destroy her relationship with her family and friends, was able to claim a committed relationship with the man she loved and let go of her longstanding guilt. Henry, having proved the loyalty of his friends and colleagues through asking for and obtaining their help, seemed to gain a new lease on life.

Once Sixes are assured of the loyalty of their essential allies, they are able to relax their fears significantly. The support of these significant others is key to healing the defective thinking that often afflicts Sixes. "I was so scared I couldn't think straight" no longer describes their mental pattern. When feeling relaxed and secure Sixes can be the most cooperative, egoless and naturally childlike of all the types.

TYPE SEVEN: THE ENTHUSIAST IN LOVE

Seven is one of the Enneagram styles associated with fear. While Fives cope with a threatening world by developing their mental capacities in isolation and Sixes cope through constant vigilance and seeking trustworthy allies, Sevens manage their fears by staying continually in motion and distracting themselves with activities and pleasures. Generally, only the healthiest Sevens are aware of how pervasive their underlying terror actually is and how useless any attempt to outrun it will prove.

Average Sevens are preoccupied with activity and options and are especially oriented toward the future and its stimulating possibilities. They find it easier to begin new projects than to follow old ones through to completion. Their natural optimism, charm and energy make them appealing companions, but these same qualities can be a smokescreen for their underlying narcissism. Sevens at this level of psychological health are subject to impulsive actions that may verge on recklessness.

Healthy Sevens display immense vitality, passionately enjoy life and are able to sustain commitments to projects and people. Often multi-talented, they are productive and fulfilled in their lives. They are especially adept at "brainstorming" ideas. Not only do they frequently display original thinking, but their enthusiasm also inspires others to creative problem solving that, in the Seven's company, becomes fun and exciting.

Unhealthy Sevens are demanding, materialistic, excessive and self-indulgent. They are subject to rages when their desires are not quickly fulfilled and tend to escape into drugs, sexual activity, overeating—whatever will offer them temporary relief from their anxiety. Unhealthy Sevens can often be manic and may be subject to panic attacks when they exhaust their resources and have to confront their underlying anxiety.

Sevens with the Self-preservation Subtype

Self-preservation Sevens, whom Oscar Ichazo calls "defenders," are highly social, unlike the Self-preservation subtype in other Enneagram styles. Sevens with this subtype seek out like-minded people to share fun, information and stimulation. They see their circle of friendships and family as a barricade against boredom, stagnation and other forms of pain. Enthusiastic about acquiring possessions as well as having new experiences, Self-preservation Sevens are often more materialistic than Sexual or Social Sevens.

"Twisted Bargain"

Sarah, 33, a Self-preservation Seven, came to me in a panic, feeling threatened by potentially serious losses in her immediate future. She and her husband, Roger, 35 (a Self-preservation One), were five years into in their marriage, the second for both of them.

They were childless by choice. "Kids would tie us down too much," Sarah said. "We want the finer things in life."

Roger and Sarah were both hard working and ambitious in their respective sales positions—he in mortgage loans and she in residential real estate. They were determined to purchase a $1.5 million home during the coming year and were striving to earn as much as possible for the down payment.

Sarah thought she could obtain a great bargain on a home through one of her contacts at the office. Jack, who was 25 years her senior, had been a real estate agent for almost 40 years and something of a mentor to her. He was preparing to list for sale his parents' elegant home as they finalized their arrangements to move into an assisted living complex during the next six to nine months.

Sarah and Roger wanted this house for themselves more than they had ever wanted anything. Knowing this, Jack suggested to

Sarah an arrangement that could make her and Roger's dream come true. For several years he had been expressing to her his frustration over his "loveless, sexless, boring" marriage to an ailing wife. Now he told Sarah that if she would agree to have a sexual affair with him over the next six months, he would sell his parents' home to her and Roger with reduced commission fees and at the below-market price of $1.5 million.

Accepting Jack's proposition would mean that Sarah would meet him about once a week for a "pleasure payment date." Jack reasoned that he had helped Sarah establish her real estate career over the past eight years and he felt she owed him. All he wanted, he said, was one last wonderful sexual fling with a healthy woman whom he cared about—not such an outrageous desire, surely.

The home was a great bargain and Sarah was almost salivating at the thought of owning it. Jack was attractive for a man of 62 and he had always been flirtatious. (Later in our sessions, after gaining some understanding of her own Seven type, Sarah said she thought Jack was also a Seven, perhaps with a Sexual subtype.) She felt she owed him for much of her success in real estate, was grateful for his mentoring, liked him as a person and sympathized with his plight over his chronically ill wife. After all, she rationalized, doing what he wanted would mean only one hour per week for six months—about 22 meetings, minus the weeks when one of them was traveling.

She agreed to his proposal.

Sarah had already had sex with Jack on two occasions when she first came to see me. At this point she was struggling with endless mental debates over the moral parameters of her decision. Was this, in fact, an act of prostitution? Should she risk telling Roger? Would he want to kill her for doing such a stupid thing? How could she live with herself if she continued the sex with Jack? Worse, how could she allow this offer of his parents' home to fall through? How would she and Roger deal with the reality of not purchasing the home?

It was difficult for Sarah to cease posing her questions long enough for me to complete her basic intake information. She was in a real dilemma. What was she to do?

As I continued asking her pointed questions about her core values and moral boundaries, her materialism became crystal clear.

She expressed her belief that standards and cultural morals were all relative; she saw no absolutes, citing many cultures where mistresses or polygamy were common. At this juncture, she was choosing to buy the house and have sex with Jack.

I explained how understanding her personality type might be helpful for such decision-making. She was anxious to take the survey and immediately confirmed the Self-preservation Seven results. She was becoming more aware of her ambitious, materialistic, self-indulgent, yet highly energetic and impatient nature.

One of her main concerns was whether she had a moral obligation to tell Roger. We analyzed endlessly, at her insistence, the pros and cons: Secret-keeping was almost never healthy—telling Roger would eliminate enormous stress. Maybe he could accept this form of "volunteer work" for a short period?

No. Not a chance. She feared Roger's reaction. Besides, what she was doing was immoral. She made a temporary commitment to tell Roger everything, knowing they might have to drop the entire transaction. But she feared his judgments and rejection.

After thinking about this for a week, she decided not to tell her husband anything. After all, she told herself, she was only doing this for their common good, so that they could purchase the house they both so desperately wanted. Telling Roger could only hurt him and possibly devastate their marriage.

"Roger's a Type One," she said, "and he has this moralistic, self-righteous streak in him."

Several months into our sessions, when her affair with Jack was well underway, Sarah burst into my office with important news: Jack's dad had suddenly died of a heart attack and his mom would be moving into the assisted living community sooner than Jack had planned. This meant that Sarah and Roger would have to speed up their plans, come up with a significantly larger down payment than they could manage at the moment and make what felt like a premature commitment to purchase the house.

Jack reassured Sarah that he would work with her on the down payment and fees, accepting whatever down payment she and Roger felt comfortable making—as long as she was willing to stick to their deal for the remainder of the six months. He reiterated his distress over his marital situation, his appreciation of her friendship and his hope that she understood his need for a sexual connection with a woman he valued.

At this point Sarah was lying awake many nights debating what she should do. But she went forward with every step necessary to purchase the house. After a 60-day escrow, Sarah and Roger became the owners of their dream home. Jack seemed happy for them, sending flowers and dinner the weekend they moved in.

There was still slightly less than two months left in Sarah's sexual arrangement with Jack and he asked how she felt about keeping the remainder of their bargain. She assured him she would never go back on her word, as she knew Jack would never go back on his. A deal was a deal.

At this point Jack decided that, for the last seven weeks of their time together, he wanted only coffee dates with Sarah—an hour each week to restore their platonic working relationship.

Sarah was grateful to be relieved of the burden of their bargain and the secret keeping. She felt Jack had been a perfect gentleman even during their sexual encounters. She said she would always value him as a friend and as her real estate mentor.

Roger and Sarah continue to live happily in their new home as they work to decorate it. To date, Sarah has chosen never to reveal to her husband the twisted bargain she made, since she believes telling him could only lead to his feeling hurt and betrayed. She loves Roger with all her heart, she says and her last five years with him have been the happiest of her life. She has been able to put her sexual arrangement with Jack in the past and now considers him a family friend. Her strong materialistic and pragmatic values have allowed her to rationalize her profound disloyalty to her husband and consider that the end justifies the means.

The marriage between Sarah and Roger has several factors predictive of success: Their lovemaps are highly compatible and their levels of personal development seem average (with Sarah sometimes unhealthy but committed to significant therapeutic growth). Both share the Self-preservation subtype, and the connecting line between Seven and One allows them to complement each other's energies.

"Foot Fetish"

Jason, 32, a Self-preservation Seven, came to his first session with me struggling to camouflage his extreme anxiety and probable depression. He had two issues: one was his sports bar predicament; the other was a potential lack of acceptance from his fiancée, Rita, 30.

Jason was a natural salesman. His easygoing, slightly disheveled good looks made him highly approachable. He had been in several sales positions (men's sportswear, commercial mortgages, currently advertising space for a radio station) and enjoyed having many irons in the fire.

His biggest iron, at the moment, was a sports bar that he and his best friend, Alex, had sunk every penny they had into creating and hoped to open for business. They had worked nights and weekends to build out the bar, a stage for live music and seating—doing most of the manual labor themselves. Jason reported that both of them were determined to make this venture a huge financial success.

The problem was that it now seemed every penny they had wasn't going to be enough. Each had invested $50,000 (Jason cashing in his 401-K savings to provide his share). Both struggled to economize wherever they could, but they had underestimated many start-up expenses and salaries for the employees during the first several months. Jason and Alex both feared that the project was about to go belly-up.

Jason's stress level was aggravated by pressure from Rita, his fiancée, who was impatient with his spending most of his free time working on the bar and having little left over for her.

First, I recommended that Jason and Alex find a third financial partner—perhaps an older, more established entrepreneur who might be interested in part ownership of a sports bar. Following much brainstorming, Jason finally saw the wisdom of owning one-third of a successful business, as opposed to hanging on to half of a sinking ship. Eventually, they found the perfect partner—the father of Alex's former girlfriend, a wealthy entrepreneur looking for an excuse to get out of the house more frequently. He was willing to invest $75,00 for only 20 percent ownership and apparently had some practical business advice to offer.

Since this new arrangement seemed to be working well, I saw an opportunity to help Jason learn more about his blind spots, the "natural neuroses" of his Type Seven personality. He was able now to see clearly how impatient and at times reckless he is with decision-making, especially when he fears losing some of his options. He loves to buy, do and have—on many levels with many things simultaneously. When his rapid-fire choices are not well calculated, he becomes even more reckless and determined to get what he wants.

By this time, Jason was beginning to see how some of his personality traits were not only getting in his way but also clashing with Rita's. They had been fighting almost daily, with intermittent screaming matches. Jason had previously avoided much discussion about Rita, under the guise of needing to settle the sports bar crisis first. However, since that crisis was now past, it was time to look at the reality with Rita.

Jason feared her judgments and her probable rejection once she found out about a certain aspect of him. He thought I would probably stop seeing him, too, once I learned the truth.

I assured him that I was not in a position to judge and that my only interest was in helping him solve problems, creating understanding and solutions.

Unable to meet my eyes, he addressed the arm of the chair he was sitting in. "I think I have a foot fetish. Looking at women's feet and toes really turns me on. I like naked feet—no socks or shoes—and I love toenail polish. Pretty feet really get me going, give me incredible erections. I look at a lot of them online."

He gave a quick glance in my direction, as if to check my shock level. "I really love Rita—her care and nurturing—but sometimes she just suffocates me, makes too many demands on my time. And she has no idea *why* I like to kiss her toes. I try to tease her, tell her it's because she's a princess and any man would be grateful just to kiss her feet. But I feel like I'm lying to her. I'm afraid she'll throw a fit when she finds out."

"What do you honestly want, Jason?" I said. "Do you want to be single and free from the pressure of Rita's demands? Or would you rather have the comfort and security of her love and the added benefit of her waiting on you?"

Jason wanted it both ways—he hoped Rita would back off and give him more space, but at the same time be constantly there for him.

I explained that a committed relationship would require real compromise, negotiation and collaboration—something he had never done with a partner. Also, if he wanted to be loved for who he truly is, he would need to learn self-disclosure and become more vulnerable with Rita.

During the weeks Jason spent pondering this issue, we also had a number of sessions dealing with his foot fetish. I explained the process of classical conditioning and how he had come to visually associate women's feet with intense sexual arousal (as Pavlov's dogs had salivated to the sound of a bell, having come to associate the sound with their feeding). Jason seemed relieved to hear that his fetish was no more than a conditioned response—and that some of it might even be re-conditioned.

However, he made it clear that he didn't really *want* to "fix" his fetish. This was not why he had come to therapy. His main concern had been his dilemma about the sports bar and he was grateful for my help in resolving that. Now he was troubled about his relationship with Rita, who was already pressuring him for more time together, more commitment, more intimacy. How could he tell her about his foot fetish? He was confused about his own feelings and what he actually wanted from the relationship.

Finally, Jason asked Rita to join him for one of our sessions. "Rita's been badgering me for a long time to let her come in here," he said, once the three of us were gathered in my office. "So here we are, Rita. What do you want from this session?"

Rita, a voluptuous woman with long dark curly hair, appeared gracious and anxious to please. "I was hoping to discuss the future of our relationship," she told him, "if in fact there *is* a future, Jason."

Jason looked as though he wanted to sink into the couch. He suddenly became defensive, pouring out a list of his challenges with the sports bar and accusing Rita of making unreasonable demands on his time.

She listened intently, then asked him to look at his own personality as described in the book I had prepared for him. His Self-preservation Seven type, she pointed out, tended to be impetuous, self-indulgent, highly materialistic, demanding gratification of his own comforts and needs, reckless at times and attempting to cover too many bases at once. But she was fair in also listing the qualities that made her love him: his ambition, determination, independence and high energy, as well as his ability to be practical and reach his goals.

Now it was time to discuss Rita's personality. She had wanted to take the C-JES survey, which Jason kept forgetting to mention to me. Certain from her reading that she was a Sexual subtype and that Jason was "one hundred percent Self-preservation," she turned to me with a question: "Is there anything you can do, Mona, to make Jason less self-centered?"

Jason flushed. "I didn't invite you here to do a bitch session," he said. "There's some important information about myself that I need to give you."

Rita was silent, looking at him expectantly.

"I have a foot fetish," he blurted out. "I enjoy it very much and I'm afraid you won't be able to understand it or accept it. That's why I always tease you about your cute toes and say I'd rather give you a toe job than have you give me a blow job." He attempted a laugh.

Rita's eyes filled with tears and she was speechless for a long moment.

"I'm so sorry that you've held all this inside," she said finally. "I can't imagine the embarrassment you must have felt. Why didn't you tell me sooner? Of course I accept you. I love you, Jason. It's okay that you're fixated on feet—how is that any different from big boobs or long legs? It seems like most guys have some kind of fetish."

Jason, obviously relieved, seemed to be fighting back a few tears of his own. "I just want you to *think* about it," he said.

Rita's response was to become more caring, more possessive, more protective and significantly more seductive with Jason—all common responses for her Type Two personality.

However, over our next few sessions, Jason became more distant and critical of Rita. Though grateful for her acceptance, he found her excessive favors and attention smothering and confining. Aware that she wanted more intimacy from the relationship than he did, Jason knew he was in no position to remain engaged or to think about marriage.

Eventually, he decided to end the engagement. He knew this would break Rita's heart and he felt especially guilty since she had been so accepting of his foot fetish. But it seemed only fair to her to end the relationship sooner rather than later. He wanted to present the reasons for his decision in a joint session with me, so that I could help him explain to her their differences and incompatibilities.

When we did this, Rita was crushed but also appreciative that Jason hadn't strung her along. She saw the situation clearly. "Once again, Jason, you've bitten off more than you can chew. Our relationship isn't all that different from your situation with the sports bar."

They agreed to part friends.

I still counsel Jason periodically on certain issues and have been pleased to see him grow in self-awareness and insight into his natural blind spots.

In summary, the most important elements for predicting relationship success were actually not in place in Jason and Rita's relationship. Their lovemaps had major areas of incompatibility; neither of them had their expectations for an ideal mate satisfied by the other. Both had average to unhealthy levels of development (especially Jason). They had different subtypes (his Self-preservation versus her Sexual) and they lacked a connecting line that would have allowed them to complement one another's differences. The only structural factor they had for relationship success was sharing the same Harmonic Group—the "Positive Outlook" Group (composed of Nines, Sevens and Twos). Their shared optimism was, no doubt, a strong point of attraction in the beginning and it was also the note on which their relationship ended in my office.

Sarah and Jason as Self-preservation Sevens

Both Sarah and Jason are highly materialistic and preoccupied with

Self-preservation issues. In Sarah's case, her need to purchase her dream house at an affordable price allowed her to rationalize deceiving her husband about the adulterous liaison that made the ownership possible. Although she assumed that her husband's desire for the house was as great as her own, her failure to either discuss the issue with him before accepting Jack's sexual proposition or disclose it afterward suggests an underlying awareness that her actions would probably have seriously damaged their relationship.

Jason's primary focus on making the sports bar a going concern reveals his preoccupation with financial security. His relationship with his fiancée was clearly of secondary importance in his life and the foot fetish that worried him was actually a minor issue compared with his inability to commit to intimacy on a deep level. It was probably a wise decision to break the engagement, given their incompatible temperaments.

Sevens with the Sexual Subtype

Sevens with a Sexual subtype, whom Ichazo associates with "suggestibility," are enthusiastic about new experiences—continually seeking new romantic partners and enjoying new ideas. They often have powerful imaginations, which they use to the fullest. Fascinated by their own flights into imagination as well as their fantasies about other people, Sexual Sevens can easily grow bored and often find it difficult to sustain commitments in love relationships or in work.

"Cybersex"

Lacy, 28, knew she was a "Sexual subtype and one hell of a Seven" as a result of a lecture she'd heard in one of my classes and some reading I had suggested about eight years prior to her decision to come in for therapy.

"I'm in big emotional trouble, Mona," she told me, "and I don't know what to do.

"I enjoy life, adventure, new challenges," she continued. "I enjoy trying almost anything new. I love men, fantasies, travel, taking risks, pushing the envelope. Now, I'm deeply in love with two men and I can't even *think* of giving up either one. Help!"

Her green eyes filled with tears and her svelte little body collapsed on my couch.

I asked her to tell me more about the two men.

The first was her fiancé of three years, Brett, 32, who was committed and loyal to her. He was proud of his expanding dental practice, had bought her a big diamond and was ready to settle down with her and start a family. Her family and friends adored him.

"I think he's a Five," she said, "and that poses a little bit of a problem, with his withdrawn nature and lack of risk-taking. But he's healthy and mature—more than I am. I'm sure he's a Sexual subtype, like me, because of our incredible, intense connection."

She laughed. "I can see you're wondering, Mona: What is this woman's problem? Well, it's the other man—my Internet love affair—Zeke. I've fallen deeply in love over the past four months— quite by accident and all by e-mail, Instant Messaging and sending pictures—with a man I've never even met. Zeke lives in Florida, as it turns out and even though he's only 18, he's exceptionally mature. He knows everything there is to know about sex and women.

"We got connected through an Internet computer game where Zeke and I were both participants. We began personal side talks and he just mesmerized me with his seductive insights and ideas for male-female connections. He had me orgasming the first time we exchanged Instant Messages—by asking me to participate in an experiment he was conducting for his sociology class at college. He made me feel so happy, so exhilarated to be a woman, so enticed by the thrill of it all—and all this without ever leaving my computer! Can you believe that?"

I encouraged Lacy to explain more.

Recently, the intense sexual feelings she had toward young Zeke and her ability to have multiple orgasms almost daily had put a serious damper on her sex life with Brett. Brett was beginning to feel her pulling away, appearing distracted, needing too much time alone for her computer games. Instead of spending five or six nights a week at his home (where she essentially lived), she was now spending only one or two. Brett began asking pointed questions about whether she had found another man. Impatient with her phony excuses for being busy, he requested they seek counseling.

Lacy had promised Brett that, once she got her own head straightened out, she would do whatever joint counseling was appropriate. He reluctantly agreed to this timetable.

Captivated, infatuated with the notion of a younger man who might be more of a soul mate than her tried-and-true fiancé, Lacy was now considering a trip to Florida to meet Zeke in person.

I pointed out that securing more information about Zeke could only be an asset. Instead of flying to Florida, I suggested some more rational and less expensive preliminary steps.

First, I suggested that she come clean with Zeke—tell him that their cybersex had become a serious threat to her engagement to Brett. She had mentioned Brett to Zeke but had failed to communicate the extent of their commitment for fear that her engagement would be a turn-off for Zeke.

Second, I thought it would be a good idea for her to begin speaking with Zeke by phone, since their real voices would inject at least some element of reality into their conversations. Even though they had e-mailed pictures to one another, all their connections so far had technically been through cyberspace.

Third, I suggested that, if they still found it important to meet in person, they fly to a neutral city—perhaps midway between California and Florida—just for the day, to see if any real chemistry existed outside of cyberspace.

When Lacy told me that Zeke hated all my "stupid ideas" and refused to talk by phone, I pointed out what a red flag this might be. However, I encouraged Lacy to hang in there and communicate her whole truth to Zeke, which she did.

Within a week everything changed. Zeke panicked at the possibility of Lacy actually phoning him. Feeling guilty over possibly contributing to the breakup of her engagement, he decided to come clean also: He was actually 68, not 18, a paraplegic and a professional writer of pornography.

He admitted his delight at being able to make Lacy orgasm so intensely and frequently. As a pornographer, he knew all the right verbal buttons to push. The pictures he e-mailed were actually those of his handsome 18-year-old grandson. He apologized to Lacy and said he would honor her request never to contact her again.

Lacy's response to Zeke's confession was floods of tears— triggered by relief and a sense of closure as well as profound embarrassment at having been duped. She recognized her own complicity in what had happened: she had been seduced through her own hunger for thrilling fantasies.

The shock of her realization set the stage for in-depth work on her self-awareness and she became more conscious of her natural neuroses and the blind spots typical of the Sexual Seven's psychic structure. She was able at this point to see her own history in a fresh perspective. Continually resisting commitment and recklessly seeking thrills, she had dropped out of college in her second year to pursue her dream of becoming an acrobat, spending over two years with a circus group. This career possibility ended abruptly when she seriously injured her ankle.

After her recovery, she worked for nearly three years as a tour guide in Asia and Africa, where she contracted a life-threatening virus that brought her back to the U.S., where she lived with her parents while rebuilding her health. Finally recovered at 25, she found a position as a travel agent and met Brett on a blind date. Now, with her sexual fantasy of Zeke crashing to earth, she was ready to move toward greater psychological health and restrain herself from recklessly following her impulses.

In the meantime, Brett was becoming more insistent that they begin some joint sessions. Lacy agreed and decided to share with him the "Internet hang-up" that had caused her "to doubt marriage, to doubt commitment to one person." She chose never to share the sexual aspect of her connection with Zeke, but acknowledged her involvement with the iconoclastic theories of an older gentleman, a person from one of her games that she no longer had any contact with.

Brett asked many questions and struggled to put it all together. Eventually, he felt Lacy's energy returning to their relationship. She was now more appreciative of him, more grateful for his love and devotion, more committed to the journey into higher consciousness and personal development.

We ultimately did numerous premarital counseling sessions to resolve typical issues such as in-laws, spending habits, expectations for childrearing and religious differences. Following many bumps in the road, Lacy and Brett were far more prepared to embark on a realistic and grounded journey into marriage.

By now, Lacy had resolved many of her old tendencies—such as living in fantasy or denial, extreme thrill seeking, fascination with glitzy future possibilities, fear of commitment and fickleness. Through the therapeutic process she became more discerning and mature in her choices.

Using our Five Factors for predicting relationship success, Brett and Lacy have four of the five, a strong foundation. First and most important, their lovemaps are highly compatible. Second, Brett is exceptionally healthy and Lacy (who had dropped from average to sometimes unhealthy in her psychological development) is successfully striving for healthier levels. Third, they are fortunate to share the Sexual subtype—both craving strong one-on-one intensity. Finally, they are connected by the complementary line between Seven and Five, which allows them to balance one other's differences.

I feel certain that Brett will provide a sense of grounded, logical and less impulsive decision-making for Lacy, while she will add adventure, creative approaches to life and a zest for living to his experience.

"Double Trouble"

Garth, 65, an intense, energetic Sexual Seven, came to me enraged over the ultimatum presented by his fourth wife, Sondra, 46. A man who enjoys gambling on horse races, card games and sporting events, Garth is protective of his personal freedom, which he defines as the ability to do and have exactly what he wants when he wants it.

Garth and Sondra (who we later discovered is also a Sexual Seven) had been married for four years, traveling throughout

Europe and Asia, seeing and betting on the finest thoroughbred horse races in the world. Each of them had considerable wealth and was financially independent.

"That's the only way I could stand to be married," Garth told me, "if the woman has her own money and never tries to tell me what to do with mine. I've lost many millions, won or earned back many millions.

"Sondra's different—divorced once with no kids, never worked a day in her life, a trust-fund baby whose parents are deceased. She has one brother whom she hasn't spoken to in ten years. She's a fun gal, always up, ready to roll—just like me. We both love horse racing—she's owned many show horses and racehorses. Me, I just love the betting part.

"But here's the problem, " Garth continued. Now she's trying to clip my wings—she's given me an ultimatum about not going on a trip with two of my single buddies to the south of France for a week. It's a private resort with nude beaches, nude women and pretty liberal use of cocaine and other drugs. I invited her to go along, but she says absolutely not—not with my two buddies, who she feels are uncouth. Okay, I can accept that. But when she says I'm not going either, that really gets my back up.

"The cocaine isn't the problem here—I've tried it several times in the past, but she trusts me not to do any more drugs. What she objects to is the women. She's afraid I'll get seduced into some crazy sexual escapade—and I just might! I'd love to have her there with me—I'd rather have sex with her—but since she won't go, I've promised to use condoms a hundred percent of the time. Which only makes her more furious."

He shook his head. "I feel I'm entitled to sexual experiences of my choice. I was raised in poverty, in the Chicago ghettos. Now that I've earned my way out, I plan to live my life to the fullest for as long as I can.

"When Sondra and I met, I explained this to her up front and she seemed delighted. We've had a fantastic life together, including a great sex life. I'm basically a monogamous guy and only want to do some crazy, out-of-bounds stuff once in a great while. The way I see it, I've earned my freedom. I've divorced and paid for three ex-wives to get them off my back. Now I'm asking this one to just get off my back voluntarily. Please make her understand, Mona—I need my options and she's starting to get on my nerves. If she's going to start issuing ultimatums about what I can and can't do, then we'll have to reconsider the whole marriage."

I asked Garth how he would feel if Sondra agreed that he could go on his trip with his two friends—in fact he could go anywhere he wanted—with only one restriction. That is that he could have no form of sexual contact with anyone other than her. It was clear to me that Sondra's ultimate boundary concerned monogamy with Garth.

After a moment of silence, he said, "Okay, I'll try not to screw other women—I haven't yet—but you need to let Sondra know it's all about my freedom. I'm willing to give her the same freedom."

Sondra joined Garth for our second session. She is a beautiful, independent, high-spirited woman with great energy. She acknowledged that Garth had earned his wealth the hard way, while she had inherited hers.

"I love Garth's spirit," she said, "his curiosity, his wit, his charm, his great imagination. I love all the exciting things we do and constantly plan for in the future. And I'm willing to try almost anything sexually with him, so long as he keeps our monogamous marriage commitment. We're both daredevils who enjoy thrill seeking—like having sex in a limo, on top of a huge Ferris wheel or on the Eiffel Tower. Isn't that enough?"

There was obviously a great commonality of personality traits and values here. In the cozy space of my office it seemed as if their intense energies might actually combust at any moment.

At my insistence, they studied their personality survey results and tried to understand the implications of their both being Sexual Sevens. Now they became a bit more serious, reflecting on their motives and blind spots. Double fun, yes—but also double trouble, since neither of them was committed to actual growth, to becoming healthier within their own structure.

At one point Sondra compared the Enneagram to palm reading and astrology as her feelings of resentment over being "boxed in as a type" emerged. Like Garth, she insisted on having her freedom—

which, to her, meant being in charge, writing her own rules, deciding *if* and *when* she would make any changes in herself. Any changes she made would not come from me—and certainly not from Garth. In her own way, Sondra was more rigid than her husband.

They both agreed that he could go on his week's venture to Europe with his two buddies, but he would not touch any other woman sexually.

He ended up having a great time on the trip—drinking too much, getting involved in a couple of experiments with drugs and participating in several lap dances from the available women. He felt he technically kept his agreement with Sondra, since his hands never touched any of them.

Sondra seemed to accept Garth's version of honoring their bargain, but she felt increasingly irritated by his need, at age 65, to continually push the limits.

"He's so self-centered, so narcissistic at times, I could scream," she said.

They went on several trips to Africa and Asia at this point and I didn't see them in therapy for about six months. Then one day Garth called, obviously enraged and insisted on seeing me that very day.

When he appeared at 10 p.m. that night for our session, it became clear why he was, once again, filing for divorce. For the first time—the only time in his life—a wife had cheated on *him*. He had accidentally discovered a love letter acknowledging the sexual liaison that Sondra had established with one of the young horse owners they had met at several of the races.

"To think, " Garth said, "she had the nerve to forbid me to party with prostitutes in France, which I didn't do because of her! Now she's the one who's having an illicit affair, with a 33-year-old stud!

"It's a good thing we never co-mingled our finances," he went on, "because I'd leave her without a penny. This way, I'll just get a simple divorce, with no contest. I don't know if I'll ever see her again, but I will miss her as a traveling companion."

As the session went on, he became more philosophical. "Mona, I wish I'd taken some of your suggestions for my own growth and development more seriously. It's all such a shame, isn't it? Especially our drinking. Sondra claimed she was drunk when she hooked up with that young man.

"We've talked so much about avoiding pain," he continued. "Now it feels like we're both stuck in more pain than ever."

Looking at our Five Factors for predicting relationship success, Garth and Sondra suffered several major problems. They were both aware of the superficial aspects of their lovemap connections, but neither of them had ever thought seriously about the characteristics they actually desired in a mate. Essentially, they were so caught up in what they had in common that they failed to see what was missing—both in themselves and in their mate. This is not uncommon when partners are the same Enneagam type.

When the partners are exceptionally healthy, the enjoyment of a harmonious worldview can be a delight. But for couples who are average in their personality development and especially for those who are unhealthy, being the same type can aggravate dysfunctional behavior. This was the case with Garth and Sondra, whose mutual blind spots and natural neuroses were made worse by their partner's validation. Choosing a partner "just like me" served in this case to intensify their mutual narcissism.

In psychological health, both Garth and Sondra were sometimes at average levels and often at low levels. As a result, they lacked the ability to perceive themselves and each other accurately and grow toward greater awareness and integration.

Being of the same Sexual Seven type, they had no possibility of a structural balancing of one another's energies through a connecting interior line on the Enneagram diagram. Had one of them been a Type One or a Type Five, they would have lost some of their compatibility but would have benefited from the different perspective that an opposing energy tends to provide, counter-balancing one another's blind spots.

Being the same Sexual subtype was in some ways an advantage for this couple, since it gave Garth and Sondra similar outlooks and areas of interest. However, both of them being less-than-healthy Sexual subtypes, in addition to being the same Enneagram type, allowed them to ignore some troubling blind spots.

Another seeming plus for this marriage was Garth and Sondra automatically being in the same Harmonic triad—the Positive

Outlook group—which allowed them to reinforce each other's tendencies to stay upbeat, happy and excited. On closer inspection, however, this similarity also had its down side, in that it kept both partners from being forced to increase their tolerance for pain and frustration (which might have encouraged them to increase their level of personal consciousness and, ultimately, of psychological health).

While proceeding with the divorce, Garth remained in individual therapy for about eight more months, resolving some of his reckless risk-taking and becoming more aware of his self-centered blind spots. Although he considered calling Sondra to see if she was up to going on a few trips with him, he never actually spoke to her again as long as he was in contact with me.

Lacy and Garth as Sexual Sevens

The intensity, suggestibility and enthusiasm for new adventures in relationship that are hallmarks of the Sexual Seven are clearly visible in the personalities of both Lacy and Garth, as well as in Garth's wife, Sondra. Lacy, being naïve as well as highly suggestible, was easily seduced via the Internet by a pornographer who misrepresented himself. She quickly decided, on the basis of her avid responses to his sexual come-ons, that she was in love with him and could not bring herself to tell her loyal fiancé what had happened. Fortunately, she sought counseling and the truth about her Internet lover (whom she never actually met) was revealed.

Garth and his wife Sondra, both Sexual Sevens, bonded primarily through their support of one other's adventurousness and risk-taking, although Sondra's insistence on maintaining a monogamous marriage caused some conflicts between them. Ironically, it was she who, on impulse, became involved in an adulterous affair that precipitated the end of the marriage. Both Garth and Sondra were inexperienced in curbing their appetite for whatever looked enticing at the moment. Sharing both the same Enneagram type and the Sexual subtype made it especially difficult for this couple to gain the perspective they needed to avoid rushing heedlessly into whatever adventures presented themselves.

Sevens with the Social Subtype

Social Sevens, the subtype that Ichazo associates with "social sacrifice," feel a particular tension between their ideals and their need to be free from the responsibilities their ideals impose. They attempt to be conscientious about their responsibilities but then become resentful about having their options curtailed. Sevens with this subtype can resemble Ones (Seven's stress point) in their dutiful behavior toward others.

"Vietnam Revisited"

Haley, 52, a Social Seven, came to her first appointment with marked anxiety and resentment. Her recent conflict with Kirk, 58, her beloved husband of 27 years—and father of their two college-age daughters, was unbearable.

"It's affected our sex life," she told me, "and our ability to talk freely and frankly with one another. We're generally very open. I think Kirk and I have a healthy marriage, but this dilemma has my head spinning."

Haley appeared to be quick-witted, bright and impatient with details. Having a big heart that naturally reaches out to worthy causes, she was involved in a number of volunteer efforts with idealistic socio-political groups. Her most important commitment was to a grass-roots organization recently established to assist all veterans—from Iraq and Afghanistan to Vietnam—in getting high quality health care.

Kirk had also been deeply invested in supporting this organization. "His heart still aches for several of his closest buddies who were killed during their years in Vietnam," Haley told me. "He's never gotten over that." She herself had also suffered deep anguish when her older brother was killed in Vietnam.

"That's why we agreed to devote so much of our resources—time, money and energy—to building this program, especially since our two girls have been away at college and graduate school. I must say we've done a great job. I've been able to attract many top-notch professionals who are willing to serve as part of the network, free of charge, once a month. I've traveled to eleven other cities and helped the start-up people get new programs rolling. But now I'm worn out and I'd like to shift my focus, without totally abandoning the network."

She sighed. "When I explained that I'd like to gradually get back to some of my other interests, such as portrait photography, my Women's Club—which I've neglected for two years and animal rescue, Kirk acted as if I had done something criminal. He went into the biggest shame-and-blame routine you can imagine. I was in shock. This is so out-of-character for Kirk—he's never done anything like this before. He truly believes I'm abandoning our agreements and turning my back on the most important cause that we as a couple have ever committed our resources to."

Haley went on to describe Kirk's flood of tears over what he perceived as her betrayal. She held him and reassured him that she would remain as the head organizational consultant, but his upset wasn't fully resolved and she was hoping he might benefit from some joint counseling sessions.

Having attended several Enneagram seminars, she knew she was a Social Seven. Kirk had never shown much interest in the Enneagram, but she thought he might be a healthy Two or perhaps a Three.

He was anxious to attend a joint session with Haley, she told me, because "he knows things don't feel right and he doesn't want to screw up almost 28 years of a great relationship, including a good sex life."

Kirk brought to our first joint session the personality survey that Haley had taken home for him. He was now extremely interested in the system and ultimately agreed with his Type Two results. Uncertain at first whether he is a Sexual or a Social subtype, he eventually settled on the Sexual. Something in the analysis of his Type Two traits triggered an avalanche of previously pent-up emotion, repressed political rage, hurt and despair over the loss of his soldier friends in Vietnam.

I worked for several months alone with Kirk, after both he and Haley were satisfied that his intense reactions were not really a marriage issue. Kirk had been repressing many aspects of his true feelings over Vietnam, specifically over the loss of six close friends who were in his army unit. Our sessions helped him resolve this repressed Post Traumatic Stress Disorder and set the stage for allowing his basically healthy relationship with Haley to become even stronger.

When Kirk later read about Haley's Social Seven personality structure, he apologized for projecting his Vietnam rage onto her and for becoming so irrational about her desire to get back to some of her other interests. He came to understand how important having options is for Sevens. More importantly, he realized that he was the one who had been trapped—in his own unexpressed anger, grief and despair.

What had always been an excellent marriage now became even better. In the course of our counseling sessions, Haley and Kirk became more conscious of one another's desires and motives. Both continue to work with the Veterans Network and they share a deeper level of compassion and empathy for each other and for the veterans they are committed to helping.

In terms of our Five Factors for predicting relationship success, Haley and Kirk have extremely compatible lovemaps and exceptionally healthy levels of personal development.

Both are mature and consistently reaching for greater levels of growth and self-actualization. As a healthy Two, Kirk wanted to give of himself and his resources for the benefit of others. Haley shared a similar altruism. As a healthy Seven, she became fulfilled and joyful—nourished not by material objects or adventures but through her selfless contributions.

Another factor contributing to their successful marriage is sharing the same Harmonic Group—the "Positive Outlook" Group composed of Nines, Twos and Sevens.

In some ways this was a simple case, but extremely satisfying for both Haley and Kirk as well as for me—primarily thanks to their high levels of health and their willingness to keep growing through confronting their differences in a spirit of love and compassion.

"*Commitment Phobic*"

Mason, 37, a tall, dark and handsome Social Seven, walked into my office looking as if he'd just completed a photo shoot for GQ magazine. His energy was engaging, fast-paced and impatient.

"I hate being an attorney," he told me, "as much as I hate being someone's fiancé—all this corporate B.S. and endless details. I don't know what I'd do without my paralegals. The whole setup makes me feel boxed in—like I can never be *really free* to pursue my interests in deep sea diving, parachuting, skiing, fishing and working for the Big Brothers organization."

He soon got to the reason for his visit: "I just broke off my fourth engagement, to the most beautiful, intelligent, wonderful girl in the universe. Any guy would be so proud to marry her, to even know her."

Nicole, 34, was everything he would ever want in a wife—if and when he could say that he *wanted* a wife! Women kept telling him he was "commitment phobic."

Mason was fascinated with the Enneagram and had researched my background as a certified Enneagram teacher prior to making an appointment. His third fiancée had thrown an Enneagram book at him at the time of their breakup, advising him to look at the chapter on Sevens. He had read and reread that chapter and announced his type to me at our first meeting. No need to take any personality survey, he said—he was definitely a Seven. The only question was whether his subtype was Self-preservation or Social. He believed his fourth fiancée, Nicole, was a healthy One with a Social subtype.

The more Mason and I talked, the clearer his Social subtype structure became. He felt reliant on the approval and sense of belonging he got from various groups—his fishing and scuba-diving buddies, a group of fellow attorneys he liked and his high-risk pilot and skydiving buddies.

He also had connections with various social organizations. For several years he had worked with Big Brothers and was committed to the idea of men supporting "little brothers" who had been deprived of a male role model.

Later, as we discussed his family background, the reason for his identification with these fatherless young boys became evident. Mason's mother had died suddenly of brain cancer when he was two years old and his father, although devoted to Mason, had remained in untreated depression, probably to this day.

"My dad's now 67," Mason said. "He's been divorced four times and still isn't over my mom. He can still cry just looking at her picture. He says no anti-depressant or therapist can ever bring her back and that's true. I don't ever want to allow myself to love a woman the way he loved my mom. I never want my life to be limited the way his has been."

Yet Mason felt enormous social pressure to marry and have a family. Every time he fell in love with another beautiful woman, he would become close to her parents, especially her mother. Then, remembering his father's experience, he would sense the danger involved in trusting one woman with his heart.

"It's beginning to feel really crazy," he said. "But I tell myself that it's *my time, my future*—whatever I do with *my life* is up to me. Right? I can't imagine restricting my life to only one woman—entrusting my whole heart and happiness to this *one* other person."

I agreed with Mason that we are each free to make our own choices about the way we use our time and our life. We had several long discussions about free will and how people make decisions. I commented that free will isn't really free for most of us—that people have traumas and experiences, especially from childhood, that unconsciously and sometimes severely limit how they are able to see things. We are often the prisoners of our history without realizing it.

Mason described his childhood, following his mother's death, including the unhappy experiences both he and his father had with the women who became his stepmothers. Mason described how each of these women had tried to use his father for her own purposes. None had seen his dad for the man he really was and none had been willing to honor his mother's memory by allowing the few pictures and mementoes of her that his father wanted to keep around the house.

"Women can be so stupid, so blind and possessive," he said. "I actually don't like—and certainly don't trust—most women."

He proceeded to tell me why, describing each of his stepmothers. The first was a gold-digger who sponged off his father and ignored Mason. The second was an overbearing woman whose two hellion daughters pushed Mason down the stairs, seriously injuring him. The third was a woman who lied about her financial difficulties and manipulated his father into responsibility for her debts. The fourth was an adulteress who was discovered by the father in bed with his best friend.

Since his father's fourth divorce, two years earlier, Mason had spent a lot of time with him. In the process, Nicole and his father had become close. Mason's breaking his engagement with her devastated them both.

"I don't want to get married," he said, "but I carry this feeling of guilt and . . . well, *shame* that I can't step up to the plate and make a marriage commitment. Am I somehow defective? Most of my friends are married or getting married. A few are already divorced and on number two.

"At this point my self-esteem is really shaky. Maybe I am a freak. Will I have greater confidence, self-worth and happiness in life if I hold to my own convictions and instincts to never marry? Or would it be better to give in to the social pressure and take the big step? Please help me figure this out."

In subsequent sessions we explored in depth Mason's background—why he had come to feel the way he does. His level of self-awareness and grasp of reality were actually quite high. We went into the possibilities for change—and what, if any, changes he might be interested in making. As it turned out, there weren't many, except for the shoring up of his self-esteem. He simply needed to release and/or reframe his guilt and shame over not wanting to be married.

I assured Mason that not everyone was cut out for marriage and that the institution obviously didn't suit everyone. In fact, there is a minority of people who are better off never being married. Perhaps he was one of them.

There was considerable relief on Mason's face as he realized I was not about to give him a sales pitch for marriage. He brought up several problems, such as his second fiancée accusing him of being gay when he broke up with her. But he never for a moment doubted his heterosexual orientation, which was confirmed by several of his gay male friends.

We spoke about the deepest fears of the Seven—loss of options, entrapment, being stuck (especially in pain), lacking the freedom to do/be/have whatever he wants. Mason concluded that the commitment of a lifelong marriage was the opposite of what he desired. What made him feel especially good was his "freedom to be free."

He was beginning to understand that being different from his peers and associates was not the same as being a "freak." He could live his life in full integrity—being clear about who he is and what his intentions are—while still being different.

His intentions were to remain a lifelong bachelor and to never father his own children (although he loved his friends' children and remained available to baby-sit them as well as continuing his work as a "big brother"). He intended to have warm, close, sometimes sexual relationships with women—but with the understanding that this would not lead to marriage.

Mason seemed to gain in self-esteem as we role-played various scenarios that would invariably come up with women. His emotional posture and aura of impatience greatly improved as he role-played the woman's part. At other times he played himself while I threw him a few curve balls as the female in the scenario.

I suggested that he might consider a vasectomy, since he was so resolute about not wanting children. The circumstances of a potential unwanted pregnancy would likely produce more anxiety in Mason than the minor pain and inconvenience of a vasectomy, I said. He acted on this within a few weeks.

Near the end of his therapy Mason requested a joint session with his dad and Nicole. He felt he owed the two of them, more than anyone, a full explanation of his decisions and intentions.

His father and Nicole showed up for the session together, both open and curious. First, Mason expressed how much he loved them both and how much he hoped they would keep up their "father-daughter connection," even though he and Nicole would not be getting married. Both seemed relieved and expressed their intention to do just that.

After summarizing his intentions to never marry or have children, Mason made a proposal to Nicole. Since she was everything any man could ever want, he would be happy to have her as his most frequent date and even as a monogamous sexual partner.

Nicole declined, but with love in her eyes. She was happy that Mason had come to terms with himself, but her intention was to marry and have children. They would remain friends and would probably see one another through his dad.

In terms of our Five Factors, I can see several elements in favor of a potentially successful relationship between Nicole and Mason: her high level of psychological health, his willingness to become healthier, their shared Social subtype and the complementary line balancing energies between One and Seven.

However, the strongest variable of all—their lovemaps—was not in their favor. Nicole's lovemap required a mate who sincerely desired a healthy marriage and family. Mason's lovemap had been so "vandalized" by previous women in his life that he was unwilling to entrust his heart and happiness to any individual woman. In addition, the "natural neuroses" of his Type Seven personality compelled him to keep his options open, to avoid becoming trapped so that one woman could never hurt him as much as his mother's death had hurt his dad.

Mason encouraged his father to enter therapy to resolve his long-term depression. I hope he will, but he has not taken any action in this direction, to date.

Haley and Mason as Social Sevens

Both Haley and Mason have struggled with the "social sacrifice" issue that is common to Sevens with a Social subtype. Both clearly felt pressures to behave in ways that validated the ideals of groups they valued. Haley felt a strong attraction to working with groups dedicated to social causes and she was deeply committed to the volunteer work she and her husband had done for veterans. But her desire, common in Sevens, to explore other options led to a conflict within her marriage, in that it brought up repressed material from her husband's experiences in Vietnam. Once his PTSD issues were resolved, their marriage resumed its former healthy footing.

Mason's traumatic experiences with his mother's early death, his father's subsequent depression and his childhood experiences with a series of unhealthy stepmothers made him reluctant to commit to marriage, despite social pressure from friends and associates. Committed to volunteer work involved with fatherless boys, he was still unwilling to risk having a family of his own. Through therapy, he came to accept his need to remain a lifelong bachelor and to restore his eroded self-esteem through reframing his choice as a valid and honorable one.

Strengths of Sevens in Intimate Relationships

- Enthusiasm
- Sociability
- Practicality
- Productivity
- Spontaneity
- Imagination
- Cheerfulness
- Versatility

Limitations of Sevens in Intimate Relationships

- Lack of Discipline
- Impulsiveness
- Unreliability
- Pain Avoidance
- Self-Centeredness
- Hyperactivity
- Self-Indulgence
- Impatience

Defense Mechanisms of Sevens

Because many Sevens felt deprived of nurturing as children, they assign a high priority to providing this nurturing for themselves. The psychological defense mechanism of *rationalization* allows them to justify their sense of urgency about seeking pleasure and avoiding pain. Rationalization involves reframing—putting a positive spin on—questionable or even immoral actions that support their accumulation of resources such as houses and money (primarily in Self-preservation subtypes such as Sarah and Jason), their craving for sexual adventure (primarily in Sexual subtypes such as Lacy and Garth) or their struggle to maintain a variety of pleasurable options while keeping the approval of their community (primarily in Social subtypes such as Haley and Mason).

In each of these cases, we see Sevens attempting to squelch their underlying fear of being limited, frustrated or in pain with no options for escape. "Don't Fence Me In" could be their theme song. Reframing everything from adultery to commitment phobia allows them to absolve themselves of responsibility for their actions and turn a blind eye to the pain they cause others in their futile attempts to finally fill up the bottomless pit of their craving.

The "Natural Neuroses" of Sevens

Sevens generally have a low tolerance for pain and frustration and they strive to avoid anything unpleasant while actively seeking pleasure. They often have issues around freedom and maintaining a variety of options. They are skillful at making excuses for things they don't want to do and may strategize to avoid or abandon tasks that threaten to become boring or difficult. Their fear of potential pain or frustration may lead them to make detours that ultimately cause them more discomfort than they would have suffered through confronting the original problem.

So determined are they to keep their energy high and their attitude positive that they may indulge in substances that help them maintain these states of mind. Many Sevens subscribe to the philosophy: "I want what I want when I want it." When the immediate gratification of their needs is frustrated, they may explode in temper tantrums.

Sevens, of course, are not the only personality type with distinctive "hot buttons." Their hyper-alertness to pain has parallels in Sixes' hyper-alertness to danger, Twos' hyper-alertness to not being needed and Threes' hyper-alertness to anything that might detract from their successful image.

How Sevens Blossom in Good Relationships

In healthy relationships, Sevens are like cheerleaders who provide constant motivation and excitement. More than any other type, Sevens are inclined to understand and practice a "win-win" philosophy.

Good relationships help Sevens realize the importance of firm boundaries, which they come to see not just as limitations on their life. Along with this realization comes an awareness of the value of self-discipline, setting goals and following through on commitments.

One of the most important things Sevens gain from a healthy marriage is learning to trust another person, as Harley came to trust Kirk over the course of their 27-year marriage. This trust in the partner's good will and support is invaluable in resolving the conflicts every couple faces from time to time. In a healthy relationship Sevens learn to be more emotionally poised, patient and prudent. They also learn that boundless self-gratification is not always a positive thing. The key to their personal development in this area is their confidence that their partner understands their fears of confinement and will support their maintaining options that are important to them. In Harley and Kirk's relationship, his being a Two—a type with natural inclinations toward nurturing—is a great plus for a Seven—who might be especially inclined to feel insufficiently nurtured in early life.

Once Sevens feel secure in the love of a mate whom they love and respect, they can tap into the joyful spirit that is the essence of their nature. Having moved beyond the sense that pleasure can be achieved only through having or doing *more*, they radiate a primal joy and gratitude that inspires all who cross their path.

TYPE EIGHT: THE CHALLENGER IN LOVE

Eights are one of the easier Enneagram types to identify because they are often aggressive, comfortable with confrontation and apparently spoiling for a fight. They are part of the Enneagram group associated with gut impulses and will (Eights, Nines and Ones). While Nines retreat from an overt contest of wills and Ones turn their wills inward to compulsive self-discipline, Eights direct their wills outward in a full-bore attempt to impose their desires on the world. The thought of being vulnerable and subject to someone else's domination is an Eight's worst nightmare.

Average Eights can be confrontational, intimidating, excessive and crude. From their point of view, their stance of intimidation is an acid test of the people they meet, and those who fail to stand up to them lose their respect. The Eight's power game is played for keeps because most Eights have an underlying fear of annihilation. In addition to their formidable wills, Eights have prodigious appetites: for sex, money, power, sometimes alcohol and other addictive substances.

Healthy Eights are archetypal leaders—magnanimous, passionate, energetic and effective. The great virtue of Eights is that they are ready, willing and eager to take action. Perhaps because they remember their own vulnerability as children, they are often protectors of the weak, willing to put themselves at risk to correct injustices. Eights are *out there*—ready to put themselves on the line physically, taking risks, starting businesses, blazing trails. We depend on them to be our pioneers, entrepreneurs and explorers.

Unhealthy Eights often appear violent, abusive, ruthless and vengeful. Their natural strength—a willingness and ability to take action—can turn into a horrifying defect when the action is powered by vengeance or expressed in physical violence.

Their extraordinary energy—often the key to Eights' immense success—can also be the key to their spectacular failures when they lose control of it. Unhealthy Eights, having no conscience about bullying and overwhelming others, may exhibit sociopathic tendencies.

Eights with the Self-preservation Subtype

Eights with the Self-preservation subtype are preoccupied, in Oscar Ichazo's words, with "satisfactory survival." Individuals of this subtype are more materialistic than others. At an average level of psychological health, they tend to be highly competitive and attempt to amass money, property and power for themselves and their families. Although they have an Eight's lustiness, they are less emotionally volatile than the other subtypes, more prone to scheming than to screaming. Since Self-preservation Eights' sense of personal security comes from their ability to control their material resources—as well as the people in their life—the threat of losing their wealth can throw them into a panic.

"I Write the Laws"

Nancy, 27, a Self-preservation Eight, is a four-foot eleven-inch powerhouse of nerve, gusto and unusual leadership ability. Mature for her years, she made it clear in our first session that she wanted me to "knock some sense" into Jon, 30, her live-in boyfriend of three years. (We later found Jon to be a Sexual Four.)

Nancy was clearly in charge of herself, everyone close to her and her environment. Having survived enormous childhood abuse from her alcoholic father, she was relieved to see him abandon the family when she was 18. Immediately after his departure, Nancy found an attorney who charged low fees; drove her weak, ineffectual mother to his office; and pressured her mother into getting a divorce and a restraining order. This was nine years ago.

Still under Nancy's dominance were her two younger brothers, now 21 and 25, whom she felt she needed to keep in line and motivated to finish college (although she had no time for college herself). Both young men still lived at home with Nancy, Jon and her mother.

By the time she was 18, Nancy had decided that she would purchase a home for her family—upgrading them from the two-bedroom rental they had lived in for many years. It took her eight years to accomplish this goal, working three jobs at a time—spending her nights as a security guard and driving a delivery truck during the day while also employed as a process-server for attorneys.

Nancy has no doubt that she was born to rule over her family. She is tough, with a no-nonsense work ethic and seemingly unlimited energy. Whenever things don't work out the way she wants, her solution is to threaten, bully or force ultimatums on anyone in her path—friends, neighbors, work associates and especially her family.

"Most people are afraid of me when I'm on a mission," she said. "They might cross me once, but never twice, because they probably wouldn't live to tell about it."

She chuckled, then turned to the practical reason for her visit: her conflict with Jon, whom she characterized as "weak, misguided and self centered." If he wanted to live under her roof, she said, he would have to live by her rules: "I write the laws in our home. Jon has to pay the same amount of rent and utilities as my two brothers, do his share of housekeeping chores and cook dinner two nights a week."

She loved Jon very much and knew how much he needed her protection. "He thinks he's an artist and he's trying to finish his Master's degree in Fine Arts, which I've pushed him to do. But he wants to sell his oil paintings instead of keeping his job as a waiter. He's got an idea that he can eventually earn his full-time living by selling his art."

My role in her scenario, she indicated, was to help toughen Jon up, wake him up to her version of the real world of dollars and common sense.

Following our first meeting, Nancy insisted that Jon join her for all remaining sessions. He is a gentle soul, painfully introverted, who obviously adores and admires Nancy. Highly artistic, sensitive and longing for acknowledgment as a painter, he was struggling with career issues while trying to adhere to Nancy's rules.

Jon didn't mind living with Nancy's family and in her home temporarily. He didn't even mind her making the rules; in fact, this gave him a sense of identity, connection and belonging. Eventually, he hoped, they would be able to buy a second home so that the two of them could live alone by the time they could afford to get married.

The key problem was what they could afford.

Jon explained that he'd been working as a waiter for over six years, just to get by and pay his share of the rent while he finished his degree. Now that he was within three months of graduation, he wanted to quit waiting on tables and work full time at getting his paintings into galleries.

Although Nancy loved what Jon created, she saw his art only as a "productive hobby, maybe with some tax write-offs." The way she saw it, if Jon wanted to quit waiting on tables, he should come to work with her. She was in the process of forming her own small business—a delivery service for small bakeries and restaurants in the area—in addition to continuing her work as a process-server.

Although Nancy had accepted the fact that she would be the primary breadwinner if she married an artist like Jon, she could never accept him becoming completely dependent on her, the way her ailing mother was.

Their conflicts over Jon's desire to work full time on selling his paintings were now coming to a boil. During our sessions Jon suffered a short period of sexual impotence. His inability to get an erection, which had never occurred before during their several years of satisfying lovemaking, threw Nancy into a panic. The more she tried to push, threaten and force him, the worse things got.

After some detailed explaining of the importance of non-demand pleasuring for them both, I was able to set up loosely structured sessions for the total giving and receiving of pleasure, with each offering the other meaningful feedback on what felt good. These 30-minute sessions were to involve no pressure for performance—no intent to create arousal or penetration. Seeing that Nancy wasn't receptive to taking direction of any kind, I asked her to make the arrangements for each session.

Both of them gained tremendous insight through their "pleasure sessions." Nancy's approach softened considerably, while Jon gained a new confidence in his body and control of his responses. Before long they were back on the road to a mutually enjoyable sex life.

However, they were still at odds over Jon's career/income choices. Through dogged persistence, I was finally able to work out a compromise: Jon would keep his job as a waiter until he finished his degree and was able to save six months worth of minimum income. At that point, they agreed, Jon would request a six-month leave of absence from the restaurant and spend this period doing all he could to produce oils and acrylics, get them into galleries and obtain commissions for his other work.

At the end of the six months they would re-evaluate the situation. If Jon was not earning more than he had at the restaurant, he could still keep selling his art but would either go back to waiting on tables or work in Nancy's delivery business—which meant committing to thirty hours per week, whichever job he preferred. They were willing to pursue this agreement and needed to end therapy due to financial constraints.

In the meantime, through our sessions, Jon had developed a profound interest in understanding himself and his personality structure. It was no surprise to me when he confirmed his Type Four survey results and recognized his Sexual subtype. He had no trouble discovering from his own reading that Nancy was a Self-preservation Eight. She dismissed the "personality crap," but admitted she was probably "Self-preservation."

A year after Jon and Nancy ended their therapy I suddenly got a call from Nancy, asking for "a couple of brush-up sessions" alone with me. During the previous year her mother had died suddenly and her older brother had graduated from college and moved to a nearby city with his fiancée. Now the household consisted only of her younger brother, Jon and herself.

Jon's selling of his art, though going fairly well, had failed to guarantee an annual income greater than he made at the restaurant. Ecstatically happy producing his own work, he never wanted to go back to waiting on tables. Nancy's delivery business had tripled during the past year and she was now in a quandary about what to do.

Jon had proposed to her and wanted to get married during the coming year. Seeing that he was so happy doing his art, she was about to make a proposal of her own—but wanted my thoughts about it first. Her proposal was this: that Jon could continue with his art production essentially full time if he would also take on the responsibility for all of her company's bookkeeping (including bill paying, ordering and issuing paychecks for her two employees). Jon was a whiz with numbers and computers, both of which Nancy hated. His taking on this task would free up some of her time to create new business, allow her to save the money she was currently spending on bookkeeping services and use these funds to offer Jon a small but significant salary.

I concluded that her proposal seemed healthy for both of them. We agreed that Jon's marriage proposal was also win-win. After four and a half years together, they both felt secure in making this commitment.

Using our five factors for predicting relationship success, Jon and Nancy's lovemaps turned out to be profoundly compatible—mostly from unconscious variables that they were completely unaware of at the beginning of therapy (related to both of them being deeply wounded through childhood abuse and neglect). Both had average levels of psychological health, with some dips into the unhealthy range. However, both (especially Jon) had made significant strides toward self-understanding and insight that brought them to higher levels of personal development.

Although they are different subtypes and do not enjoy the complementary balancing of energies (since Eight and Four do not share a connecting line), they benefit greatly from being in the same Harmonic triad—the Reactive group (composed of Sixes, Fours and Eights). Both measure their love and concern for each other by the intensity of their own, as well as their partner's, responses.

Their connection continues to deepen—sharing the emotionality of the Reactive triad while having their unconscious lovemap criteria deeply fulfilled.

"Big Black Hole"

Bernie, 71, a Self-preservation Eight, had been twice widowed, twice divorced and "654 times rejected by young, pretty women" when he came to me at the insistence of his best friend and business partner, Steve. Unwilling to feel vulnerable, Bernie had great difficulty acknowledging that he was "cracking up on the inside."

Surprisingly, Bernie was aware of the Enneagram and his Eight type through several business seminars he had attended nine years earlier. He described himself as a "workaholic, insensitive, hard-ass bully—and proud of it.

"There's a big price to pay for that kind of control," he continued, "and I'm beginning to think it's too high. I don't have any close friends except Steve. And that's only because he's a big fat Type Two who loves feeling needed and appreciated for all he does. Hell's bells, I do appreciate him—if he didn't keep rescuing my ass, I'd probably be dead. We've had fifty years of friendship—met in college and later became partners in our tractor business. We both know neither of us could have been successful without the other."

Bernie went on to describe Lucy, Steve's wife of 53 years: "She asks me to dinner about three times a week and that's the only time I eat right. I think Steve and Lucy feel sorry for me. Now *I'm* starting to feel sorry for me. Oh, shit!"

He said he felt like he was "breaking apart inside." Yes, he had lots of money and a beautiful home. He used to have a "strong-as-steel" body, which he no longer took care of. He refused to answer his mail or return phone calls for weeks at a time. Steve now handled all that remained of their business responsibilities.

Bernie's fourth wife, Mary Ann, had died of a stroke at age 61 three years earlier, after four years of marriage. "I felt so guilty the day Mary Ann died," he said, "because we'd just had a big fight. As usual, she got scared, backed down and it looked as if our life would resume under my control, the way it always did. I probably caused her to have that stroke."

His first wife, Victoria, had died in a car crash caused by Bernie's drinking and driving too fast. They were both 28 at that time and he considered her the love of his life. Although he remarried and divorced twice in his 40s, he never really got over Victoria's death.

He considered his second and third wives gold-diggers: "I divorced one of them for stealing money from my accounts; the other divorced me because I canceled all her credit cards after she charged $42,000 in one month. My luck with women has never been good. I've bombed out every time."

For a moment he became pensive, then informed me that he believed he was sterile. Though he had never been impotent, he had never used any form of contraception in his life and, in all of his sexual escapades and four marriages, never once had he created a pregnancy. "It was never an issue after Victoria was killed; I wanted kids with her, back when we were 28, but never gave it much thought after her death. Seems like I would have made a pretty bad father, anyhow. Maybe never having had a family is making me more depressed."

Hearing him for the first time use the word "depressed," I invited him to tell me more about what had him feeling so down. He described a huge black hole, with himself free falling endlessly into it with nothing to hang on to, no place to land.

He abruptly changed the subject and said I couldn't help him with this. I reassured him that he had all the control in our sessions and that I could only help with those issues he chose to share with me. I suggested that, since he had refused any form of medication or therapy up to this point, he might actually feel better if he wanted to experiment with a trial period using anti-depressants.

I explained that many people develop a chemical imbalance in the brain with normal aging and/or in response to a crisis such as the death of a spouse. Since none of this was his fault, he might benefit from just an evaluation for medication.

To my surprise, Bernie agreed to see the M.D. psychiatrist I recommended. Within three weeks after starting on a prescribed dose of anti-depressants, Bernie was feeling better. For the moment, he seemed more open and willing to discuss the big black hole—the total void in his "meaningless life." He had no family—no wife, no kids, no one to love or care about him. His only "family" was Steve and Lucy, their three married kids and grandkids, who included "Uncle Bernie" for all holidays and family events.

"Even then," he said, "I feel like the fifth wheel on the wagon. They love me, but I'm truly an orphan. I've been thinking about what a complete asshole I've been all my life. I've bullied, intimidated and strong-armed people into doing whatever I wanted. I certainly wouldn't want to be in a relationship with me."

I responded to Bernie's rare self-reflection with encouragement, inviting him to share more with me and to finally allow himself to feel vulnerable—something he had never done.

"It's been a long, hard road, " I said, "keeping this all inside. Denying the fact that you've even had feelings." I continued to support everything he chose to discuss, with careful listening and acute attention to even subtle changes in my own tone of voice, so as not to imply any judgment or blame.

I sensed that he was actually beginning to trust me enough to feel vulnerable in my presence. We worked for several more months on his willingness to be more open, more connected, more real with people. He agreed to "practice" on Steve and Lucy, their kids and grandkids and several neighbors he had neglected. He even decided to go on several fishing trips with local groups.

We developed a daily schedule for his eating, exercising, reading the mail and returning e-mails and phone calls. Even though he did none of this on a regular basis, he was apparently feeling significantly better. Although I'm not a big advocate of medication, in Bernie's case it was a godsend.

Eventually he was able to discuss in depth his feelings of guilt, shame and loss related to Victoria's death. He had been drinking some, driving too fast—as usual—when he swerved to avoid another car and hit the edge of a brick fence, instantly killing the love of his life.

He acknowledged that he never recovered emotionally from that accident. "A big part of my life just seemed to end—to die—at age 28. I never allowed myself to really love or really care about much of anything after that. Just buried myself in work, material objects, controlling everything and everyone, forcing people to do things my way. What an ass! That's part of the big black hole."

From the age of 50, until he married Mary Ann at age 64 (she was 57 at the time), Bernie was a confirmed bachelor. They had met in an Enneagram seminar several years earlier. That was where Bernie discovered he was an Eight. Mary Ann was a Type Three. "I think we both used the Enneagram the wrong way," he said, "to justify our dysfunctional patterns, to make excuses for why we acted and thought the way we did. To justify not growing, not becoming more conscious."

Bernie paused. "I can't say I really loved her. I just wanted to feel normal and she, being a Three, wanted to look good. So we got married. Our fighting seemed endless and I still feel guilty for the big screaming match we had the day of her stroke. But you and Steve have convinced me that I didn't actually *cause* her stroke and I guess that's good."

In the weeks that followed, Bernie seemed more open and willing to deal with the realities of his life and the big black hole in his soul. Then, suddenly, he decided to end therapy because he felt better and also because he was becoming "much too vulnerable." I invited him to come back for additional sessions whenever he felt ready.

About seven months went by without my hearing from Bernie. Then one day I received a call from his friend Steve. Bernie had committed suicide; he had started drinking heavily again, went off his anti-depressants, withdrew and refused all forms of help.

In terms of Bernie's last marriage, with Mary Ann, there was no real substance to hold them together. Not only were their lovemaps highly incompatible but Bernie judged every woman by the "gold standard" of his first love, Victoria. Both Bernie and Mary Ann were unhealthy in their personality development. They did not share a common subtype (his being Self-preservation and hers Social), were not in the same Harmonic triad and lacked a connecting Enneagram line that might have helped balance their differences.

Nancy and Bernie as Self-preservation Eights

The issues of "satisfactory survival" with an emphasis on material-ism are evident in both Nancy and Bernie. Nancy's focus on pur-chasing a house for her family, creating a successful business and insisting that everyone in her household abide by her rules is a classic Self-preservation Eight agenda. Fortunately, her boyfriend felt comfortable with her agenda; their mutual love and caring made it possible to create a compromise that allowed him the creative space he needed for his art while securing the business support Nancy needed to expand her customer base.

Bernie's attempts at "satisfactory survival" failed on the most basic level. His confrontational stance and insistence on control in both personal and business relationships left him with extremely limited human connections. Ultimately, his despair and depression were too great for even loyal friends and a devoted therapist to overcome. Bernie asserted his ultimate need for control in the act of taking his own life.

Eights with the Sexual Subtype

The Sexual subtype, which Ichazo associates with "possessiveness," is intense and flamboyant. Eights with this subtype often defy social norms and they seem to delight in flouting the rules. In intimate relationships, Sexual Eights are inclined toward possessiveness of the beloved, from whom they expect complete surrender. If the Sexual Eight suspects that anything is being withheld, accusations and recriminations are likely. If the Eight is unhealthy, physical battering may become part of the picture.

"Cross Dressing"

Alice, 45, a Sexual Eight, is a robust, athletic woman. When she first came to see me, it was important for her to establish her dominance and control over each part of our conversation. She had an opinion about everything; she was willing to buck the system, be the "bad guy" when required and show how much she cared about particular individuals, especially her screwed-up husband.

Harry, 49, a Self-preservation Nine, had been married to Alice for 21 years. He reported feeling relieved that both their sons, ages

18 and 20, were finally enrolled in local colleges, although still living at home. Alice insisted on having the first half of our initial session with me alone. She instructed Harry to stay out in the waiting room so she could "set Mona straight about some things without being interrupted." In the end, setting me straight took her the entire session.

Alice wanted me to know how much she had "protected Harry on every front throughout their marriage. He's very passive," she went on, "refuses to stand up for himself and is actually a cross-dresser—a transvestite." She and Harry had met and fallen in love in a large lecture class that I taught on Human Sexuality at Orange Coast College 24 years earlier. They had alphabetically assigned seats that were next to each other. Our class included panels of transvestites who "really opened my eyes," Alice said.

When they met, Harry was recovering from a two-year traumatic marriage. "I instinctively wanted to protect him," she said, "to make it all okay. Plus, he was so handsome, so kind, sweet, sensitive and apparently appreciative of my strength and bluntness.

"It took Harry a full year into our monogamous dating relationship," she went on, "to reveal that he's a transvestite. He cross-dresses only in private. He sleeps in women's negligees whenever possible and fully dresses as his female self—that's with hair and makeup—at least once a week, when the boys are both gone for the night or when we occasionally rent a motel room. But now he wants to change the game plan and start going out occasionally as a female. That's why we're here, Mona—I can't stand the thought of any public exposure."

For our second meeting, I insisted that Harry have half the session alone, to allow him equal time. He seemed greatly relieved and thanked me profusely. Harry made it clear that he completely trusted me, thanks to my many years as a sex therapist and his previous experience with me as his college professor. He remembered my classes vividly—especially our panel of transvestite speakers.

Harry went on to explain that, although he loved Alice and felt indebted to her for her fierce and loyal protection of him and his cross-dressing secret, he needed to express more of his female self, perhaps by being in a group with other transvestites. Alice had done a wonderful job of shielding the boys and all their friends from the truth, but now Harry needed validation for his "Harryetta" side beyond what Alice had already provided him.

Alice was enraged that Harry would risk appearing anywhere in public cross-dressed. She alone had been his tower of strength for over 23 years. During our early sessions, she argued fiercely for her position while Harry avoided eye contact with her and zoned out completely.

When I spoke with Alice alone, it was clear that she had genuinely accepted and integrated Harry's transvestitism into their marriage. She was not at all intimidated. Her love and acceptance of Harry were clear. Having previously had absolute control of his whereabouts, of when and where he would cross-dress and with whom he would communicate, she was now deeply threatened by Harry's recently expressed desire to find like-minded souls with whom he could relate.

When I spoke with Harry alone, it became evident that he was truly lonely for some form of social interaction and feedback— simple validation that he could "pass" as a female. It seemed to him that other transvestites would be the best choice. He remembered the panels of guest speakers from my class and asked me for phone numbers.

I gave him the phone numbers for my most trusted contacts— actual cross-dressers who had done a terrific job explaining to my class what transvestitism is all about. They were connected with an organization that met over an hour's drive away, on the other side of Los Angeles. I suggested to Harry that if he chose a group a fair distance from their home, Alice might be more agreeable.

Harry insisted that I do all the talking in our next joint session. "You know Alice," he said. "If it doesn't look like it's under her control, it just won't work. You'll need to deal with her fears—really help her see that I'm more than just a thing she possesses."

In our next session, I did do most of the talking, beginning by complimenting them on their 21 years of marriage, their enlightened and sex-educated understanding of transvestitism and the raising of their two great sons. I told them how moved I was by the fact that they met and fell in love in my lecture hall and, finally, how honored I felt that, all these year later, they chose to see me when this impasse emerged in their marriage.

I moved on to summarize my understanding of the profound dilemma each of them felt: Alice feared that "Harryetta" might risk being found out by friends, neighbors or their boys and that Harry might take stupid chances through exposing his secret to people beyond her control. She agreed that this was a fair summary of her feelings.

Moving on to Harry's problem, I said that he honestly needed to be with other straight men who shared his compulsion—to compare his appearance with that of other transvestites. For many years he had needed validation, confirmation and feedback from people other than Alice. He could no longer live inside their tight little bubble. But he wanted Alice to participate with him in finding an appropriate outlet.

Harry thanked me for my clarity and went on to say that, until recently, he had been too frightened to let Alice know about his deepest longings.

Hearing Harry explain his real needs, Alice softened somewhat—a rare occurrence in her life and even more rare in their marriage. She became more open, less dictatorial and confrontational. Having been diligently studying her Eightness and her Sexual subtype, she consciously tried to back off from being, in her words, "such a controlling bitch."

Harry, too, was struggling to move beyond his habitual Nine passivity—trying to speak up for his own needs and feelings and avoid simply going along with whatever others wanted.

I advised them together to contact a well-known and respected transvestite organization for heterosexual men and their wives. I knew the group met once a month, with the men cross-dressing and the wives and girlfriends joining the gathering as their guests. The meeting place was at least 55 miles from their home, in a secluded area of a huge, out-of-the-way hotel. I suggested they tell their sons that, at least once a month, they were planning to have a romantic overnight "date." They later told me that their sons were genuinely pleased that Mom and Dad were getting some romance back into their relationship.

Preparing for their "date," they would pack up Harryetta's extra suitcase, rent a room in the same hotel, where they would have a grand time together at the meeting as Alice and Harryetta, then later have a grand time making love that night as Alice and Harry.

After much explaining, negotiating and collaborating, this case resulted in genuine success. Everyone felt it was a triumph. Over the past several months, I have continued to counsel Alice and Harry on various minor issues and they are both making rapid strides in their personal development. They still attend the monthly transvestite meetings, as their "date night."

The two factors that allowed their marriage to thrive are the two most important: 1) Their lovemaps (especially many of the unconscious criteria) are truly compatible and 2) their greatly improved level of psychological health during the course of therapy. Although they both started with average to unhealthy levels of development, both were willing to consciously push themselves into greater awareness and integration. Their egos diminished as their compassion for their partner expanded.

Alice and Harry's journey was more difficult than it would have been for a couple who had the benefit of sharing a common subtype, being in the same Harmonic group or being connected by a line balancing complementary energies. Nevertheless, they got to their destination in fairly good form, through love, dedication and hard work—which seem to be inherently necessary for significantly improved levels of health.

"Ladykiller"

Derek, 26, a Sexual Eight with a giant chip on his shoulder, came to see me at the insistence of his mother, Cindy, who had been my client three years earlier. Derek knew his personality type from having taken the Depth Analysis survey at the same time his mother did, at her insistence.

However, according to Cindy (a Sexual Two), Derek had apparently forgotten all he learned about himself. Cindy, who was divorced from Derek's father when he was 6, had been a single parent for Derek and his 22-year-old sister since then.

"I'm worried," she said, "about Derek's behavior toward women. His most recent girlfriend—his fiancée—broke up with him because she said he was too rough, chauvinistic, demanding, jealous, hateful, opinionated and controlling. I have to say I agree with her. Now he thinks he can badger her back into the relationship."

Morgan, also 26, is "a sweet, quality girl," Cindy said. "I had hoped Derek would wise up and learn how to really love a woman. But he hasn't and now he's blown it again. This is the seventh girl that's walked out on him. What kind of a husband can he ever be, if he doesn't radically change now?"

Cindy left after fifteen minutes so that Derek could talk with me for the rest of the session.

He was obviously belligerent toward his mother when he came into my office—an outspoken "bad boy." I thought at first he was joking, but it soon became clear that he actually believed "what women really want is a strong, tough guy who can put them in their place and command their respect and submission."

I asked Derek to explain more of this to me, to help me understand why a young woman as great as Morgan would break up with him.

"It's because she's f-ing stupid," he said. "She can't see when I'm right about things and tries to backtalk in a way that just makes me want to put her down. When will she ever learn that she can't win those arguments with me?"

Cindy had previously explained that Morgan, who is probably a Sexual Three, was sick and tired of Derek and that there was no possibility of her going back to him. But Derek, who was used to getting his way through force and intimidation, found it impossible to accept this.

I asked him to summarize his history with girlfriends—in case there was a pattern that I could see. He suddenly appeared sheepish as he acknowledged that his many breakups—seven altogether—probably had something to do with him being too strong, too masculine.

Was there anything about his strength that he wanted to change? I asked.

"Not really," he said. "I want to change *them, not me*. I think most girls want to be dominated—want to feel secure with a guy's power."

I agreed that feeling secure was a desirable thing for most people, but I had to disagree about being dominated. Much research had shown that the majority of women (and men too) want to be heard—to feel understood, not dominated.

This was news to Derek. How in the world would he ever be able to make a girl feel heard? This would be impossible, he concluded, because the girl either tries to talk over him or she withdraws and won't listen at all.

I explained the concept of active listening—of mirroring back the other person's main point, from their perspective. Sometimes this means redoing the mirroring—"I heard you say...."—until the partner is satisfied that you got it right. Then partners take turns, with the other becoming the "active listener."

Derek and I role-played many hypothetical conversations that he might have with a girl. He was catching on to the attitude of give and take, so I suggested that he begin by practicing active listening on his mom and younger sister.

Cindy later told me that she was amazed by Derek's openness to such a skill. Since I had indirectly assured him that active listening would guarantee him more sexual partners, this may have increased his motivation. We continued with many basic principles for building self esteem and good communication—for example making "I statements" rather than "You statements," plus learning not to personalize what the other person says by remaining non-defensive, objective and open-hearted.

Derek seemed to learn concepts quickly, but he still had a profound need to *win*—to maintain some type of control. We discussed his competitive need to win and how, by definition, it forced the other person to lose. I asked Derek to imagine how the woman felt in his presence when he would so aggressively win. How did he feel when another person "won" some point over him and *he* was the loser?

He began to establish a bit of empathy for the loser, a role he was determined never to play. Then, I asked, why would he even think that a woman who was looking to him for affection—perhaps even love or protection—would find it pleasant to be the loser? This seemed to make sense to him.

I went on to explain that one of the most important factors for increasing feelings of love and romantic involvement was *how the partner feels in your presence*. Obviously, if she feels heard, valued and understood—like a winner who has something worth listening to, her feelings of positive attachment increase. If she feels discounted, shouted at, put down, not seen as worth listening to, then feelings of love and romance are greatly diminished.

It was as if a light bulb had turned on in Derek's mind. "Oh my God," he said, "I've made these girls feel like a piece of crap when they're around me. I guess I'd want to break up with me too, if I always felt like the loser."

With this realization, Derek was motivated to change—mostly because he wanted great sex. He'd already had some meaningful positive feedback from his sister and his mother on his new communication abilities.

Now, with his new skills and insights, he decided to invite Morgan to one of our sessions, telling her he sincerely wanted to apologize. Morgan refused and told Derek never to call her again.

Now that he was feeling the consequences of his previous actions and attitudes, Derek was seriously motivated to change his perception of women and his views about what they really wanted.

During the course of our sessions, he did meet a new woman whom he was extremely attracted to—Veronica, 24, who later determined on her own that she was a Sexual Five. She was more withdrawn, self-contained and analytical than any of Derek's previous girlfriends—but expressed some direct interest in getting to know Derek.

He and I agreed that he would explore this relationship with a distinctly different attitude as well as significantly improved communication skills. He had by now virtually mastered active listening and making "I statements." He also read the chapter on Type Fives in Riso and Hudson's *The Wisdom of the Enneagram*.

As I write these pages, Derek is continuing to date Veronica. Although I have not yet met her in person, it appears that trust and mutual respect are evolving in the relationship. In contrast to his old style, Derek has not demanded anything. He reports holding off on all sexual advances and seems determined that Veronica will have to feel heard, honored and valued before he makes any suggestion involving sex. This is a new approach for him, a total contrast to his former way of operating.

Derek continues to grow and feels proud of the changes he has made. His strength is being demonstrated in more loving ways. At times, however, he has found it challenging to maintain his new attitude—especially when he loses his temper.

His previous relationship, with Morgan, had become quickly and intensely sexual. Using our Five Factors for predicting relationship success, the only positive one he had with Morgan was their common Sexual subtype. Their lovemaps were highly incompatible and Derek's unhealthy personality development quickly brought the relationship to a halt. They did not enjoy the benefits of being in the same Harmonic triad or of being connected by a direct line that could have balanced their differences.

Derek relayed to me what Morgan had said to him the night of their final breakup: "Derek, you're a control freak and you stupidly think this makes you a real 'ladykiller.' What you actually are is a killer of ladies' hearts and spirits. I hope you've learned something from our relationship and I want nothing more to do with you, ever."

These words obviously made a profound impression on Derek. As much as he had resisted his mother's insistence that he get counseling, he was glad he'd been able to explore the results of his aggressive actions.

He now felt he had another chance with a quality girl—Veronica, who is different from any girl he has ever dated. She has concluded from her own reading that she's most likely a Five and she and Derek have acknowledged their common Sexual subtype from worksheets I provided. Their lovemap expectations for their ideal partner appear highly compatible, which is of greatest importance. Derek's level of psychological health has grown enormously and Veronica has consistently seemed fairly healthy in her own development. Derek's ability to practice greater self-discipline and to contain his own reactions has markedly improved.

In addition to their common Sexual subtype, Derek and

Veronica are connected by a line balancing their complementary Eight and Five energies. I am hopeful that this relationship will work out better than Derek's previous ones.

Alice and Derek as Sexual Eights

Alice and Derek, in different ways, showed the "possessiveness" that is characteristic of Eights with a Sexual subtype. Alice wanted to control her husband and limit his cross-dressing to risk-free situations. However, because of her deep love for him, she finally came to understand his need for validation from a transvestite group outside of her control. The two of them reached a compromise that offers little risk of exposure while satisfying Harry's need for connection with other heterosexual men who cross-dress.

Derek, much less healthy, was so belligerent and disrespectful in his attempt to dominate his fiancée that she broke their engagement and refused to have anything further to do with him. His mother, concerned about his pattern of bullying girlfriends until they broke up with him, insisted that he enter therapy. My work with him enabled him to develop considerable empathy for women and learn the communication skills required to develop a romantic relationship. His careful approach to his new girlfriend suggests that a lasting connection might now be a possibility for Derek.

Eights with the Social Subtype

The Eight Social subtype, which Ichazo associates with "friendship," focuses on being part of an aligned group, usually as its leader. Eights with this subtype have a quality of complicity, of being willing to let their hair down among trusted friends. The characteristic Eight anti-social attitudes are generally less evident with this subtype. Devotion to social causes is often important to Social Eights, as is the role of protector for the group, especially against outsiders and other groups.

"AC/DC"

Jolene, 56, a tall, handsome, athletic Social Eight, came to me extremely distraught over the loss of her long-term love, Ellie. Ellie, 57, had always been fiercely devoted and loyal to Jolene, who considered Ellie the one person she could completely trust. (We learned much later in therapy that Ellie is a Sexual Six.)

Jolene and Ellie had met in college when Jolene was 18 and Ellie 19. They played competitive college basketball and ice hockey together and became best friends. Ellie had always been openly gay and her parents and three heterosexual siblings were supportive of her lesbianism.

On the question of sexual orientation, things were not so simple for Jolene. Although greatly attracted to Ellie sexually, she declared in no uncertain terms that she was straight and saw marriage and children in her future. However, the two women remained best friends and spent virtually all their free time together over the following five years, with frequent and consistent sexual contact.

Ellie was granted a Master's degree in Sports Medicine and achieved her dream of working in a sports clinic. Jolene switched her major from physical education to broadcasting, completed her own Master's degree a year and a half later and found a good job as a reporter specializing in women's sporting events.

In the meantime, they remained close friends, with many phone calls and weekend visits. Ellie continually expressed her desire for their relationship to remain sexual, but Jolene resisted, asserting that she was straight and wanted to get married. Despite this conflict, they remained extremely close emotionally, spending vacations and much of their free time together.

When Ellie dated a woman, Jolene told me, she felt irrationally betrayed and deeply hurt. However, Jolene felt free to have sexual partners of both sexes: she had short-term relationships with two males and two other females, none of which she told Ellie about. When Jolene was 26, eight years after meeting Ellie, she suddenly fell in love with a male colleague, Oscar, 30, probably a Social Four. It seemed he and Jolene had a great deal in common: he was a talented up-and-coming broadcaster, she a powerful reporter for women's sports. The relationship became sexual almost immediately and they began living together.

Jolene and Oscar married two years after they met and over the next three years had two children, a boy and a girl. Jolene became the strong driving force within the family and derived great satisfaction from her role as protective parent and cheerleader for Oscar's broadcasting career.

Oscar, however, was profoundly insecure about every aspect of himself. Jolene continually protected him, networked on his behalf and created strong allies for him in broadcasting. Despite his persistent self-doubts, Oscar eventually found a position with a major network. At that point, he began to snipe at Jolene about her being "uncultured, insensitive and crude." After years of doing everything she could to build him up, Jolene saw this as the last straw. She filed for divorce, confident that she could handle herself as a single mom and survive on her own.

In my office twelve years later, acknowledging the trauma of her divorce from Oscar, she expressed pride in her achievements since that crisis: putting her two kids through college, seeing both of them marry fine people during the past year, gaining success in her current career as a writer on women's sports—all this with little help from her ex-husband.

"The part I'm not so proud of," she said, "is the two long-term sporadic affairs I had during my marriage—one with a married male colleague (which was mostly about sex) and one with a beautiful female athlete (whom I've remained great friends with to this day).

"I'm also not very proud of the way I treated Ellie," she said. "I was so terrified of being gay and never having a family that I jumped into the relationship with Oscar. For all his talent, he was such a neurotic jackass—I figured I could make a big difference for him socially. And I did. But I neglected Ellie. We still telephoned, then e-mailed for a number of years, sending photos of the kids, then only notes and Christmas cards. I never felt right about introducing her to Oscar. She never met my kids, in person, until they were 13 and 15."

Within a year after her divorce, Jolene was contacting Ellie daily, trying to reconnect and pursue "the real love of my life." Although Ellie had been in a solid relationship with another woman for over three years, she eventually gave way to Jolene's persistent seductiveness, broke off with her partner and reestablished a passionate sexual relationship with Jolene.

Jolene's son and daughter were both accepting and loving toward "Aunt Ellie," but experienced considerable confusion over their mother's announcement of her lesbian orientation. Jolene and Ellie didn't actually live in the same household until both children were away at college—five years before Jolene came to see me. At that point Jolene and Ellie's romantic love affair was progressing smoothly, with only a few major bumps. Both were active in organizations for lesbians and gays as well as a local church.

Then one day, about two months prior to my first session with Jolene, Ellie intercepted a love letter from an obviously married man who had been having an affair with Jolene. This revelation was earth shattering for Ellie. She insisted that Jolene go to a hotel that night and never sleep in their home again. Jolene understood the intensity of Ellie's feelings about fidelity and betrayal. She rented an apartment, hoping that joint counseling might eventually lead to reconciliation.

Ellie, however, felt there was no possibility of any further romantic or sexual relationship between them. Jolene, devastated by this, told me she had only been trying to deal with her own demons: she never wanted to be "held down" by being totally gay or totally straight. In truth, she is bisexual—AC/DC. She only feels free when she has access to both male and female partners—which allows her to feel powerful and autonomous.

The more we talked about Jolene's "neuroses," the more she realized she had been living in complete denial about her sexual acting out. We had profound discussions about sexual orientation, freedom of choice, loyalty, attachment and bonding. Eventually, Jolene saw that she actually is part of that small percentage of people who fall exactly in the middle of the Kinsey Scale—halfway between heterosexual and homosexual.

Jolene seemed a bit stunned to realize that being bisexual didn't give her license to violate other commitments and expectations for a monogamous relationship. She was anxious to invite Ellie to join our sessions. However, I advised her to hold off until she had a better grasp of her own deeper motives. Understanding her Eight type, as a result of taking the personality survey and her Social subtype were meaningful steps for her.

Eventually, Ellie did join us for numerous sessions and quickly verified her Sexual Six personality. Both were greatly relieved to have "objective X-rays" of their psychic structures, in order to make our discussions more productive and less volatile. Ellie was dating other women, including her former lover (whom she had left for Jolene). She felt she could no longer trust Jolene in the sexual arena, although it might be possible to re-establish the foundations of their friendship.

As I write this, they have resumed some private and social time together. But Ellie is adamant about their relationship never again becoming sexual. She wants Jolene to be free to explore her "AC/DC issues," wherever that exploration may lead, but also insists on protecting her heart from additional hurt, fear and insecurity.

Currently, Jolene has chosen a six-month period of celibacy and sobriety in order to explore her internal issues with greater clarity. She had a period of indulging in too much alcohol, which we successfully resolved. Her children have been understanding and compassionate. They both want "Aunt Ellie" to be part of their extended family forever.

Looking back on Jolene's marriage with Oscar, there were serious discrepancies in their lovemaps. Jolene was unaware of many unconscious aspects of her own lovemap, including the gender of her mate (which turned out to be *either* male or female, but she was unable to accept this prior to our therapy). Both Jolene and Oscar were average to unhealthy in their psychological development. Jolene has made significant progress and continues to make self-affirming choices in her life. Oscar and Jolene did share a common Social subtype and were in the same Harmonic Group, the Reactive triad (Fours, Sixes and Eights), which accounted for much of their initial attraction. However, there was not a solid enough foundation of lovemap compatibility and personal development for their marriage to endure.

On the other hand, Jolene and Ellie enjoyed the benefits of Ellie's lovemap being very clear and fulfilled by Jolene as a mate.

Unfortunately, Jolene was deeply confused and conflicted for many years (both consciously and unconsciously) regarding her lovemap criteria and sexual orientation.

Since Jolene has become healthier in her personal development, she can now enjoy greater connection with Ellie's essentially healthy level of consciousness. They have the advantage of being in the same Harmonic triad, but do not share a common subtype or a connecting line to balance their differences.

The ultimate future of their romantic/sexual potential remains unknown. Jolene claims it will happen and Ellie claims it will never be possible. Regardless, they have evolved an honest, deeply bonded sense of loyal friendship and family ties, which include Jolene's two children.

"Therapy or Jail"

Frankie, 32, a powerfully built Social Eight, had been living with his fiancée, Isabella, 29, for over three years. They had a one-year-old son together, yet Frankie had refused legal marriage until Isabella could demonstrate that she was fully adjusted to his chauvinistic views. She later verified her own personality type: a Self-preservation Two.

Frankie's mother, Ventura and their attorney had set up a court-ordered twelve-month anger management program for Frankie, requesting me as the therapist/administrator. Frankie's only alternative was to serve time in jail.

In our first session it was clear that Frankie resented being in my office and had no intention of answering any direct questions. It was evident that he welcomed confrontation and trouble. Up until now, Frankie and his gang had had some close calls and a few scrapes with the law, but nothing serious. This time it was definitely serious.

I explained that private therapy was not the same as a prison sentence and that I actually worked for him and would do only what he requested.

Frankie wanted complete control of our conversation. He explained that since the age of 12 or 13 he had been the leader of a tight gang of males who had grown up together and had made a pact never to move away and never to betray or deceive their "brothers." Now, twenty years later, the "brothers" had a meeting every Friday night and Frankie said all seven of them were prepared to die for one another.

In response to my query about his one "serious incident with the law," Frankie told me that some guy had challenged his gang and he had to put him in his place. He offered to bring his mother to our second session to explain the details.

We spent the remainder of our first session discussing Frankie's partnership with Isabella and his belief that issues such as contraception and childbirth were entirely the woman's problem. Isabella had been a real pain-in-the-butt on the subject of contraception—every form she tried made her ill. Their precious son, Juan, had been the result of contraceptive failure (omission).

Any suggestions I made regarding condoms or vasectomy brought out Frankie's combative side and he categorically dismissed these subjects as "women's business." He seemed proud of his control of Isabella and made it clear that he would never tolerate any kind of disloyalty or insubordination from her. He felt compelled to continually test his mate on every issue—including sexual favors, her loyalty to all gang members and his refusal to do any form of housework.

He ruled their family just as Isabella's chauvinistic father had done all her life. If she gave Frankie any trouble, he would threaten to put her and the baby out on the street. "I'm a lot of hot air sometimes," he said with a chuckle.

In reality, Frankie was willing to lay down his life for Isabella and little Juan. No one would dare mess with them for fear of having to deal with him. Isabella felt secure and entitled to Frankie's powerful protection. As a Self-preservation Two, she felt deserving of financial and social rewards commensurate with everything she did for Frankie.

Frankie was aware that his mother and I had been casual friends for over 25 years. She was an administrative secretary at the college where I was an instructor and Frankie was sure that she had given me a "bad rap" on him.

I acknowledged that his mother and I had had many conversations, mostly over lunch, about our families and childrearing; I knew Ventura fairly well—and told Frankie I was aware that she had "a headstrong, good-looking son" of whom she was "very proud." She had told me that Frankie owned his own business and had a beautiful fiancée and an adorable baby boy.

Frankie appeared relieved to hear this, then made some defensive comments about never having gone to college. I assured him that college wasn't for everyone and said I thought he was smart to own his own tile company. His education was all on the job and he would no doubt make more money than his dad (a school principal), his mom or even his younger sister, who was a librarian. He was the only entrepreneur—the only one running his own show and he didn't need college for that. After this conversation, Frankie seemed to relax a bit.

As we had agreed, he invited his mom to our second session. Ventura was relieved that we were proceeding with what their attorney had negotiated with the court. She felt they were fortunate to have me qualify as an anger management specialist, so that Frankie wouldn't have to attend one of the standard court-appointed programs. The bottom line was that our 52 weeks of required sessions (with written quarterly reports for the court) were approved in lieu of jail time, which could have been devastating for Frankie's growing tile business. His sentence was for assault, destruction of private property and disturbing the peace.

Ventura explained that Frankie and his six still-bonded gang members had been out of line—drinking and behaving boisterously in a local restaurant/bar.

At this point Frankie forcefully took over the conversation. "This pipsqueak guy walked over to us and told us to 'shut the hell up.' We were holding our usual Friday night meeting on important issues and having a great time. Two of my guys grabbed this jackass by the neck. I couldn't allow anything to happen to them, so I stepped in and told this dude he'd have to deal with me. We were about the same size—I'm only five-ten, but I'm solid muscle. I told him I'd make him sorry he'd ever messed with us."

Evidently the bar owner had already called the police when he asked all those involved to leave his premises. Frankie rolled up his sleeves and marched outside, followed by all six gang members. Frankie taunted the other guy into taking the first punch, whereupon

Frankie knocked him out cold. In the process, he destroyed the owner's parking lot sign.

Police arrived just after Frankie had knocked the other guy out. Frankie commanded all his men to go straight home, while the police arrested him. He was taken to jail and released the following day after Isabella borrowed $5,000 from her father to bail him out.

Ventura expressed great support for her future daughter-in-law and said that Frankie had better wake up soon. Given the financial and social messes her incorrigible son had created over the years, it was a miracle that he'd managed to stay out of jail thus far. Now, she felt, it was time for Frankie to grow up and give up his gang.

"That will *never* happen, Mother," he said fiercely. "All but one of us have kids of our own now and the gang will last forever—at least until we all die."

Frankie refused to take the personality survey, saying he didn't need any "tests" to tell him who he is, but he acknowledged after a look at my one-page description of subtypes that he was "certainly Social." Both Isabella and Ventura took the survey as if they were Frankie and both results pointed to a classic Type Eight.

I knew that Frankie would never consider giving up his position of power, his extreme loyalty to the gang or their Friday night powwows. Realistically, I could only expect to expand his consciousness and incorporate more reason and purpose into the gang's continued existence.

As I explained different aspects of his Eightness, both pros and cons, he became increasingly proud of himself. He actually was a powerful leader, a good host, a skillful controller of people.

We included Isabella in numerous sessions, for which she seemed grateful. She was popular with all of Frankie's gang and offered much advice and support to their wives and girlfriends. Frankie and Isabella seemed proud of one another in social situations. It became clear that their lovemaps were deeply compatible and mostly fulfilled, especially when socializing with their gang of friends.

I offered many examples and ideas of how Frankie could become an even stronger gang leader through including Isabella and the other women and children in some of their weekly meetings. Frankie finally came to like the idea of having the "real gang," the seven guys, meet every other Friday night (rather than every week). On alternate weekends they would plan Sundays to include the women and children in a group activity—a picnic at a public park, a soccer game, a visit to the zoo or an amusement park.

Frankie presented this idea to Isabella; it made her so happy that she cried. He reported that all six of his men had agreed that this plan would resolve many of their own problems at home.

I pointed out that Frankie would most likely always have to shoulder the responsibility of leadership for his group; no one could do it but him and it was clear that all gang members agreed on this. Now that his "men" had entered their 30s, there would be additional leadership responsibilities—not only for socializing, including women and children, but also to advise them on important issues such as health insurance for their families (only one man had insurance through his work), starting college funds for their kids and retirement funds for themselves.

As the months went on, Frankie took on a maturity I had not fully expected. For example, in one of their Friday night men's meetings he called in a professional financial planner whom I had recommended, to talk about insurance and ways of saving and growing their money. All of them were impressed and began making small but significant changes.

Frankie by now was feeling extremely good about himself as "king of the gang." I concurred and pointed out that Isabella was the "queen"—always by his side and supporting all his good ideas. I proposed to Frankie that, as the gang leader, he would also need to deal with the idea of legal marriage. I had previously advised Isabella *never* to push this issue, but rather to allow Frankie to reach his own conclusions. He was now becoming more aware of his role modeling and responsibility not only for the gang members but also for his young son.

Was it smart not to be legally married to his son's mother? After we looked at all sides of the issue, Frankie suddenly decided, as a result of his own training, on a highly traditional Catholic view of marriage. Yes, he said, they "should get married in the church and have the holy sacrament, never to be annulled in God's eyes."

Isabella was ecstatic about this idea, though she had never had any intention of leaving the relationship, married or not. Frankie actually proposed to her in my office, requesting that their wedding take place the following summer.

Their relationship has continued to mature and develop in direct proportion to Frankie's increased level of psychological health. Never once did he consider giving up the gang or outgrowing it. Rather, he felt a profound need to "grow the gang" as its leader. His heart got bigger, his mind became more conscious and his ego became much smaller.

Our twelve months went by quickly; I wrote the quarterly reports for the court and all Frankie's requirements were satisfied. Frankie and Isabella are now happily married and expecting their second child.

I still see them occasionally for minor issues and upsets. For example, Frankie never did deal with the issue of contraception. Isabella has confided in me that, since he feels contraception is the woman's problem, she has made plans to have a tubal ligation with the birth of their second child. She feels no consultation with Frankie is needed.

In using our five criteria for assessing long-term relationship success, Frankie and Isabella's marriage appears strong. Their lovemaps are exceptionally compatible, with each feeling proud and safe with the other. Isabella has many of Ventura's good qualities and Frankie's personality and chauvinism give him a strong resemblance to Isabella's father, with whom she is deeply bonded. In addition, their culture, religion and local subculture all support their expectations for one another.

Frankie's level of psychological development progressed from unhealthy to average and sometimes exceptionally healthy levels. Their development as individuals was clearly reflected in their marriage and their intimate communication improved tremendously. In addition, they are connected by the balancing line between Twos and Eights, which allows them to complement one another's different energies.

Jolene and Frankie as Social Eights

Jolene and Frankie, in different ways, are both highly engaged with the focus on friendship that characterizes Eights with a Social subtype. Jolene, struggling with her unacknowledged bisexuality all her adult life, has regarded her enduring friendship with Ellie as "home base" throughout her ordeal. Her successful effort, after her divorce, to re-sexualize her relationship with Ellie led to fierce conflicts when she could not resist the temptation to also have a sexual affair with a man. Jolene's highly sexual nature, complicated by her genuine bisexuality, strained her lesbian relationship and deep friendship with Ellie. This may have made it impossible for Ellie ever to resume the sexual aspect of their relationship, although the friendship seems likely to endure.

Frankie's commitment to his gang of "blood brothers" had remained unshakable over a 20-year period and his difficulties with the law arose out of that connection. Ordered to participate in a court-approved anger management program, he gained insights through therapy that helped deepen his commitment to his fiancée and son, enhanced his natural abilities as a leader and broadened his vision for the development of his gang. In the end, he not only married the mother of his son, he also contributed enormously to the maturation and social responsibility of all the men in his group, perhaps transforming them from a "gang" into a "cohort."

Strengths of Eights in Intimate Relationships

- Confidence
- Magnanimity
- Willingness to confront
- Decisiveness
- Self-reliance
- Courage
- Protectiveness
- Concern for justice

Limitations of Eights in Intimate Relationships

- Insensitivity
- Aggressiveness
- Vengefulness
- Arrogance
- Domineeringness
- Intimidation
- Excessiveness
- Refusal to acknowledge weaknesses

Defense Mechanisms of Eights

It is not unusual to find that in childhood many Eights experienced physical assaults or other attempts to crush their will by force. As a result, their central issue is survival: eat or be eaten. Other Eights may have grown up in a power vacuum, needing to compensate for or be responsible for passive or dependent parents; thus they learn early on to make autonomous decisions. Given either of these perspectives, it's not surprising that Eights can come on too strong and be loud, forceful, hostile or excessive.

Even at their healthiest, Eights avoid self-analysis. Their primary defense mechanism is *denial* of anything that might limit their own feelings of strength and power. As a result, they are generally more comfortable facing physical danger than their own vulnerability. Feelings of softness and love are difficult to acknowledge, since these emotions have the potential to make an Eight look weak or vulnerable.

Eights' built-in insensitivity to their own potential destructiveness can cause significant problems in their intimate relationships. Self-preservation Eights may focus so intensely on survival issues such as acquiring material security in the form of houses and businesses that they deny the right of their partners to have other priorities (as we saw, for example, with Nancy). Sexual Eights such as Alice and Derek may be so single-minded about possessing and controlling their partners that they deny the damage they are doing to the other's self-respect. Social Eights such as Frankie often focus on leadership and group obligations while denying or dismissing the negative effects of their compulsions on their families.

The "Natural Neuroses" of Eights

Eights have such powerful needs for control and autonomy that they often trample on the rights of others. In an effort to avoid facing their own vulnerability, they can develop a cynical, calloused view of the world and the mindset of the outlaw. While they may have profound compassion when others need their help or protection, they often demonstrate a complete lack of empathy for anyone who challenges them in any way.

An excess of testosterone is often a factor pushing Eights toward an eagerness for physical confrontation. They see their "bad boy" or "bad girl" image as a compliment to their power, autonomy and nerve. Socialization may mitigate the physical aggressiveness of Eight females, but in general Eights have less need than other personality types to be influenced by social norms. Their sheer physical energy and sensory-motor dominance can make them feel entitled to violate laws and expectations and walk over anyone who might interfere with their lusty appetites.

How Eights Blossom in Good Relationships

For all their power and protective force, even healthy Eights often have problems with intimate relationships. To a stressed Eight, other people look overwhelming, as though they might engulf the Eight if he or she were to allow any contact at all. Eights' solution is to retreat, to isolate themselves and regroup for another assault on the world.

The "one up/one down" position can create enormous conflict for individuals of this type. Eights who have a poor track record in sustaining intimate relationships (such as Bernie and Derek) often lack the ability to relate to others as peers, as equals. This usually requires considerable self-discipline and a profound willingness to change.

When Eights feel secure they become more outgoing, generous and protective of others—but from a position of strength: the powerful benefactor who can afford to give something away. We see this in the cases of Nancy, Alice and Frankie, who displayed generosity and caring when they perceived their devoted partners as needing their protection.

Eights generally acquit themselves well in a crisis that requires them to put themselves physically on the line as a way of protecting others. This is evident, for example, in Frankie's insistence on taking on the sole burden of his gang's confrontation with the law. Having a strong survival orientation, Eights are the natural warriors of the Enneagram and they blossom when they feel appreciated for their willingness and ability to take action.

TYPE NINE: THE PEACEKEEPER IN LOVE

Generally accommodating, serene and self-effacing, Nines are driven by a strong desire to maintain harmony in personal relationships. One special attribute of Nines is their ability to make others feel "seen," accepted and appreciated. Their open, empathetic, non-judgmental attitude can make them immensely likeable.

Nine is part of the Eight-Nine-One Enneagram triad associated with gut impulses and will. Where Eights try to dominate others and impose their will and Ones turn their will inward toward compulsive self-discipline and perfectionism, Nines avoid an open contest of wills and maintain harmony with others by evading decisions and action. Their will sometimes manifests itself in passive-aggressive behavior, creating difficulties for others through an inappropriate failure to act.

Nines generally have difficulties asserting their will, and one way to assess their level of psychological health is to examine their ability to take purposeful and effective action. Average Nines are pleasant, conventional and unpretentious, but frequently unable to take proactive steps. They often have a rich fantasy life that allows them to avoid facing immediate conflict and real problem-solving.

When Nines are healthy, they transcend the style's natural sluggishness to act in decisive and positive ways while retaining their peaceful, unselfconscious, comforting qualities.

Unhealthy Nines can be willfully blind to the reality of their lives, gripped by addictions, numb, disoriented and delusional. They may find it difficult to distinguish reality from fantasy.

Nines with the Self-preservation Subtype

Self-preservation Nines, whom Oscar Ichazo associates with "appetite," are creatures of habit, absorbed with food, television, reading, gardening and other simple pleasures. Although individuals of this subtype may be highly talented, they are rarely ambitious, preferring the reassurance of routines and comforts to significant challenges. Self-preservation Nines also tend to be the most socially conventional of the Nines.

"What's Eating Me"

Karen, 33, a Self-preservation Nine, came to me in the hope that I could talk her husband into not divorcing her. She was pretty and easygoing, with huge blue eyes, curly blonde hair—and an obese body.

"I weigh 300 pounds," Karen announced in our first five minutes together, "at least twice what I should be. But that's no reason for divorce after ten years of a good marriage."

Her husband, Reggie, 41 (later identified as a Social Seven) enjoyed his work as a salesman for sporting equipment. His success afforded the couple enough income so that Karen never felt any pressure to work.

"I give Reggie whatever he wants," Karen said, "freedom to attend all his sports events and go out with his friends, oral sex, no hassles. We've never had a real fight."

Under my questioning, it became clear that the reason Karen and Reggie had never had a real fight was that she was terrified of conflict and avoided confrontation at all costs. She was happy to sleep and watch TV whenever Reggie went off with his many male friends to games, competitions and hunting or fishing trips.

"It never occurred to me that Reggie would have an affair on me," Karen said, "and he never has. But now he acts as if he wants out, says he wants a chance to experience sex with other women before he dies—especially with someone who weighs less than 300 pounds."

Tears were rolling down her cheeks as she confessed, "I just like to eat. I love fast food, hate to cook—too much hassle. My metabolism requires a lot of sleep. I don't like getting all revved-up about things the way Reggie does."

Despite their extreme differences, Karen felt they complemented each other and had an excellent marriage. For most of their twelve years together (ten of them married), they had navigated their differences into many forms of compromise and collaboration, including their mutual decision not to have children.

During the first year of their marriage Karen found herself unexpectedly pregnant. Reggie wanted her to have the child, but she panicked and told him a baby would be too much work and trauma to her system. In the end, Reggie reluctantly agreed to the abortion.

I gently tried to move forward with the real reasons for Reggie's threat of divorce. "It's all about my weight," she acknowledged. "He's so angry he calls me a 'fat slug.' I guess that's true, since I've never exercised and I've gained at least 120 pounds over the decade of our marriage."

She had tried many diet programs and nothing worked for her. Then she asked her oldest sister, a physician specializing in OB/GYN, to research the possibilities for gastric bypass surgery. Through medical colleagues Karen's sister located a surgeon who specialized in these procedures. Despite her parents' and Reggie's concerns about the surgery, Karen made an appointment with the surgeon for a consultation.

In the meantime, Reggie had reached the point of almost zero sexual interest in Karen and had turned to occasional Internet pornography—something he didn't really want but considered preferable to an affair.

After months of therapy and at my prompting, Karen agreed to invite Reggie to join her for one of our sessions. Her description of her husband had been quite accurate: he was a handsome, energetic, athletic young black man who loved his beautiful blonde wife—minus about 150 pounds.

"I'm so fed up," Reggie said. "We've wasted years and thousands of dollars on Karen's weight problem. I still love her and I'll always love her, but I'm so turned off to her visually I could scream. Maybe it's time for me to leave the marriage."

Karen burst into hysterical sobbing. Her fat body, she said, was not a good enough reason to get a divorce. She still felt she could fix it, with the radical measure of stomach bypass surgery.

I asked how Reggie felt about this procedure. He explained that he had initially opposed it, believing it would only provide another excuse for Karen's overeating. But after reading more about it and attending a consultation with the surgeon Karen's sister recommended he had changed his mind. It could be their one remaining hope.

Karen declared that if he would support her getting the surgery—which would make it literally impossible for her to overeat because of her stomach cavity being so reduced—she would promise to lose 100 pounds in one year from the date of the surgery. She requested that I write a formal contract for both of them to sign.

After some hesitation, Reggie agreed. His signing implied his support for Karen's effort to lose weight and his agreement not to mention divorce again for a year. If Karen failed to meet her weight-loss goal of 100 pounds after a year, she said she would not object to Reggie's filing for divorce.

Within a month, Karen had successful gastric bypass surgery under her sister's close scrutiny. When I saw her three weeks after the surgery she had already lost eleven pounds—the first time in her life she had ever lost weight. She was immensely proud of herself.

Reggie, she reported, was "cautiously pleased" with the immediate results. She actually felt nauseated, she told me, when she attempted to overeat. Now that she was physically unable to stuff down her fears and anxieties along with huge amounts of food, she declared that it was time to look at *what was eating her* rather than what she was eating.

Over the following months I continued to see her every two weeks and we worked diligently to deal with her core-level fears: fear of conflict; fear of being destroyed as a result of open disagreement; fear of direct confrontation, which made her freeze up and become unresponsive; fear that confronting her real problems might be annihilating; fear of losing the tiny bits of peace she had left.

"I'm the queen of denial," she concluded. "If I could just learn to deal with myself—and rise above my fears—I think I could 'get a life,' as Reggie would put it."

Karen became an excellent client and we decided every two weeks during our sessions what small steps and risks she would attempt. Her confidence grew quickly and she felt enormous pride in her accomplishments. She discovered that she actually did have passion—for raising cats and flowers. She made their home look beautiful again through her gardening skills and hired a housekeeper. She also developed a small business breeding Siamese kittens, to supplement the family income.

After three months, Karen was noticeably thinner, having shed 35 pounds in all. By the end of six months she had lost 65 pounds and was feeling confident about achieving her 100-pound loss inside of a year. She mentioned that her ideal weight, at 5'6", would be 140 to 145 pounds and achieving this began to seem possible.

As the twelve months came to an end, Karen had lost 115 pounds and at 189 pounds she looked infinitely better. Reggie, who had joined us for several sessions during the year, acknowledged that he had long since abandoned the idea of divorce. He now wanted the marriage and actually wanted to have sex again with Karen.

She felt confident that she would lose another 50 pounds or so and stabilize at her healthy weight. A spirit of good will again pervaded Karen and Reggie's relationship. Over the past year I've continued to counsel Karen periodically on specific issues, fears and personal goals.

What made Karen and Reggie's relationship an ultimate success? The main contribution was Karen's weight loss, which uncovered many other issues that, in turn, allowed Reggie to restore some of the criteria in his own lovemap that had initially attracted him to Karen. It was of major importance for Reggie to be socially acceptable and financially successful. He has always wanted to be the sole breadwinner and dominant force in the marriage, which was fine with Karen. Her lovemap had always been fulfilled by Reggie. Now they were both satisfied with their spouse and had a mutually fulfilling sex life.

Karen's level of psychological development, originally unhealthy, improved to the point where she could evaluate herself as "being too much of a Nine." Both Reggie and Karen are committed to a lifelong journey of pursuing higher levels of psychological health. And both seem to understand what that actually entails.

Although they do not share the same subtype and are not connected by a balancing line to complement their differences, they do enjoy the benefits of being in the same Harmonic Group (the "Positive Outlook" Group: Nines, Sevens and Twos). Nines and Sevens often have good rapport because they share a tendency to see the "glass as half full" and avoid negative thinking.

"The Price of Peace"

Lance, 58, a stocky Self-preservation Nine, set an appointment with me only because of his wife's "paranoid insistence" that he had lost control of his company, its staff and its CEO. His wife, Marlene, 55, a Self-preservation Three, was distraught over what she felt was Lance's avoidance of all conflict and his inertia about taking action on reported graft by his employees.

Lance had inherited a small plastics manufacturing company when his parents were killed in a boating accident ten years earlier. He had been a high school social studies teacher for many years and had never wanted to own any kind of business. Yet he was relieved at the opportunity to leave teaching, because he had always felt his students took advantage of his good nature and permissive approach to discipline. He enjoyed being free now to putter around the house and yard and avoid anything strenuous.

Prior to our first appointment, Marlene explained that she was anxious to begin marriage counseling, which she saw as a way of getting Lance into some depth psychotherapy. "I'm worried sick," she told me. "Lance is allowing us to be robbed blind and I'm afraid we'll lose the company. His dad—whom I was close to and loved very much—was a brilliant businessman. Unlike Lance, he kept his thumb on the pulse of all company decisions and policies. Lance does absolutely *nothing* to hold anyone accountable for anything."

Marlene and Lance were together for our first few sessions. She pushed to do the personality analysis, which the friend who referred her to me had highly recommended. They had no difficulty validating Lance as a Self-preservation Nine and Marlene as a Self-preservation Three. Their twenty-year marriage was the second for both. Although they had no children together, both seemed extremely proud of Marlene's two daughters, each of whom had produced two sons. Lance spoke about how much he loved "the little guys, so long as they go home before bedtime."

Lance acted increasingly withdrawn as Marline presented vivid, detailed descriptions of how he was losing the business. When they filed their income tax for the previous year she had become so alarmed that, on the advice of their CPA, she employed an independent accountant to do a detailed analysis of the company's books. The findings indicated that their general manager, Monte, whom they had trusted for many years in the role of CEO/CFO and their comptroller, Hal, had siphoned off hundreds of thousands of dollars over the past decade—and perhaps longer—since the death of Lance's parents.

Marlene was justifiably upset. Having worked long and hard for many years as a high school teacher and physical education coach, she had dreamed of early retirement. Now she felt the situation demanded that she go to work at Lance's company—so that she could have some hands-on control of the books, expenditures and bonuses.

Lance had refused to even discuss such a move. He had total trust in Monte and Hal, whom his dad had hired. Not only did he believe them to be good, honest employees, they had been running the company for almost 30 years. Lance especially appreciated that they never "bugged" him with company finances, personnel issues or manufacturing problems. They simply handled everything.

"If Marlene ever got her nose into the business," he said, "she would be in my face all the time, with one crisis after another." Besides, Monte had managed to keep the company relatively small and to maintain their big specialty customers over the years. "That's how I like it," Lance said, "no muss, no fuss. I'm sure Hal and Monte have done a great job. They just send me my 'net profits' check each month and that's good enough for me."

Unable to contain herself any longer, Marlene said Lance's attitude was "ridiculous and myopic." She had personally employed the outside auditor after their tax accountant said he thought there was something fishy about the books. After scrutinizing their profit-and-loss statements for the past ten years and the books Marlene had access to, the auditor concluded that sums of approximately $100,000 to $150,000 per year in expected net profits were unaccounted for.

This loss amounted to well over a million dollars in net profits—and that represented only what Marlene could trace. Her sense of financial security and her goal of early retirement from teaching were now in jeopardy. She confronted Lance with the facts and accused him of not loving her enough to take a stand against the fraud that had been squeezing profits from their company.

Lance reassured her of his love and commitment to their marriage. He certainly didn't want any trouble—least of all the upset of a separation or a divorce. He just didn't want any trouble with *anyone*—including Monte and Hal.

Marlene made it clear that she had never actually considered divorce or separation. Lance, she said, was "the nicest man I have ever known." They had a good sex life, a great family and grandkids and they got along fine. There was just this one giant problem: Lance's complete denial, avoidance and inertia regarding the profits missing from his business and the employees responsible for this.

Although Lance had never actually studied the "findings" from Marlene's independent auditor, he said he knew "how anyone can twist numbers around." It was clear that he did not feel able or willing to take an adversarial stand against Monte and Hal. At one point he admitted that he was petrified of ever firing Monte (or even Hal). "Monte," he said, "has done all the hard, dirty work, taken the brunt of all employee crises and product problems. If he's siphoned off some of the profit, I think he probably deserves it."

As our sessions progressed, it became obvious that what Marlene wanted most was to maintain her secure marriage with Lance, take early retirement at the end of the current school year and simply share in the rightful profits of the business.

It became equally clear that Lance's preferred scenario was peace and calm, the freedom to "numb out" and not confront fraud, corruption, Marlene's anger or anything else.

In one of our discussions I proposed a solution I thought they both might find acceptable: Marlene could take early retirement at the end of the school year and become a company employee—in name only—with a possible salary of $90,000 per year. Also, they would hire her independent auditor, not to confront Monte or Hal (which greatly relieved Lance), but simply to help them restructure the company financially, based only on *future* projected profits, in order to incorporate Marlene's salary. Her job would be "consulting on difficult clients," which meant that she would essentially do nothing. Monte always handled these situations for Lance, anyhow.

This way, Lance would have no reason even for a discussion— much less any form of conflict or confrontation—with Monte and Hal. Marlene and her auditor would simply have a meeting with the two men, directly exposing the findings of the audit but making no reference to the past or to any concern about fraud. This proposal would become effective in June (three months away), the date Marlene had set for her retirement from teaching.

Marlene was moved to tears of relief at my suggestion. She admitted she had no urge to file fraud charges against Monte or Hal and no feeling of insistence that they should be fired or jailed. What she really wanted was the continuation of her marriage with Lance, emotional and financial security and the freedom to quit teaching.

Lance's relief at my proposal made him break out in a cold sweat. Above all, he wanted to avoid confronting anyone— especially Marlene. "If she's happy, I'm happy," he said. He made it clear that he wanted no involvement with the financial restructuring of the company. Marlene, her independent auditor and their tax accountant would handle everything. Any "hidden profits" left over after Marlene's $90,000 salary would be silently left to Monte and Hal.

We were all in agreement.

I continued counseling Lance and Marlene on various communication patterns and issues around mutual empathy, but the "great divide" had been closed. They continued to enjoy their marriage, a good sex life and some new levels of satisfying communication as well as romantic ventures that I was able to suggest.

As we examine the Five Factors for predicting long-term relationship success, three of the elements are strong for Lance and
Marlene: Their lovemaps are especially compatible, with both feeling satisfied that their expectations for an ideal mate have been
met. They have the natural advantage of sharing the same Self-
preservation subtype. And they share the connecting line between
Nines and Threes, which allows their energies to complement one
another.

Unfortunately, Lance was unable or unwilling to grow significantly in his internal levels of personality development. He
remained at average and often unhealthy levels within his Type
Nine structure. Marlene remained at average levels, becoming
occasionally healthier and less materialistic in order to preserve the
marriage that was a high priority for her. Lance and Marlene did not
share the same Harmonic Group, the last of the Five Factors.

As far as I know at this time, both Lance and Marlene have
remained satisfied in their marriage, with no "shakeups" in Lance's
business.

Karen and Lance as Self-preservation Nines

Both Karen and Lance are classic examples of the Self-preservation
subtype of Nine. In Karen's case, "appetite" (the key word associated
with this subtype) was literally the root of her marital problems. Her
tendency to stuff down her fears along with the fast food she craved
had ballooned her weight to extreme obesity and put her marriage
in jeopardy. Once she was forced to confront her husband's sexual
aversion to her fat body, she took decisive action in having gastric
bypass surgery that effectively reduced her weight and restored the
basis for her essentially good marriage.

Lance's fear of confrontation and upheaval that might require
him to change his comfortable habits of life is especially common
in Self-preservation Nines. So terrified was he of conflict, that he
was willing to forego financial profits to which he was entitled, in
order to avoid a confrontation with his cheating employees. Financial security is generally of high importance to Self-preservation

subtypes of all Enneagram types. Thus Lance's willingness to give up the money shows how high a price a Nine may be willing to pay to keep the peace.

Nines with the Sexual Subtype

Sexual Nines, whom Ichazo associates with "union," are focused on merging with another person, connecting so completely with their beloved that their lives become inseparable. Often attracted to dynamic people, Sexual Nines draw energy from their partner that counters the Nine's own inertia. Nines with this subtype may be more aggressive than other Nines in seeking out a suitable life partner and doing whatever is necessary to preserve the relationship. This one-on-one intensity is characteristic of Sexual subtypes in all Enneagram styles.

"I Should Have Said No"

Polly, 39, a Sexual Nine, first set an appointment to see me as a result of her best friend, Eva, giving her the gift of two therapy sessions as her 40th birthday present. Lithe and slender, Polly was dressed in a low-cut red jersey dress that effectively displayed her attractive figure.

Since her last divorce, she said, she had felt lost and disconnected from any purpose she might previously have had in life. Yet she also insisted that she felt fine and denied that she had "any real problems." The incongruity of her statements made me understand why her friend had been anxious for her to begin therapy.

As I took the standard history, it became obvious that Polly had felt truly happy only when she was merged in intimate connection with a man. This was her primary source of identity. Married and divorced three times, she reported believing that each husband, in turn, was "The One" she would spend the rest of her life romantically adoring. She was still determined to find her ideal man, convinced that marriage was her "right path in life." Many of the memories and desires she described appeared unrealistic, even bordering on delusional.

Polly seemed nervous and embarrassed as she described her three ex-husbands. Her first, Bryce, had been a strong candidate for professional baseball; she was "completely and totally in love" with him when she found he had been having a torrid sexual affair with one of her girlfriends during the entire second year of their marriage.

On the rebound, she met Chad, a dashing, tall-dark-and-handsome specialty sports car salesman. She completely merged with him and enjoyed her new identity as the wife of a successful businessman. Chad's huge financial success afforded Polly the opportunity not to work and this three-year period (when she was 30 to 33) was the happiest in her life, she reported.

Then one day a police officer phoned Polly, asking some probing questions about Chad. It turned out that he had been selling cocaine in large quantities, sometimes to minors, for over ten years. After he was sentenced to six years in prison he rejected Polly, blaming her for not being smart enough to find him the right attorney.

They divorced during the first year of his prison sentence, after which Polly felt disoriented and unable to establish any clear identity for herself. Fortunately, her divorce attorney was able to secure for her ownership of the home they lived in, which she sold in order to live off the equity.

Although Polly had held several office jobs and worked in department stores, she felt her "true career" was as a soul mate for her husband. "I've been a real doormat," she said, "going along behind the scenes, making sure my man wasn't upset by anything. There were a lot of times in my relationships when I should have said no, but I couldn't face the conflict, the possibility of being pulled apart from my mate."

So she rarely said no to anything—especially in her last marriage, to Rodney, whom she described as "bigger than life." He lived in a luxurious home overlooking the ocean and presented himself as a wheeler-dealer investor and commodities genius.

They lived together in Rodney's home for almost a year prior to their one-year marriage. Polly later found out that Rodney did not own the home but had been house sitting for a college friend who was temporarily living in Europe.

"I should have said no in the beginning," Polly said, "when Rodney insisted on using my credit cards, running up massive 'loans' to himself. He kept explaining that some of his larger deals were so secret they could only be conducted under someone else's name. I allowed him to run up $43,000 on my credit cards and later found out he owed over $120,000 in his own name."

The reality of her situation began to sink in when Polly inadvertently found several threatening overdue billing statements addressed to Rodney.

One day Polly returned home to find her husband gone. He had left a note stating that he didn't "have the time or interest to hang around doing all the bankruptcy B.S." He had decided to move to Mexico to do some big deals with a friend of his and he wouldn't be coming back. He instructed Polly to do whatever she wanted— to file her own bankruptcy or leave the country herself.

Polly was distraught. Now, three years later, she was still in shock, still entangled in legal red tape. Her attorney had told her she was legally divorced, but negotiations over complications from the credit card debt were still ongoing.

Was Polly now ready to face her level of denial? To admit how she had idealized these men? Could she acknowledge that her lack of a real sense of self had made her utterly dependent on these relationships?

I sensed that Polly was fragile and that we needed to proceed gently. I inquired about whether she felt she had played a part in the breakup of her relationships.

"Of course I didn't know about all the business fraud, the cocaine dealing or the affairs," she said, "but I am guilty for never saying no—never taking a stand for my own needs or desires."

I invited Polly to do the depth personality analysis and she was eager to take it. She wept off and on and reported "numbing out" as she read about her Sexual Nine structure, especially the unhealthy aspects. Without much prodding from me, she came to the conclusion that she had to find her true self. She wanted to find a real job that she could commit to, so that she could become emotionally and financially independent—"or at least not completely at the whim of some crazy man."

As the weeks went on, Polly became increasingly interested in establishing written goals and expectations for herself.

There were several books that contained important insights for Polly at this point: *The Assertive Woman* by Stanlee Phelps and Nancy Austin; *Are You the One for Me?* by Barbara DeAngelis; and *Why Do I Think I'm Nothing without a Man* by Penelope Russianoff.

Polly was open to the use of clinical hypnosis for reframing her identity and restructuring aspects of her self worth. I made recordings of the post-hypnotic suggestions so that Polly could listen to them nightly as she was falling asleep.

We worked hard on defining Polly's overall vision for her life— the things she really wanted in herself and in a relationship. Her specific short-term and long-term goals and expectations eventually became congruent with her overall vision for herself. The three things Polly wanted most were:

• To become more conscious of her choices and behavior as well as her personality type. Toward this end, the Enneagram was especially helpful.

• To find a career position that allowed her to feel creative and involved. Eventually, she achieved this goal through becoming a buyer of women's clothing for a large department store.

• To establish an independent sense of herself, apart from being in an intimate relationship with a man. Polly evolved significantly into greater levels of discernment, the ability to self-soothe and a conscious awareness of her lovemap and long-term goals. This allowed her to be far less dependent on a man for her worth and value.

There were many rough periods in the course of Polly's therapy—times of painful decision-making and doubts about possibly making mistakes in rejecting certain romantic possibilities.

Polly had unconsciously believed that she needed a man who

was exciting, a party boy with lots of glamour. She was completely unaware of her more basic values and expectations, such as honesty, stability, responsibility and commitment. When this was brought to her consciousness, she realized that she was trying to recapture the love, security and feeling of being merged that she so desperately needed following the death of her extroverted, show-off father. He had been suddenly killed while racing cars when Polly was 13. As more of her unconscious desires and expectations for her ideal mate became clear to Polly, she recognized the truth about her beloved dad—that he had been reckless, glitzy and involved in wild business schemes that frightened her mother.

However, throughout her teenage years she felt that the way for her to feel secure again was to someday find a husband just like Dad—that this would provide her with solid grounding and a real sense of identity.

As Polly learned more about the Enneagram, she concluded that her dad might have been an unhealthy Sexual Seven or possibly a Three. (Her mother, with whom she had never bonded, she thought was probably a Self-preservation Five.)

As Polly analyzed her three husbands, she concluded that Bryce, with his sexual affairs, was probably a Sexual Three and Chad (whose impact on her was the strongest of her three husbands) was a Sexual Seven. Rodney, the "scam artist from hell," she decided, was probably a low-level Social Three.

"It all makes more sense," she said, "now that I can see how profoundly I wanted to replace my upbeat, dazzling dad with another man who would give me that same feeling of being merged, bonded and emotionally secure. I now understand how dangerous that was and how much I need to create this security within myself."

We continued therapy for a short period, during which Polly rejected several handsome playboy suitors. Several months after we stopped therapy, Polly phoned to tell me she had "met a great guy— not especially handsome or flashy, but very respectful— a fabulous man who seems to have all the same values and expectations I do. I think he's a Sexual Type Six. If he's a keeper, I'll bring him in for premarital counseling."

Looking back on the Five Factors for predicting relationship success, it seems obvious that the first two—the most basic elements—were seriously askew in Polly's marital choices: her lovemap and her low level of psychological health. Although her three husbands all met the surface criteria of her lovemap, she had not yet looked deeply enough into herself to uncover the more important aspects of her expectations for her ideal mate. Her unconsciousness about her own and her partners' desires and values proved to be the major pitfall in all three of her marriages.

Her average-to-unhealthy level of psychological development was also a crucial factor in her disastrous choices. This is where the Enneagram made an especially profound contribution to Polly's growth. Her new level of persistence and commitment also made a huge difference in her psychological health, bringing her ultimately to a fairly high level.

Although Polly probably shared the Sexual subtype with two of her husbands, the same Harmonic Group with Chad (the Seven) and the direct balancing line with the two Threes (Bryce and Rodney), none of these advantages could compensate for her lovemap not being fulfilled with any of them or for the lack of psychological development in both herself and her spouses.

"Nothing Happened"

One of the most frustrating dilemmas in all my years as a psycho-therapist came from the case of Arnie, 26, a Sexual Nine and his sweet wife, Becky, 28, who accompanied him to every minute of every session. Their vocal patterns were almost identical and they had similar physical gestures and facial expressions. They even looked alike—both with fair complexions, dark brown hair and large brown eyes set off by stylish glasses. Both reported their three-year marriage to be one of total compatibility and absence of conflict. I had an eerie sense that these two individuals had essentially merged into one entity.

Seemingly an unlikely couple to be seeking marriage counseling, they finished each other's sentences and were on the same page with every topic that arose during my intake history questions. When I inquired why they were here, they looked at each other and said they weren't sure, although I knew this to be untrue. Charlotte, 39, their former roommate and a long-term client of mine, had referred them.

A few hours after Arnie's call to set an initial appointment for Becky and him, Charlotte phoned me to explain her referral and confirm that Arnie had made the call under pressure from her. Charlotte wanted me to know that on numerous occasions late at night she had caught Arnie using her computer, masturbating to the worst kind of pornographic filth, while Becky was sound asleep.

Arnie had grudgingly made an agreement with Charlotte to seek therapy with me, in exchange for Charlotte's not telling Becky about these incidents.

Well aware of how confidentiality works, Charlotte simply told me that these were the facts and that she firmly believed I could help Arnie—before something worse happened. Charlotte also reminded me that these were the housemates she'd had to move away from due to the extreme filth in their house.

Since Arnie and Becky acted as if they had no immediate reason for seeing me, I asked if they would allow me to divide our session into 15-minute segments so I could get to know each of them better as individuals. Then we would end each session together for 20 minutes.

They both objected to this idea and began clutching each other's hands. I moved forward with considerable questioning as to what they desired to change in themselves or in their marriage—to no avail. I ended up asking them to think about this issue and I requested that, before our next meeting, each of them make a list of everything they might want to improve and any kind of marriage enrichment they felt might benefit them.

In the following session I asked about their lists. The only thing Becky had written down was that they should remember to call her parents every Sunday, as they had promised, since they both nearly always forgot. "We have no problems," she said. "Arnie is the most perfect husband in the world."

Arnie simply "forgot" the assignment and mumbled that they didn't have any problems. All he could think of that might improve their marriage was to do more diligent research on how and when to trade in their old car, which was giving them problems and find a new one that was "maintenance free."

I asked them direct questions about budgets, joint money, checking accounts and household chores. Who did what? They both essentially avoided direct answers by reporting complete satisfaction with their present system. Never did either of them mention any need or desire to change anything regarding household chores, cleaning, dishes, laundry or maintenance.

They agreed that it was probably better that their previous housemate, Charlotte, had moved out, even though it was difficult to pay the rent by themselves.

I asked them to respond to true/false statements on a worksheet that I often use for couples' communication and enrichment. In every instance, they simply agreed with whatever the other had said. No conflict, no disagreement, no flaws in their perfectly idealized view of each other.

I pressed on with more specific questions from the worksheet about their sex life. They said it was wonderful, they had never had any problem. Both seemed amused at the fact that they were usually too tired to make love. But sometimes on the weekends, if they didn't go out, they could manage to stay awake. They reported complete satisfaction with the quality and frequency of their lovemaking, which was approximately once or twice a month.

Since they were "only seeking enrichment" from our counseling, I asked if they had used outside sources of stimulation to enhance their sexual experience—such as pictures, sex toys, vibrators, adult films or DVDs in soft-core or hard-core. Both replied with an emphatic "No," saying that they never found sex toys or any form of pornography necessary or even desirable.

I explained that as relationships—especially long-term marriages—evolve there is often a tendency for people to change, perhaps to become bored with the same monogamous sexual patterns and that the day might come when they would want to add some new dimension to their intimacy. Perhaps a vibrator might become desirable to help Becky orgasm more frequently, since she had commented that she had reached orgasm only twice in her life. Or perhaps some of the excellent new lubricants would add a dimension of more pleasure for both of them. They listened politely, but with little interest.

"Even the use of a sex film that you could rent or buy," I said, "could be an added way of keeping the sexual energy within the relationship, as opposed to one or both of you getting into the habit of masturbating so consistently that the erotic energy might get siphoned off from the marriage." Again they listened, but no indication of engagement or even curiosity.

Arnie made no eye contact with me during this session, which was unusual for a Sexual subtype. Their complacency and need to appease each other were deadening. I felt I had hit a brick wall and could go no further.

I had previously inquired about how Arnie knew they were both Nines. He responded that he had taken an online survey from the some institute that their former roommate, Charlotte, had recommended. Also, Becky later took the same online survey and got a score within one point of Arnie's. I realized that their results were most likely correct and that both of them being Nines explained a lot. Their quick recognition of their common Sexual subtype also made perfect sense.

I took this opportunity to explain how highly compatible this made them and how few conflicts or fights they would have. Both confirmed this by saying they had never had a fight—not even an argument.

There was, I continued, also a downside to their being the same personality type as well as the same subtype. This match would make them doubly blind to their natural neuroses, since neither would have a different viewpoint that might serve as a corrective to the other's misperceptions.

In the end, after short-term marriage counseling, I had the profound frustration of knowing that the state of filth in their home, as well as Arnie's Internet involvement with S & M chat rooms and pornography, had never been addressed. In spite of all my direct questions, they resisted any reference that might suggest they could be subject to any kind of conflict.

I had done my best and felt we should end our sessions. But

I invited them to return to therapy, either together or individually, if and when a problem arose. I saw little likelihood that Arnie, who appeared most in need of individual counseling, would seek it without Becky's presence as a kind of safety shield. Neither of them could allow the slightest chink in their collaborative armor and thus in the course of our therapy sessions essentially *nothing happened.*

In terms of the Five Factors for predicting success in an intimate relationship, Arnie and Becky had three positive elements: lovemap compatibility, sharing of the Sexual subtype and both being in the "Positive Outlook" Harmonic Group.

The problem of both partners being at low levels of psychological health, as well as Arnie's tight secret regarding his Internet activities, could certainly upset their serene situation at any moment. Thus, their seeming peace and compatibility were precarious. In addition, they had no balancing connective line that might have allowed them to complement each other's strengths and weaknesses.

Being the same type as well as the same subtype, as we saw also in the case of two Sexual Sevens in an earlier chapter, can produce more dangers than advantages, especially when the partners are less than healthy in their psychological development. The psychic structures of Arnie and Becky were, in effect, "Siamese twins." Despite their surface compatibility, their compulsive merging ultimately crippled both partners individually as well as their marriage, preventing any possibility of meaningful change.

Polly and Arnie as Sexual Nines

Polly and Arnie, in different ways, offer powerful examples of the pitfalls of the Sexual Nine's compulsion to merge with a beloved partner. Both, in a sense, were confronted with the challenge of claiming their individual identity through acknowledging their personal needs and desires. Polly, the veteran of three disastrous marriages, had merged her identity each time with that of a man who resembled the glamorous and irresponsible father she had lost to an accident when she was 13. Finally recognizing her destructive pattern, through the help of therapy and the Enneagram, she was able to reclaim her identity, set clear goals for herself and explore the possibility of a relationship with a different type of man who was psychologically healthier.

Arnie and his wife, both Sexual Nines, had a less positive outcome. Because their sharing of the same type and subtype reinforced each other's need to merge without any hint of conflict, they were unable to acknowledge troubled areas of their marriage, even with the help of an experienced therapist. Although their tight merging might seem to immunize them to disharmony, it also effectively immunizes them to personal growth as individuals and as a couple. Since they are so unprepared psychologically to deal with the conflicts that confronting their actual differences would entail, it is likely that they will do their utmost to avoid ever being forced into that situation.

Nines with the Social Subtype

Social Nines, whom Ichazo associates with "participation," want to be liked by others and avoid conflicts. They often become involved in groups but may resist taking large amounts of responsibility. Social Nines have a strong desire to "fit in," and often avoid deviating far from group norms.

"It's All About Him"

Sunny, 33, a Social Nine whose blonde, blue-eyed good looks matched her name, felt ready to have children. But she was uncertain whether she was prepared for the responsibility of child rearing and whether her husband, Vince, was the right person to have a child with.

Her sweet nature came through despite the confusion and sense of futility that reflected her disenchantment with herself and her marriage. Vince, 30, whom we later learned was a Self-preservation Seven, was the busy and upwardly mobile owner of a small furniture business.

"He's the only man I've ever met," Sunny told me, "who loves shopping more than I do." His excitability and impatience were often at odds with her easy-going nature. "We fight a lot," she said. "Actually, he's the one who does the fighting, I just acquiesce. His business and his health are always the center of his attention and I'm usually left out in the cold."

All their activities, including their trips, centered on Vince, who could not bear to be deprived of anything he craved. "For example," she said, "he really loves pecan ice cream. Thursday night we ran out. Vince was so upset he made me drive to the market at 10:00 p.m. to get him more, explaining that he had some important paperwork to attend to. I swear, it's all about *him*. He's totally self-centered."

Sunny was ambivalent about almost everything in the marriage—not only about having children with Vince but also about his compulsive investments (such as the oriental antiques that had nearly driven them into bankruptcy) and his preoccupation with his health. While he was still a good-looking guy, she was afraid his addiction to junk food would eventually catch up with him.

His critical attitude toward her had left her conflicted and uncertain about her own direction in life.

"On the one hand," Sunny said, "I could go back to work at the bank. I was a branch manager, but I hated the pressure, hated reprimanding the tellers. So I quit when Vince said I could work for him at the furniture store. But he ended up yelling at me for errors I made and for not being aggressive enough with the customers. I tried so hard to please him and everyone else who worked there. It was a real mess. He told me never to set foot in the store again. Now he refuses to even let me help him with the bookkeeping, as though I've suddenly become incompetent."

One recent event in their life had been the "last straw" that led her to seek a therapist. Vince, bored with their sex life, had decided that he wanted them to try "swinging—having sex with another couple, exchanging partners." Sunny had no desire for this, but couldn't bring herself to clearly say no. They were referred to another couple in a nearby city through Vince's contacts.

But the foursome didn't work out: the other woman was a whiner and the husband arrogant and pushy. "Vince was angry about the whole experience and tried to blame me—which led to our worst fight ever. As usual, he did all the actual fighting and I just caved in."

Sunny was beginning to look more deeply into her own values and what the marriage really meant to her. She felt free to question anything with me, but said she could never initiate a discussion with Vince on his values around monogamy and fidelity. He would simply "blow up," she said.

Although she felt the need to fit herself into Vince's world, she was also becoming alarmed about what that world really consisted of. "In Vince's world, I'm never enough, I'm never okay," she told me through tears. "He makes me feel worthless and insecure."

I reminded her that no one can actually "make you feel" anything without your consent. I offered her several techniques for keeping negative energy outside of her own system. One of these was the "Invisible Bubble," a procedure through which she could visualize herself encased in an invisible bubble that would automatically deflect any arrows of negativity directed at her by another person—leaving her unaffected.

Another exercise I recommended was a technique known as a "mudra" to Yogi masters who practice it. This involved forming small circles with both hands through touching the tips of her thumb and middle finger. This closing in of the energy meridians could help preserve her inner calm in the face of a psychological assault from outside. These approaches seemed to help her significantly.

Although we'd had similar conversations several times before, this time a light seemed to turn on in Sunny's mind. What if she stopped giving Vince any more consent? What if she refused to allow him to hurt her again?

She suddenly had a glimpse of her own power and her potential for becoming a self-actualizing person. Then, just as abruptly, she regressed to her old ambivalent, numbed-out self.

I spoke to her calmly but sternly about her recognition of her own power and her ability to say no—about "not acting so much like a Nine," as she put it. This made her smile as she recognized that her feelings of powerlessness and resignation were normal for her personality structure and her history with Vince. I also pointed out that she was on the verge of enormous personal growth—which could be unnerving for anyone.

She was trembling. "Will you hang in with me if I try to do this?"

I promised to be truthful and to gently confront her about remaining proactive toward her long-term goals—especially her desire to "find her spine" and "be able to say no."

In the following weeks Sunny grew more confident through doing minor experiments: saying no to a telephone solicitor or someone at the grocery store. She was feeling more secure about her own right to make decisions.

One decision was to insist that Vince take the same personality survey that had revealed her to be a Nine with a Social subtype. She was certain about his being a Self-preservation subtype. Vince grudgingly took the test and came for the first time to a joint session with Sunny for the interpretation.

During the session he was defensive about his personality tendencies but also amused at how accurately the Self-preservation Seven qualities described him. When it became clear that his Type Seven game had been "called," the chip on his shoulder became more evident. He declared that he had "decided to attend this one session as a favor to Sunny" but didn't have time for all her nonsense. He wanted to make it clear that she was not welcome to work in his business ever again. "She's just too spineless, too people-pleasing, too indecisive—obviously not cut out for sales."

He turned to me. "Can't you train her to do things on her own? I hate it when she tries to hold me back or force me into social situations. I'm tired of carrying her. This has to change."

During the next months Sunny did indeed decide to make some major changes. Mostly on her own and in consultation with friends and family—but outside of therapy—she decided to divorce Vince. She researched attorneys and went to consult the one she liked best without asking anyone's advice. She was becoming proactive (rather than reactive).

In one of our sessions I had urged her to read Steven Covey's *The 7 Habits of Highly Effective People* and to choose three of his seven habits to focus on. Becoming proactive was the one she most wanted to master.

"Vince acted as if he didn't really care much about the divorce or my moving out," Sunny told me. "But he focused intently on the financial arrangements." She opted to have him deal directly with her attorney, who she felt confident would be fair as well as protective of her rights.

With the short-term alimony Sunny received, she decided with her "new spine" to attend X-ray technician school and become certified. She felt good helping people, especially in the medical field. Vince's making fun of her need to be helpful now seemed to have no effect on her.

She made arrangements to rent a room from her sister, who needed the extra income and some good company. Things have continued to move in a positive direction for Sunny. The road hasn't always been smooth and sometimes, as she put it, she "would go completely Nine-ish" and space out about decision-making. But in general, she has continued to grow and become significantly healthier in her development.

When we consider the Five Factors for relationship success, Sunny and Vince shared only the fourth element: being in the same Harmonic Group—the "Positive Outlook" Group composed of Nines, Sevens and Twos. In their case, this essentially meant that they never really confronted their problems. They tried to sustain a positive attitude without the substance, communication or nurturing to support a healthy relationship.

Both Sunny and Vince expressed profound disappointment in the person their spouse really was, as compared to the ideal in their lovemap. Vince wanted a highly active, risk-taking businesswoman who could "help handle the store and train employees." Sunny wanted a strong, caring social companion who listened, supported her emotionally and valued traditional family life with children.

Sunny and Vince both had somewhat average and often unhealthy levels of personal development. But she was striving to become healthier, while Vince made no effort, rationalizing that he "didn't have time for meaningless personality surveys and therapy sessions."

They suffered from different subtype orientations—his Self-preservation versus her Social. Finally, they had no complementary line that might have helped balance the energies between Nine and Seven. Divorce, in the end, emerged as the best option for both of them.

"The Clown Who Cried"

Ollie, 54, a Social Nine, was a bit overweight, with a round cherubic face—the kind of man people naturally want to hug, although Ollie himself never initiated such contact. He described himself in our first session as "stuck between jobs and between marriages. All my options look equal to me and none of them look good."

Amiable and eager to please, Ollie knew from some reading he had done that he was a Nine, but had not understood the subtypes. From my brief explanation and written description of the three subtypes, Ollie pegged himself as Social in less than a minute.

"That's me," he said. "I'm always looking for the approval of the group. I want to belong, but I hate it when there are too many 'shoulds' and 'have-tos' put on me."

His career history was first as a professional clown, working with circus routines and performances for private parties. His favorite jobs had been with huge traveling circus acts. "I truly loved the people—giving the whole group laughter."

But he had to give up clowning, at the insistence of his first wife, after she gave birth to their daughter and became pregnant with their son. "I cried over the loss, then went to work in sales—mostly for food and party supplies."

His marriage to his first wife, Edith, whom he now believes to be a Self-preservation Eight, lasted only four years. "After our son was born," he said, "Edith became a control freak and started having an affair. She just wanted out, so we got a divorce. Since my two kids were so young at the time, she demanded that her new husband legally adopt them. I was so desperate to keep the peace and not hurt the kids that I agreed to the adoption.

"Looking back, it was a good thing in some ways. Her new husband was a big investment guy, loaded. He's always liked me. I'm no threat to anyone. They've invited me for many family holidays, so I could be with the kids."

Ollie had done a few years of therapy that allowed him to make peace with his decisions about his children. "AA helped me complete that," he said. "I had about two years of very heavy drinking in my early 40s and did the 12-step program."

He met his second wife, Virginia, in the program. They married at her insistence and divorced a year and a half later after her relapse into drinking. Ollie himself never had another drink, but he felt used and humiliated over his inability to buy Virginia all the things she wanted. "When she found out how little money I really had," he said, "she wrote me a Dear John letter, left town and filed for divorce."

The breakup of Ollie's second marriage left him feeling more ashamed than ever, scattered and insecure, with low self-esteem.

Now, ten years later, Ollie reported, he often had periods of depression and feeling isolated from every group and every job he was in. Although his son, now 28 and his daughter, now 30, kept in fairly close contact with him, he said, "I go into periods of such profound depression that I'm a walking zombie—just numbed out. I met a nice woman from my old company, Lynn, whom I've asked out several times, but I just feel too flat to take the relationship anywhere. Recently, I've worked hard to repress some really dark periods of shame and rage. What good would it do to let those feelings out?"

I was beginning to see that Ollie's real issues had not yet surfaced. None of the topics we had discussed seemed to be what was troubling him so deeply. I gently asked him about this and told him that it was typical for clients to begin therapy talking about issues they had already resolved. That way they could build rapport and see how much they could trust me with their deeper, more complicated and unresolved issues.

Tears filled Ollie's eyes and he sheepishly admitted having "held back my darkest secrets." He went on to explain that his "god-awful, hellish flashbacks to childhood" had all but paralyzed him from time to time over the past few years.

"That's why I came in, Mona. I wasn't sure until this very moment if I could tell anyone the whole truth. It's so brutal."

I assured Ollie that I was experienced and professionally

prepared to handle highly volatile matters, but—much more importantly—my heart was open and willing to merge with the pain I felt in him and to guide us through whatever rough waters lay ahead.

Ollie sobbed uncontrollably for several minutes—which felt like hours for us both. I simply held the space for him and his vulnerable silence. Finally, he said, "It was my rotten dad and my older brother, Ike. Dad was a monster and he taught Ike to be just like him. They both molested and raped children. Boys, girls, it didn't matter. My little sister's becoming deaf was probably their fault.

"They would both grab me, pin me down and start their humiliating practices by forcing me to give one of them a blow-job while the other watched. If my dad was drinking, he would proceed to rape me anally. I passed out from the pain on several occasions. I just wanted to dissolve, to disappear.

"They threatened me," Ollie continued, "told me if I ever breathed a word to anyone, they would kill me—just throw me in the river in a bag. And I believed them. My mother never intervened. She probably knew the truth, but was frightened to death of my dad's temper."

This pattern began when Ollie was about 13. He learned to "fly under the radar," not to cause any trouble or be visible, even at school. When he was 16, he heard of a traveling circus visiting a nearby town, packed his few clothes and hitchhiked to the circus, determined to get a job. He lied about his age, saying he was 18 and that both his parents had been killed, so he had to make his own living.

"I got a job selling hot dogs, sleeping under the bleachers. This old man, Gus, who was a lifelong carnie, took me under his wing and allowed me to sleep on the floor of his rat-infested trailer. I promised I would never cause him any trouble and I never did. Gus taught me everything he knew about being a great clown. He died about two years later and had written on a napkin that I was to inherit all his possessions, which meant the broken-down thirty-year-old trailer and his few clown outfits.

"I was attracted to the clown business because it made me feel like I belonged. I felt merged with the crowds who came to the circus. But after a while I was doing the clown roles mindlessly, just disengaged from everything."

After two more years, Ollie left the circus when he turned 20 and enlisted in the army. He developed severe stomach problems, Crohn's Disease and constipation; had various surgeries for severe hemorrhoids; and finally got a medical discharge. "I think it all related to the sexual abuse from my dad and brother," he said. "I thought I was so smart, having repressed everything, but as they say, *the body doesn't lie.*"

Once he was out of the army, Ollie started getting sales jobs and doing clown gigs on the side.

He has never seen his parents, his brother or his younger sister since he left the farm in 1967. He came to me because he could no longer avert the flashbacks of his abuse or repress the rage that now flooded his mind. Keeping the lid on his emotions allowed him only the option to go numb, become unable to focus and disengage from life.

I assured Ollie that he had been an extremely brave young man to venture out on his own at age 16 and succeed in supporting himself. He had also learned a clever trade—the clown business. He was a real survivor, who had made many right choices to save himself. His self worth immediately improved as I explained the distinct differences between survivors and victims and between shame and guilt.

There were rough periods that followed in Ollie's therapy. Over the next year we did extensive role-playing and reverse role-playing. Ollie wrote "total truth letters" to his dad, to his brother Ike, even to his mother for her "supreme neglect." We did many sessions with deep hypnosis and used the Callahan Techniques, tapping neurologically sensitive spots on the body to resolve anger, anxiety and shame. I had Ollie read Roger J. Callahan's book, *Tapping the Healer Within*, as well as *Shame and Guilt* by Jane Middleton-Moz.

First, it was important for Ollie to feel cleansed through fully expressing all the negative emotions he had held in for more than four decades. At times, the process was so painful that he wanted to quit therapy, yet he knew there was "light at the end of the tunnel." He persevered, with great encouragement and positive reinforcement, as I acknowledged his many victories. His ownership of the full truth, the circumstances and consequences surrounding each flashback and his own violent fantasies—all seemed to culminate eventually in him taking a stand for himself.

He was coming into his own "personhood," as he called it. He did matter and he now felt a need to be heard. No longer wanting to dissolve and disappear, no longer needing to "remain under the radar," Ollie was at last ready to claim his life and his value. His self-image improved enormously and he resumed dating Lynn, the woman from his old company whom he'd previously had "no energy to pursue."

Ollie has continued to improve in many ways: taking care of his health with better food and exercise, making advances in his sales career and beginning to think of buying his first home. He now feels, at age 55, that he might have a future, after all.

He was anxious to bring Lynn (42 years old, divorced with no children) in to meet me and "get the real scoop" on him. He insisted that we tell Lynn all about his childhood abuse. I presented Ollie's entire history to her as a series of heroic steps that helped him survive. I also explained that, in spite of Ollie's own pain and depression, he had always kept in contact with his two children and remained friends with their stepfather and his former wife. I emphasized what good character and strong values this required. Listening to all this, Ollie smiled and nodded agreement. His heart was healing and his self-worth had enormously improved.

Later on, Lynn took our personality survey, which confirmed that she is a Social Six. She too had suffered some childhood abuse—"only minor, compared to Ollie's"—and always identified with the underdog. She had quickly and deeply bonded with Ollie, becoming his confidante and "safe haven."

In many ways, their relationship seems to be off to a good start, with the maximum four of our Five Factors for predicting relationship success seemingly present. Their lovemaps appear highly compatible, with clear expectations for their ideal mate being met; Ollie's level of psychological development has moved up from his former unhealthy-to-average levels, to sometimes highly healthy levels. He and Lynn share the Social subtype and they are connected by the balancing line between Nines and Sixes, which shows their ability to complement each other's differences. We'll see how it goes.

Sunny and Ollie as Social Nines

Both Sunny and Ollie exemplify the Social subtype's common desire to fit in with others and avoid making waves that might jeopardize their place in society. For Sunny, this meant enduring psychological abuse from her husband in order to maintain a status quo that was deeply unsatisfying, assuming (as many Social Nines do) that any action on her part could only make her situation worse. In the end, her husband's violation of her deep lovemap values about marital fidelity, together with the process of therapy, gave her the courage to become proactive in seeking and obtaining a divorce and pursuing a satisfying career.

Ollie spent decades of his life struggling to repress his natural rage and shame at the horrendous sexual abuse he suffered as a child. Although he took pleasure in making people laugh through his work as a clown, his strategy of "flying under the radar" allowed him to remain unnoticed most of the time in social situations. Ultimately, after two failed marriages and a period of alcohol abuse, he came to a point where he could no longer accept the pervasive numbness that was his only alternative to facing his true feelings. With the help of therapy and enormous self-disclosure, he gained the courage to come to terms with his past, develop a sense of self-worth and take steps toward achieving a potentially fulfilling relationship.

Strengths of Nines in Intimate Relationships

- Agreeableness
- Patience
- Flexibility
- Peacefulness
- Willingness to accommodate
- Unpretentiousness
- Ability to reserve judgment
- Calmness in a crisis

Limitations of Nines in Intimate Relationships

- Fear of conflict
- Indecisiveness
- Absent-mindedness
- Resistance to change
- Stubbornness
- Passive-Aggressiveness
- Self-doubt
- Laziness

Defense Mechanisms of Nines

Even though they may have deeply bonded with both parents, Nines frequently felt their parents had little time to give them close attention and care. Thus, in order to gain love and approval, they needed to stay out of the way and cause no problems or tension. As adults, therefore, Nines are often willing to go to great lengths to maintain their feelings of stability and peacefulness. They accommodate others, smooth over conflicts and make few demands, so as to avoid jeopardizing their relationships. While Nines are busy keeping others happy and maintaining a harmonious status quo, they pay little attention to their own desires and may feel hidden resentment about this sacrifice.

The Nine's primary defense mechanism is *narcotization*—numbing out and going unconscious to their personal needs and desires. This numbing out—through overeating, abusing alcohol or other substances, television watching, gardening or participating in mindless amusements—can help them disown the pain of their resignation and frustration. Nines often have amnesia about anything in their history that was negative or disturbing.

The self-forgetting of Nines can make them seem not present for their own life. They grow when they can move into purposeful action—as Karen, the 300-pound Self-preservation Nine, did in choosing to have gastric bypass surgery; as Polly, the Sexual Nine, did in gaining insight into her over-accommodating pattern with her three husbands; as Sunny, a Social Nine did in taking a proactive stance toward divorcing her psychologically abusive husband and seeking training for the job she wanted; and as Ollie, another Social Nine, did in confronting his true feelings about the abuse he suffered as a child.

The "Natural Neuroses" of Nines

Nines' sins are generally those of omission: they neglect duties, forget their promises and make path-of-least-resistance choices. Sloth is the "deadly sin" associated with Nines, but many people with this style are not lazy in the usual sense of the word. Rather, they are often so exhausted from the continuous push-pull of their thoughts and feelings that they become immobilized. The result is a mental, if not physical, lethargy and a desire for peace at any price.

Nines tend to be out of touch with the faculty of will in themselves; they have a difficult time asserting even the simplest preferences and often do not know what they truly want or need at any given moment. They often feel resigned to their lack of power to effect change in the world. However, their passive aggressiveness—their refusal to act in situations where action is crucial—reveals the stubborn force of will beneath their inertia as well as their resentment about not being acknowledged. Many of them could benefit from old-fashioned "assertion training"—in which assertion is recognized as a desirable halfway point on the continuum between passivity and aggressiveness.

How Nines Blossom in Good Relationships

The ability of Nines to be non-judgmental, accepting and understanding of all kinds of people can express itself in many ways—for example in their natural talent for mediation. When they are in situations or relationships where their gifts are recognized and supported, they can realize their great potential for making personal connections and facilitating understanding between people.

When Nines have a life partner who supports and encourages them to find their voice and express their personal needs and desires, they are often able to assert themselves and take action toward achieving what they want. For example, Karen, a Self-preservation subtype, was able to reach her goal of losing 100 pounds in a year, thanks in large part to her husband's commitment to supporting her efforts.

Polly, a Sexual subtype, used the supportive relationship with her therapist to help her assess her troubled marital history and take steps toward a more self-directed life.

Sunny, a Social subtype, used not only her therapy sessions but also the advice of trusted friends to make a proactive decision to divorce her psychologically abusive husband and train for a career of her choosing.

Even Ollie, a Social Nine whose childhood abuse had been a serious handicap throughout his life, was able, with therapeutic support, to gain sufficient insight to begin a relationship that has the potential to give him the love and appreciation he needs to further his psychological growth.

Part III

❧ Love That Lasts ❧

*I*n my many years as a therapist, I've continually marveled at two basic—and seemingly contradictory—realities of the human condition:

One is the incredible ability of people to change and grow, moving beyond their defense mechanisms and neuroses into higher levels of psychological health and happiness.

The other is the utter unwillingness or inability of people to make essential changes that could enrich their lives and allow them greater fulfillment and freedom.

I remain in awe of the different ways we, as humans, define problems and the myriad solutions we find. What one individual regards as a problem, another might well perceive as a solution. What one person or couple sees as a major crisis, another might experience as a blessing. Examples can include even such drastic events as discovering that a child is autistic, personal bankruptcy from a failed business, having a home burn to the ground or diagnosis of a life-threatening illness.

Being in the trenches with problems like these for many years has brought me to the humble realization of how much we *don't know* about human beings and the overall human condition. Even in the best of circumstances, it appears to me that relationships are usually not fully resolved or healed, but rather managed, negotiated or re-created in a more adaptable, fluid state.

Yes, people and relationships can change—for better and for worse. However, the basic principles for creating and sustaining a satisfying intimate relationship tend to remain the same: commitment, trust, safety, integrity, excellent communication, the willingness and ability to learn about one's self and one's partner and to nurture and support that partner regardless of one's personal agenda.

In addition to acknowledging these tried-and-true principles, I've attempted in this book to offer a theoretical framework—Five Factors that can bring us closer to predicting whether a committed relationship or marriage is likely to endure over time.

In my own practice, these Five Factors have been a powerful tool not only for the prediction of long-term relationship success but also for the management of the pesky problems that can plague even healthy relationships.

The highest number of predictive factors that any relationship can have is four of the possible five. This is the case because the fourth and fifth factors cannot coexist in the same relationship. Given the structure of the Enneagram, two people cannot be in the same Harmonic Group while simultaneously having their types connected by a direct complementary line balancing their differences.

Of course no one enters a love relationship consciously seeking any of these Five Factors. However, as the dynamics between two people unfold, they may discover any combination—or the total absence—of these predictors.

You may be wondering if it's possible for a relationship to survive with only one or none of these factors. Yes, it is possible—through sheer will power, commitment, fear of being alone or fear of change. But it's not likely. Usually, with only one or none of these predictors, there are so many levels of problems and clashes that the relationship essentially breaks under its own weight. The difficulties and lack of a healthy connection leave even an intact relationship, at best, basically dysfunctional.

As you will remember from Part I of this book, the paradigm of the Five Factors lists them in order of their importance. So, for example, it's more vital to have your lovemap criteria at least somewhat fulfilled by your partner than to be in the same Harmonic Group or be connected by a complementary connecting line between your personality types.

1. The Lovemap

I've observed over the years that partners who basically meet each other's expectations and ideals for a mate possess the most crucial factor for predicting the success of their relationship. Compatible lovemaps—including both conscious and unconscious aspects—is perhaps the only one of the Five Factors that, standing alone, could provide sufficient basis for a satisfying and sustainable relationship.

However, when compatible lovemaps are combined with any of the other four predictors, chances for long-term relationship success increase proportionately. When two or three of the four factors are in place, resolving problems becomes easier—and the number of difficulties will undoubtedly be fewer, to begin with.

The most challenging part of dealing with a client's lovemap is in the excavation of the unconscious aspects, where defense mechanisms such as repression, denial, rationalization and/or avoidance may take over. For example, I recall a beautiful young woman client, Laura, 33, who had a loving, healthy fiancé who was a successful young physician. Her problem was that she could not feel any romantic attraction toward him.

As I pursued the deeper aspects of her lovemap, it became clear that as a child Laura had felt loved only when her father beat her, which he did for any minor offense. Since this was the only attention she received from him, the beatings became, in her mind, the mark of his caring for her. Thus, her unconscious belief was that being beaten was the *real proof of love*. Since it would have been unthinkable for her kind, gentle fiancé ever to lay a violent hand on her, she concluded that they had "no chemistry" and thus should break up—which they ultimately did. If, instead, Laura had pursued the therapeutic correction of her "vandalized" lovemap, the relationship might have had a good chance of success.

Even in healthy relationships a deeper knowledge of your lovemap and your partner's can lead to greater understanding and enrichment. Coming to understand the unconscious aspects of the lovemap may also reveal a gap between your expectations and the reality of your relationship. Information of this kind can pave the way for correction of a person's lovemap that may have been vandalized or distorted in some significant way, as Laura's was. This process becomes the real substance of therapeutic intervention.

Couples who wish to explore the compatibility of their lovemaps may find it helpful to discuss their attitudes toward such subjects as having children, financial agreements, paid employment, household chores, sexual practices, fidelity, where to live and work, personal integrity, religion and divorce. Many clients who have come to me for premarital counseling have found it helpful to explore these issues in the presence of a third party, such as a professional therapist, who will confront them with relevant questions.

2. Levels of psychological health

The second most important predictor of relationship success is the psychological health of both partners. The greater your own and your partner's level of maturation, self-actualization and capacity to move beyond your personality type's natural neuroses and blind spots, the greater the likelihood that you will create a long-term loving relationship.

If only one partner is psychologically healthy and the other resists real growth or change, the relationship has less chance of survival—or of becoming functional. In addition to the criteria precisely and insightfully described for each personality type in various Enneagram books, I would like to add some criteria for psychological health that apply equally to all personality types:

• *Objectivity:* the ability to avoid taking personally what your partner does or what happens in a given situation; to resist taking offense even when your partner is being argumentative or obnoxious.

• *Self-soothing:* the capacity for self-containment of your immediate emotional reactions. This includes internally managing your reactivity and choosing appropriate times and places to discuss your upset with your partner.

• *Self-validation:* reliance on your own assessment of your merits and your own internal compass, rather than on the praise or criticism offered by others. This means not allowing others—including your partner—to define your worth.

• *Congruency:* internal and external consistency; what you think is reflected in what you say and what you do. Believing something and behaving as if you believed something different is incongruent.

• *Withholding judgment:* working on the assumption that expressing your personal opinions and value judgments about others—including your partner—is not necessarily helpful or even appropriate unless specifically requested. Your own perceptions do not constitute the "gold standard" for others to live by.

• *Humility:* understanding that you do not have all the answers; remaining open to others' perceptions and opinions.

• *Discernment:* the ability to resolve differences and dilemmas with objectivity and wisdom rather than opinions or excuses.

• *Pro-activity:* choosing to take positive action toward your own goals rather than simply reacting to others' actions or obstacles in your path.

• *Living by principles:*
    • Keeping commitments (rather than offering excuses)
    • Focusing on what is important (rather than what is emotionally urgent)
    • Using wisdom (rather than relying on mere facts)
    • Focusing on ideals (rather than limitations)
    • Choosing effective action (rather than seeing yourself

as a victim)
- Seeking truth (rather than relying on myth or deception)
- Forgiving (rather than holding grudges)
- Self discipline (rather than seeking immediate gratification)

These elements constitute a sampling of the qualities that make up the highest levels of personal development for all of us. With these qualities present in both partners, the probability of relationship success grows exponentially, regardless of personality differences.

The Enneagram provides a brilliant roadmap for the specific patterns of development related to each of the nine personality structures. Many of the books listed in our Bibliography can be helpful.

3. Subtypes

The third most important element for predicting relationship success is both partners having the same subtype. Although there has been much discussion among Enneagram enthusiasts about which types go best with which other types, I've observed that the role of subtypes is actually more crucial. I'm continually amazed at how couples seem to suffer deeper conflicts due to subtype differences than from the broader differences between their personality types. This phenomenon has only begun to receive the attention it deserves.

All nine types appear to be about equally divided into the three subtypes, which are basically a set of biases and filters that distort— or at least color—everything we think and do. These subtype biases are mostly buried in our unconscious. Part of my work as a therapist is to help clients recognize which of the three subtypes— Self-preservation, Sexual or Social—is primary in their experience, which is secondary and which is least developed. Differences in the primary subtype for a couple can lead to enormous conflicts and disruptions in communication.

As I've worked with couples over the years, I've observed that those who share the same subtype have an easier time problem solving and establishing empathy, common values and congruent goals. There is a need for more exploration in this area and it has been encouraging to see a number of Enneagram researchers moving in this direction.

As you have seen in many of the cases presented in these pages, when partners are of different subtypes they often become painfully aware of the contrasting priorities between themselves and their beloved:

• Partners of *Self-preservation* subtype people tend to see them as self-centered, not sufficiently invested in the relationship, lacking in passion, overly concerned with materialistic or security needs and emotionally detached.

• Partners of *Sexual* subtype people generally consider them too intense, demanding of attention, high-maintenance and co-dependent—or at least highly dependent on the partner's time and attention for their well being. They can feel like "energy sucks" to their partners, due to their relentless demands for intimacy.

• Partners of *Social* subtype individuals often resent their intense concern about what others think, their high level of involvement in outside activities, their responsiveness to social pressure and the diversion of their energies into too many groups and pursuits. Their scattered focus of attention can make them seem distracted or simply spread too thin.

There are, of course, many exceptions to these generalizations. I've simply summarized above the most common complaints from individuals who have partners with different subtypes.

4. Shared Harmonic Group

The fourth most important factor I've observed in successful and enduring relationships is shared membership in one of the Enneagram Harmonic Groups described by Riso and Hudson. Individuals in the same group share unspoken agreements about general approaches to life and the "best" way to behave.

• Individuals in the *Positive Outlook* Group (Nines, Sevens and Twos) agree that keeping an upbeat attitude and pleasant demeanor is important. Congenital optimists, they find it especially difficult to deal with individuals of other types who whine, criticize or "catastrophize." However, they often fail to confront real problems and ugly conflicts effectively, if at all.

• Members of the *Competency* Group (Threes, Ones and Fives) share unspoken priorities about getting the job done in the most effective and efficient way possible. They tend to be the most capable of focusing on goals and enduring whatever pain and self-sacrifice may be necessary to achieve them. Emotional balance and stress reduction find little importance on their agendas.

• People in the *Reactive* Group (Sixes, Fours and Eights) share underlying assumptions about the value of intense responses from a partner, sometimes bordering on fury or aggression; they see this reactivity as a measure of investment in the relationship. There is sometimes an unspoken agreement among these types not to bother with self-soothing, since it might compromise expressing their passion about an issue.

5. Shared connecting line

Sharing a direct connecting line is fifth in importance as a predictive factor for long-term relationship success. Many of the cases in this book exemplify the way a line on the Enneagram diagram connecting two types signifies complementary or "opposite" energies that can help balance a couple's differences. For example, a marriage between a Six and a Nine may benefit both, as the Six's keen awareness of potential dangers tempers the Nine's tendency toward unthinking reliance on habitual ways of doing things and the Nine's idealization of the partner counterbalances the Six's tendency toward self-doubt.

Another example of this balancing connection: in an intimate relationship between a One and a Seven, the One's natural sense of order and values may help the Seven manage and prioritize myriad options, while the Seven's exuberance and playfulness may temper the One's tendency toward rigidity and judgment.

Other factors affecting long-term relationships

In my experience, many other variables such as addictions (e.g., alcohol, drugs, sex), eating disorders, sexual orientation mismatches (one partner in a heterosexual marriage being predominantly homosexual) and gender dysphoria (one partner desiring transsexual surgery) can raise huge red flags for long-term relationship success. These realities are not necessarily related to the lovemap or personality type.

Nevertheless, couples in such situations sometimes manage to stay together, influenced by such factors as religious beliefs, family pressures, economic factors, cultural mores, disabilities, guilt and/or a sense of responsibility. Occasionally, couples may agree to live together as functional roommates and/or as good friends for the sake of their children or for a variety of other reasons, such as advancement in a public service career or politics. While appreciating the will power and commitment that sustain such liaisons, I am saddened by the utter misery for so many of the men and women who remain in these dead-end situations.

The role of the therapist

I continually remind myself that in my work as a therapist I can be only as effective as my clients allow me to be. For those who are open to growth and change, I can offer a variety of tools—such as various forms of therapy (e.g., Gestalt, object-relations, rational-emotive and bioenergetics), marriage counseling, clinical hypnosis, Callahan's Thought Field Therapy (TFT), sex therapy, Enneagram analysis and a wide variety of other clinical perspectives and concepts—to help them achieve greater satisfaction in their individual lives and relationships. But the choice to *apply* these tools always rests with the client.

In nearly all cases, the therapist must defer to the client's needs and goals and avoid imposing his or her own values. For example, in the chapter on Type Nine, in the case of Lance and his wife, it was essential that I focus on their priorities (Lance's no-conflict agenda and his wife's desire for retirement and financial security), without encouraging them to impose legal sanctions on the managers in Lance's company who had obviously committed serious financial fraud.

A therapist's skill is linked to his or her own psychological health and it's important for all of us who work in the trenches with clients to apply to ourselves the criteria listed above under "Levels of psychological health." The personal qualities we embody in our therapeutic relationships with clients can serve as a model for the attitudes and values they might find useful for healing their wounds or enhancing their lives. If we exemplify these healthy attributes in our relationship with them, they may also find it possible to emulate these qualities in interactions with their partners.

Most of my clients have come to me through recommendations from other clients. If you feel that either individual or joint therapy might be helpful for you, asking for recommendations from friends and colleagues who have worked successfully with a therapist could lead you to the right person.

Although professional licensing, advanced degrees and years of experience are no guarantee of a therapist's skill, consideration of these factors can increase the odds of your finding a person who can offer you the best kind of help. In general, verification of the licensing of a Marriage and Family Therapist (MFT), Licensed Clinical Social Worker (LCSW) or Clinical Psychologist is a positive factor. In addition, many therapists now have websites that describe their licensing, training and experience.

By this point, you will have understood my enthusiasm for the Enneagram as one of the more powerful therapeutic tools, especially helpful in couples counseling. If you are seeking a therapist with this specialized knowledge and experience, you can find on the International Enneagram Association's website (www. internationalenneagram.org) a list of practitioners in various locales who incorporate the Enneagram in their therapeutic work.

Personal growth and relationships

I hope some of the cases described in this book will strike a chord with you. However, it would be a mistake to assume that resemblance of your own situation to that of the clients I've discussed means that your outcome will essentially be the same as theirs. Every person is unique, as is every relationship and set of circumstances.

A loving and enduring intimate connection is something sought by almost everyone and, for those who have it, a treasure to be cherished. If you are now in an such a relationship, I hope that reading about the varieties of cases discussed here has offered you useful insights into your own distinctive pattern of living in the world and connecting with your partner. Above all, I hope you have found a sense of the potential for growth even within troubled relationships.

If you are one of the many individuals seeking to fill the "hole in your soul" with a satisfying relationship, I hope you have found some practical help in recognizing your deepest wants and needs through understanding your personality type and digging out the less conscious aspects of your own lovemap. More importantly, I hope the self-knowledge you have gained supports your sense of worth and your level of consciousness, whether or not you ultimately find a compatible life partner.

With or without an intimate partner, we all struggle with conflicts—both within and outside of ourselves. Through our approaches to these challenges we shape our spirit, our values and our essence. As we grow in self-awareness, we have more to offer and a greater ability to attract a naturally right mate.

As we resolve our conflicts, we also have more heart substance to deepen and widen the circle of loved ones who are our parents, children, sisters, brothers, grandparents, extended family, in-laws, friends, colleagues, clients, teachers, students, leaders, followers, fellow humans both known and unknown to us. As our circle of compassion widens, we have the potential to become the radiant and loving beings we were born to be.

Appendices

APPENDIX A: CJES Survey

The Coates-Jacobs Enneagram Survey (CJES) consists of 135 statements about the preferences, behaviors, motivations and perceptions of people. The Survey is designed to determine your ENNEAGRAM PERSONALITY TYPE.

This Survey is not a test or any measure of ability, growth, maturity or mental health. The CJES Survey simply determines your CORE TYPE on the Ennea-gram circle. All 135 items are of equal value, so there are no "right" or "wrong" answers.

Directions: Part I

Directions: Part II for rating your choices are located at the end of the Survey.

As you read each statement, respond only by HOW YOU HAVE GENERALLY FELT, THOUGHT AND ACTED. Please respond based on your deeper desires and tendencies – the REAL YOU. Statements in the Survey are organized into groups of three. Circle only the number of the statements that fully describe you. **There may be some or many of the groups where none apply to you.** In cases where two or all three statements describe you, decide which ONE most identifies you; circle only ONE PER GROUPING. If you find it necessary to circle two or all three statements in the same group, do so only ONCE. If only PART of a statement describes you, DO NOT circle it. In many of the groups, you will circle NONE.

Statement Groups: There will be many groups in which you circle none.

Responses should be guided by how you've been most of your life.

1. I'm often viewed as tough and others hesitate before tangling with me.
2. I tend to remain calm in a crisis; I don't get upset like others do.
3. I feel a moral responsibility to set things right when people are clearly in the wrong.

4. I tend to be self-sacrificing and feel good when I'm helping others.
5. I enjoy receiving recognition and acknowledgment (awards, rewards) for my efforts.
6. I feel different from others and often express myself in unusual ways.

7. I'm an independent person who prefers privacy and my own quiet time.
8. When possible, I consult others when making decisions; I feel secure having their support.
9. Needless rules, limitations and not having enough options can frustrate me.

10. It is important for me to feel in unison with others and to avoid conflict.
11. I know how things should be done and don't like to accept imperfections, especially in myself.
12. I spend much of my free time helping others because it feels good to be needed.

13. I know that projecting a successful image is important for my career and lifestyle.
14. I can get so preoccupied with my fantasies and memories that others may think I'm impractical.
15. I try to take a detached view of problems, seldom discussing them with others.

16. I feel a responsibility for making the groups I'm in function effectively.
17. I enjoy being on the go, having a full calendar and refuse to "miss out" on life.
18. I get things done, even if I have to "strong arm" a few people.

19. I frequently criticize myself and sometimes others, for not doing better.
20. I see myself as affectionate and at times very possessive of my loved ones.
21. I want to make a good impression on others in order to reach my goals and get the recognition.

22. I'm a sensitive person and I use my own feelings and intuition to resolve my problems.
23. I prefer to keep my thoughts to myself, so I can resolve problems in my own mind.
24. I am cautious and feel anxious when I have to make important decisions without reassurance from others.

25. I don't really mind going to extremes or bending a few rules to create an exciting adventure for myself and others.
26. I trust my own strength and courage; when it comes to taking a stand, I won't compromise.
27. I'll do almost anything to prevent conflicts and arguments.

28. I usually come out "on top" because I'm able to stay in control of the situation.
29. I am ambitious and push myself to "hit the mark," regardless of the competition.
30. I plan new adventures and excursions often before the current one is over.

31. I feel unique and often misunderstood by others.
32. I seek harmony and ease in my life, sometimes to the point of ignoring problems.
33. I prefer to sit back and observe others rather than get involved in small talk or their emotional issues.

34. I want to have a special place in others' lives; knowing what's going on with them helps me feel close.
35. I strive for precision, correctness and to be above criticism from others.
36. I am frequently concerned or apprehensive about things in my life.

37. I tend to daydream and get "lost" in pleasant thoughts and memories.
38. I have highly refined tastes and often feel others lead rather drab lives.
39. In social situations, I prefer to get others talking rather than tell them about myself.

40. I'm an excellent troubleshooter and contribute to the safety and well being of others.
41. I constantly strive to be a good person who is reliable, efficient and trustworthy.
42. To love and be loved are more important than most anything else in my life.

43. When my plan of attack isn't working, I can change my strategy and simply "do what it takes" to attain my results from another direction.
44. I look on the positive side of problems; others sometimes view me as too optimistic or too unrealistic.
45. I am strong-willed and don't hesitate to protect my loved ones and friends.

46. I know what's right and wish everyone else worked as hard as I do to achieve it.
47. My deep concern for people makes me want to help them in any way I can.
48. I value loyalty and people doing their duty the way I do.

49. I am shrewd and straightforward; I can really come down on people if I have to.
50. I stay busy, juggling activities and keeping up with many different interests.
51. I am a self-starter who drives to the "finish line" regardless of how much work it takes.

52. I often feel self-conscious and vulnerable around people; others seem more "at ease" than I am.
53. When someone asks how I feel, I often don't respond because I am a very private person.
54. I have trouble saying "no" because I dislike getting into disagreements with others.

55. I prefer to be left alone to investigate the things I find interesting.
56. I am a "go-getter" and a producer who is more concerned with success than most other people.
57. I believe in right and wrong and it irritates me when people are careless, sloppy or inaccurate.

58. I often feel lonely because people do not make the effort to understand me.
59. I am dedicated to people and to the groups I am part of and I want others to be this way.
60. I know how to push to get what I want, especially if I am pushed.

61. I am people-oriented, nurturing and I want to feel close with others.
62. I can be complacent at times, appearing indifferent and just going along with the flow.
63. I have fun with most people because it's only common sense to make "the best" of everything.

64. Other people describe me as earthy, blunt and street-smart.
65. At times I focus on how I feel so much that I become self-absorbed and impractical.
66. To feel secure, I work hard to maintain my commitments and responsibilities.

67. I stay on the go, don't look back and try to avoid painful situations.
68. I do what is comfortable much of the time and find it disruptive to change my patterns.
69. I make many sacrifices for others and sometimes let them know when they take me for granted.

70. I like starting new projects and I'm fairly good at coaching others to keep them up and running.
71. I have very high standards and I am often frustrated when people don't live up to them.
72. I avoid getting too close and personally involved with most people.

73.   I should consider my own needs more instead of being so concerned about everyone else's.
74.   I prefer lots of friends and excitement; I don't want to miss out on experiences that would be fun or interesting.
75.   I find myself acting as a "go-between" because I am a calming influence on others.

76.   When I make a significant purchase, it is based on well-researched data and need, rather than on impulse.
77.   I get aggravated when things are not done in the best possible way.
78.   Without even thinking about it, I adapt to others and adjust myself accordingly.

79.   I work differently than the average person and require more freedom from convention; I need to follow my own style.
80.   I value rugged individualism and my ability to control my own territory.
81.   I really want to trust authorities but sometimes find myself doubting them.

82.   I am often irritated with others when they lack ethics and integrity.
83.   I sense there is something missing in my life because most people appear happier or more fulfilled than I am.
84.   I am free with money and spend more on fun "binges" and impulses than others would.

85.   It pleases me when people honestly depend on my help and appreciate me.
86.   My ability to concentrate and focus on specific tasks, without direction from others, is one of my assets.
87.   I am a powerful survivor and a protector of those who are weaker than myself.

88.   I am usually very good at "keeping the troops" on purpose, so we win our intended goals.
89.   Sometimes I get over-committed, work in circles and get myself into a frenzy, which creates more anxiety.

90. My friends might describe me as quiet or unresponsive as opposed to assertive or confrontational.

91. I take on many responsibilities and worry or feel "on guard" much of the time.
92. I sometimes put off important decisions because all choices seem to have equal priority.
93. I have definite goals and like acknowledgment when I have met or exceeded expectations.

94. I spend a considerable amount of time searching for authenticity, the REAL me and comparing myself to others.
95. I am constantly in motion and on the go, doing multiple jobs and activities.
96. I am constantly trying to improve myself and the world around me.

97. Some people see me as aloof, detached and not very sociable.
98. I know how to say no and I don't back down or get intimidated by authorities.
99. I think and act too much from my heart and not enough from my head.

100. I am diligent and idealistic, correcting wrongs when I can.
101. In a relationship, I can be too self-sufficient, hardheaded and forceful just by being my blunt, practical self.
102. I appreciate all sides of an argument and consider pros and cons equally.

103. I can get too involved in others' problems and make myself too emotionally available.
104. When I withdraw from others to search more deeply for myself, I often end up more confused.
105. Because it is extremely important for me to excel, I'm usually prepared to "do what it takes."

106. I'm not a "joiner" and do not belong to, nor seek, membership in many organizations.
107. I have no problem enjoying creature comforts and rewarding myself in a variety of ways.
108. I often have contradictory reactions to authority, resulting in my appearing either defensive or insecure.

109. When I know I'm right, I want to tell people and show them how to do the job correctly.
110. I'm emotionally sensitive and get drawn into the drama of relationships.
111. When I want something, I go for it; I see no reason to be deprived of things I enjoy.

112. I enjoy going to the aid of people in emotionally difficult situations; I like people to need me.
113. I keep my plans to myself and prefer that others don't know what I'm doing.
114. I am more comfortable being in charge and in control than I am with having someone else in control.

115. Being great at what I do and being known for outstanding achievements, is very important to me.
116. I am suspicious of others' motives at times; I continually scan the environment for possible danger.
117. I am comfortable with the familiar and feel reassured when things are calm and peaceful.

118. I'm more skeptical and better suited than other people to sense danger or threatening circumstances.
119. I simply do not allow things to get to me or disturb my peace of mind.
120. Even though I may be depressed or upset, it's extremely important for me to present a self-assured, confident image.

121. I spend time fantasizing and "reviewing" past conversations and events.
122. I tend to think that if "a little is good, more is better," and I lean toward excess in certain areas.
123. I am critical of others when they are imprecise, inefficient or out of line.

124. I keep my acquaintances separate (as in business, sports, family, hobbies); many of them have never met each other.
125. I respect courage and strength, as well as the ability to use force when necessary.
126. I feel compelled to help others and sometimes over-do my giving with few rewards coming back.

127. Other people see me as orderly, precise and maybe a bit stiff and rigid.
128. People lean on me for protection because they know when "the going gets tough," I get tougher.
129. My presence is not threatening to others because I'm basically calm, diplomatic and reassuring.

130. I have a strong desire to assist others and to be important in their lives.
131. I very much want to be treated as an individual who is different from others.
132. I want to make a great impression to be successful and avoid looking bad.

133. Others find me hard to read and distant because I don't seek out their opinion or approval.
134. I "push the limits" and create adventure rather than waste time doing nothing or being passive.
135. I often get approval from my superiors for preparing well and following the organization's policies.

Directions: Part II   *Rating Your Choices*

Now that you've completed the Survey, go back over the items you circled
and weigh how much each item describes you. Write 1, 2 or 3 in the left margin
beside the circled items.

> *1* = *generally descriptive of me.*
> *2* = *strongly descriptive of me in most situations.*
> *3* = *absolutely descriptive of me almost all of the time.*

APPENDIX B – CJES Self-Scoring Sheet

1. After completing the CJES, transfer your weighted ratings for each of your selected statements to the corresponding spaces below. (Note: Some of the numbers below are purposefully out of order.)

1 ___	2 ___	3 ___	4 ___	5 ___	6 ___	7 ___	8 ___	9 ___
18 ___	10 ___	11 ___	12 ___	13 ___	14 ___	15 ___	16 ___	17 ___
26 ___	27 ___	19 ___	20 ___	21 ___	22 ___	23 ___	24 ___	25 ___
28 ___	32 ___	35 ___	34 ___	29 ___	31 ___	33 ___	36 ___	30 ___
45 ___	37 ___	41 ___	42 ___	43 ___	38 ___	39 ___	40 ___	44 ___
49 ___	54 ___	46 ___	47 ___	51 ___	52 ___	53 ___	48 ___	50 ___
60 ___	62 ___	57 ___	61 ___	56 ___	58 ___	55 ___	59 ___	63 ___
64 ___	68 ___	71 ___	69 ___	70 ___	65 ___	72 ___	66 ___	67 ___
80 ___	75 ___	77 ___	73 ___	78 ___	79 ___	76 ___	81 ___	74 ___
87 ___	90 ___	82 ___	85 ___	88 ___	83 ___	86 ___	89 ___	84 ___
98 ___	92 ___	96 ___	99 ___	93 ___	94 ___	97 ___	91 ___	95 ___
101 ___	102 ___	100 ___	103 ___	105 ___	104 ___	106 ___	108 ___	107 ___
114 ___	117 ___	109 ___	112 ___	115 ___	110 ___	113 ___	116 ___	111 ___
125 ___	119 ___	123 ___	126 ___	120 ___	121 ___	124 ___	118 ___	122 ___
128 ___	129 ___	127 ___	130 ___	132 ___	131 ___	133 ___	135 ___	134 ___

COLUMN TOTALS:

___	___	___	___	___	___	___	___	___
A	**B**	**C**	**D**	**E**	**F**	**G**	**H**	**I**

2. Add each column (A through I) vertically, writing the total for each column on the "Column Totals."

3. Transfer these numbers to the "TOTALS" spaces at the bottom of the next page.

4. Mark your TOTALS for each letter by circling the proper dots above each total; then connect these points. Your highest score is most likely your primary (or core) Enneagram Type (*the number indicated beneath each letter*).
Notice your proportion of traits in all nine Types.

CJES Enneagram Graph

	A	B	C	D	E	F	G	H	I	
25	•	•	•	•	•	•	•	•	•	25
24	•	•	•	•	•	•	•	•	•	24
23	•	•	•	•	•	•	•	•	•	23
22	•	•	•	•	•	•	•	•	•	22
21	•	•	•	•	•	•	•	•	•	21
20	•	•	•	•	•	•	•	•	•	20
19	•	•	•	•	•	•	•	•	•	19
18	•	•	•	•	•	•	•	•	•	18
17	•	•	•	•	•	•	•	•	•	17
16	•	•	•	•	•	•	•	•	•	16
15	•	•	•	•	•	•	•	•	•	15
14	•	•	•	•	•	•	•	•	•	14
13	•	•	•	•	•	•	•	•	•	13
12	•	•	•	•	•	•	•	•	•	12
11	•	•	•	•	•	•	•	•	•	11
10	•	•	•	•	•	•	•	•	•	10
9	•	•	•	•	•	•	•	•	•	9
8	•	•	•	•	•	•	•	•	•	8
7	•	•	•	•	•	•	•	•	•	7
6	•	•	•	•	•	•	•	•	•	6
5	•	•	•	•	•	•	•	•	•	5
4	•	•	•	•	•	•	•	•	•	4
3	•	•	•	•	•	•	•	•	•	3
2	•	•	•	•	•	•	•	•	•	2
1	•	•	•	•	•	•	•	•	•	1

COLUMN
TOTALS:

___   ___   ___   ___   ___   ___   ___   ___   ___

A   B   C   D   E   F   G   H   I

APENDIX C
BIBLIOGRAPHY ᴄᴏ𝒙

ENNEAGRAM BOOKS

Baron, Renee and Elizabeth Wagele. *The Enneagram Made Easy: Discover the 9 Types of People.* (New York: HarperCollins, 1994).

_____. *Are You My Type, Am I Yours? Relationships Made Easy Through the Enneagram.* (San Francisco: HarperSanFrancisco, 1995)

Bartlett, Carolyn. *The Enneagram Field Guide: Notes on Using the Enneagram in Counseling, Therapy and Personal Growth.* (Nine Gates Publishing).

Daniels, David N., M. D. and Virginia A. Price, Ph.D, *The Essential Enneagram: The Definitive Personality Test and Self-Discovery Guide* (San Francisco: HarperSanFrancisco, 2000).

Naranjo, Claudio, M.D. *Character and Neurosis: An Integrative View.* (Nevada City, CA: Gateways/IDHHB, Inc., 1994).

_____. *Ennea-Type Structures: Self-Analysis for the Seeker.* (Nevada City, CA: Gateways: IDHHB, Inc., 1990).

_____. *Transformation Through Insight: Enneatypes in Life, Literature and Clinical Practice.* (Prescott, AZ: Hohm Press, 1997).

Palmer, Helen. *The Enneagram: Understanding Yourself and the Others in Your Life.* (New York: HarperCollins 1991).

_____. *The Enneagram in Love & Work: Understanding Your Intimate & Business Relationships.* (New York: HarperCollins, 1995).

Riso, Don Richard with Russ Hudson, *Personality Types: Using the Enneagram for Self-Discovery.* (Revised Edition) (Boston: Houghton Mifflin, 1996).

Riso, Don Richard and Russ Hudson. *Understanding the Enneagram: The Practical Guide to Personality Types.* (Revised Edition) (Boston: Houghton Mifflin, 2000).

_____. *The Wisdom of the Enneagram: The Complete Guide to Psychological and Spiritual Growth for the Nine Personality Types.* (New York: Bantam, 1999).

Rhodes, Susan. *The Positive Enneagram: A New Approach to the Nine Personality Types.* (Seattle, WA: Geranium Press, 2009).

_____. *Archetypes of the Enneagram: Exploring the life themes of the 27 subtypes from the perspective of soul.* (Seattle, WA: Geranium

Press, 2010).

Searle, Judith. *The Literary Enneagram: Characters from the Inside Out.* (Portland, OR: Metamorphous Press, 2001).

Wagner, Jerome, Ph.D., T*he Enneagram Spectrum of Personality Styles: An Introductory Guide* (Portland, OR: Metamorphous Press, 1996).

_____. *Nine Lenses on the World: The Enneagram Perspective.* (Evanston, IL: NineLens Press, 2010).

GENERAL REFERENCES

Beattie, Melody. *Codependent No More: How to Stop Controlling Others and Start Caring for Yourself.* (New York: Harper & Row, 1992).

Brizendine, Louann, M.D., *The Female Brain.* (New York: Morgan Road Books, 2006)

Callahan, Roger J., Ph.D. with Richard Trubo. *Tapping the Healer Within: Using Thought Field Therapy to Instantly Conquer Your Fears, Anxieties and Emotional Distress.* (Lincolnwood, IL: Contemporary Books, 2001).

Carlson, Richard. *Don't Sweat the Small Stuff—and it's all small stuff.* (New York: Hyperion, 1997).

Covey, Stephen R. *The 7 Habits of Highly Effective People: Restoring the Character Ethic.* (New York: Simon & Schuster, 1989)

DeAngelis, Barbara, Ph.D. *Are You the One for Me? Knowing Who's Right & Avoiding Who's Wrong.* (New York: Island Books/Dell, 1992).

Dyer, Dr. Wayne W. T*he Power of Intention: Learning to Co-Create Your World Your Way.* (Carlsbad, CA: Hay House, 2004).

Friday, Nancy. My Secret Garden: Women's Sexual Fantasies. (New York: Pocket Books, 1974).

Hendrix, Harville, Ph.D. *Getting the Love You Want: A Guide for Couples.* (New York: Henry Holt & Co., Inc., 1988).

Hite, Shere. *The Hite Report: A Nationwide Study on Female Sexuality.* (New York: Macmillan, 1976).

Hudson, Frederic M., Ph.D. *The Adult Years: Mastering the Art of Self-Renewal* (Revised Edition). (San Francisco: Jossey-Bass/A. Wiley Co., 1999).

Keirsey, David and Marilyn Bates. *Please Understand Me: Character & Temperament Types.* (Del Mar, CA: Prometheus Nemesis, 1978).

Lewis, Thomas, M.D., Fari Amini and Richard Lannon. *A General Theory of Love.* (New York: Random House, 2000).

McGraw, Philip C., Ph.D. *Relationship Rescue: A Seven-Step Strategy for Reconnecting with Your Partner*. (New York: Hyperion, 2000).

_____. *Self Matters: Creating Your Life from the Inside Out*. (New York: Simon & Schuster, 2001).

Middleton-Moz, Jane. *Shame and Guilt: Masters of Disguise*. (Deerfield Beach, FL: Health Communications, 1990).

Money, John. *Lovemaps: Clinical Concepts of Sexual/Erotic Health and Pathology, Paraphilia and Gender Transposition in Childhood Adolescence and Maturity*. (New York: Irvington Publishers, Inc., 1986).

Offit, Avodah K., M.D. *Night Thoughts: Reflections of a Sex Therapist*. (New York: Congdon & Lattès, Inc. 1981).

_____. *The Sexual Self*. (New York: Congdon & Weed, Inc., 1977).

Paget, Lou. 365 *Days of Sensational Sex: Tantalizing Tips and Techniques to Keep the Fires Burning All Year Long*. (New York: Gotham Books, 2003).

Phelps, Stanlee and Nancy Austin, *The Assertive Woman* (Fourth Edition). (Atascadero, CA: Impact Publishers, Inc., 2002).

Russianoff, Penelope. *Why Do I Think I Am Nothing without a Man?* (New York: Bantam, 1984).

Whitfield, Charles L., M.D. *Boundaries and Relationships: Knowing, Protecting and Enjoying the Self*. (Deerfield Beach, FL: Health Communications, Inc., 1993).

WEB SITES

Judith Searle: www.judithsearle.com
Carolyn Bartlett and John Reynolds: www.insightforchange.com
Mary Bast: www.breakoutofthebox.com
Roger J. Callahan: www.SelfHelpUniv.com
Tom Condon: www.thechangeworks.com
David Daniels, M.D. and Helen Palmer: www.enneagramworldwide.com
Enneagram Monthly: www.ennea.org
International Enneagram Association: www.internationalenneagram.org
Andrea Isaacs: www.EnneaMotion.com
Don Richard Riso and Russ Hudson: www.EnneagramInstitute.com
Jerome P. Wagner: www.enneagramspectrum.com

THE AUTHORS

Mona Coates, Ph.D., is a psychotherapist and college professor emeritus of Sociology-Psychology/Human Sexuality, licensed marriage and family counselor, certified hypnotherapist, nationally certified sex therapist and sex educator. She has produced several cassette programs, conducted a wide range of seminars and professional workshops, directed two sex education films and co-produced and hosted her own television show, "Sexuality Today." She is the author of the *C-JES (Coates-Jacobs Enneagram Survey)* and The Self-Scoring Book and a former Board Member of the Southern California chapter of the International Enneagram Association.

Judith Searle's books include *The Literary Enneagram: Characters from the Inside Out; Getting the Part: Thirty-three Professional Casting Directors Tell You How to Get Work in Theater, Films, Commercials and TV; Lovelife*, a novel; and *In the Teeth of Time: Poems 1971-2004*. She is a former Board Member of the International Enneagram Association and former chair of its Southern California chapter. www.judithsearle.com

CPSIA information can be obtained at www.ICGtesting.com
Printed in the USA
BVOW020625021012

301879BV00001B/101/P